THE GATES
OF GAZA

THE GATES OF GAZA

A STORY OF BETRAYAL, SURVIVAL, AND HOPE IN ISRAEL'S BORDERLANDS

AMIR TIBON

Little, Brown and Company

New York Boston London

Little, Brown and Company
Hachette Book Group
1290 Avenue of the Americas, New York, NY 10104
littlebrown.com

First Edition: October 2024

Little, Brown and Company is a division of Hachette Book Group, Inc. The Little, Brown name and logo are trademarks of Hachette Book Group, Inc.

The publisher is not responsible for websites (or their content) that are not owned by the publisher.

The Hachette Speakers Bureau provides a wide range of authors for speaking events. To find out more, go to hachettespeakersbureau.com or email HachetteSpeakers@hbgusa.com.

Little, Brown and Company books may be purchased in bulk for business, educational, or promotional use. For information, please contact your local bookseller or the Hachette Book Group Special Markets Department at special.markets@hbgusa.com.

ISBN 9780316580960
Library of Congress Control Number: 2024937640

Printing 1, 2024

MRQ

Printed in Canada

CONTENTS

Israel, the Palestinian Territories, and Neighboring Countries

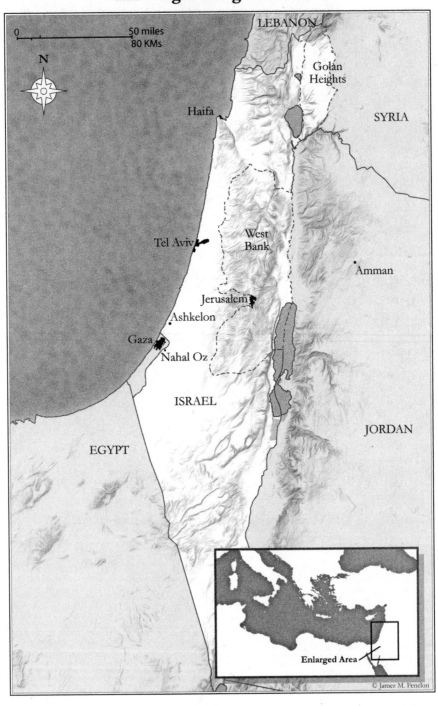

Gaza and Surrounding Israeli Communities, including Nahal Oz

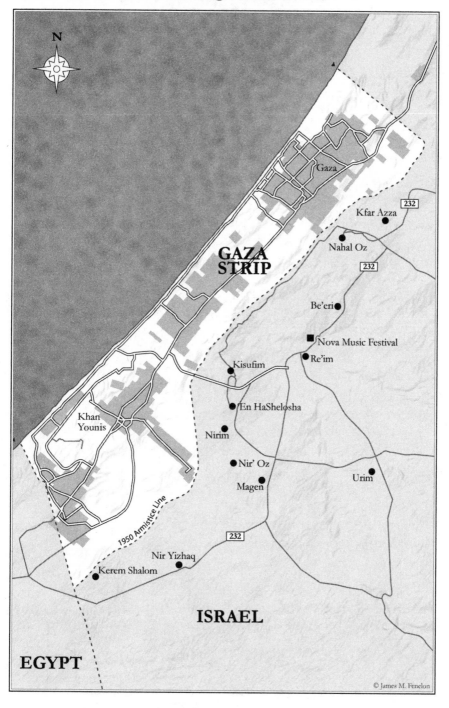

© James M. Fenelon

"This is dawn at Nahal Oz, a *kibbutz*, a collective farm, on the Israeli side of the Gaza border. . . . This kibbutz is manned by youngsters, straight out of the army, because it is so close to the Gaza Strip, and potentially part of the front. Just a few miles away, Israeli troops patrol the border, but the Nahal Oz area is the responsibility of those who work the land. Often, the men on the tractors carry rifles.

"At about four every afternoon, the work in the fields ends, the tractors and horses return to the barn, the men and the women return to their quarters. There is a tin shower building for men, another for women. They sing in the barn at dawn and they sing in the shower at dusk. After the evening meal, the perimeter lights are turned on, and about one-third of the men go on guard duty."

—**Edward R. Murrow,** *CBS News,* **March 13, 1956**

THE GATES
OF GAZA

CHAPTER 1

"THEY'RE HERE"

6:29 A.M., OCTOBER 7, 2023

AT FIRST, THERE WAS ONLY a whistle. A short, loud shriek coming through our bedroom window, indicating the descent of a mortar from the skies above our house.

I didn't wake up immediately. The noise, otherworldly but familiar, somehow blended into my dreams.

Miri, my wife, was quicker to realize the danger. "Amir, wake up, a mortar!" she said, elbowing me.

In an instant, I was wide awake, adrenaline pumping. We both leapt out of bed and, wearing only our underwear, frantically sprinted out of our bedroom and down the hall, toward the open doorway of our safe room.

One second, two seconds, three seconds. We reached the room and shut its heavy iron door.

No sooner were we enveloped in darkness than a large explosion rocked the building. We had made it just in time.

That first explosion was followed by a second, and a third, and then more and more. It was a barrage of mortars—a heavy, deadly rain falling all around us.

"Did you hear an alarm?" I asked Miri, whispering into the void of the blacked-out room.

"I just heard it about to fall, that's what woke me up," she replied. There had been no siren—nothing to warn us but the whistle.

We were beginning to catch our breath, but as we did, we felt the vibration of another explosion nearby and then another. I looked at my blue Torgoen watch and saw that it had now been five minutes since we ran to the room, and the bombardment hadn't let up.

For the first time since we'd sprung out of bed, I looked at my phone, which I'd brought with me from the bedroom. I wanted to know what was happening—in our community, in our broader region, in our country. Clearly, something unusual was going on.

We were surprised and disoriented, but not fearful, certainly not panicked—not yet. As residents of Nahal Oz, a small community of just over four hundred people located on the Israeli border with the Gaza Strip, we had experienced situations like this before. Nahal Oz, which was founded in the early 1950s, is less than a mile from the border fence, making it officially the closest Israeli community to the Palestinian coastal enclave that runs along the Mediterranean Sea.

Nahal Oz is surrounded by green fields and natural beauty, but in recent decades, it has become one of the most bombarded places in Israel, as terror groups from Gaza have launched thousands of rockets at it. When you live here, occasional rocket or mortar fire is something you grow used to. Unlike most of Israel, which is covered by the Iron Dome missile defense system, Nahal Oz doesn't enjoy such protection; it is so close to Gaza that the system's automatic interception hardware doesn't have enough time to calculate the route of an incoming mortar.

In every home in Nahal Oz, and in other Israeli communities along the Gaza border, there is a special room: an aboveground bunker built of thick concrete that is supposed to withstand a direct hit from mortars and even from certain types of stronger, heavier rockets. This room, the safe room that we ran into that morning, also has a metal plate that can cover the window and prevent shrapnel from flying in, as well as a shrapnel-proof door that serves the same purpose. This standard-issue safe room has a clear security function, but most families on the border use it for another purpose: this is where our children go to sleep at night.

Nahal Oz is so close to Gaza that when a mortar is launched toward the community, you have only seven seconds to take shelter. When you're inside the house, that means running to the safe room and shutting the door. For families with small children, the choice is clear: if there's a mortar attack during the night or early in the morning, it's much better for the parents to run to the children's room than the other way around.

So far, our two daughters seemed undisturbed by all of the drama. Galia, a blond-haired, blue-eyed three-and-a-half-year-old, was dozing peacefully, still hugging her favorite doll. Her little sister Carmel, one year and nine months old, had briefly raised her head and glanced at us with sleepy green eyes when we'd first dashed into her room but then found her pacifier and returned to her dreams.

This wasn't the first time they had experienced this kind of situation: their parents running into their bedroom as explosions mounted in the background. We never made a big deal out of it, so neither did they. It was part of our lives and theirs—a frenzied but familiar routine in Israel's borderlands.

As the mortars kept falling around us, we felt safe inside the room with its heavy door locked and its only window sealed with a solid metal plate. This was a simple square of iron, the exact same size as the concrete aperture, attached to the wall with hinges. We typically kept it pulled back from the window, since we wanted our girls to be able to enjoy sunlight and fresh air in their bedroom—but in times of need, it could be rolled shut to cover the window within seconds, as we had done upon entering the room this morning.

With the door closed and the plate covering the window, it was pitch-black inside the room. But we used our phones for light and now settled onto the floor to wait out the bombardment. As soon as we had done so, however, we read on our phones that Hamas, the Palestinian terror group controlling Gaza, had not just attacked our community but also fired mortars and rockets at dozens of other places across Israel. We hoped that the girls would continue to sleep peacefully in their beds for a little longer, but we knew that, for us, the night was over. We had to start packing.

———

I had first visited Nahal Oz nine years earlier, in August 2014. Israel and Hamas, which had taken control of Gaza seven years earlier, were fighting a long, bloody war that summer, and I had driven down to the Gaza border area from Tel Aviv, where I lived back then, to report on the hostilities. In my work as a journalist, I had previously covered wars in Syria, Ukraine, and Iraq's Kurdish autonomous region; it was discomfiting to witness the widespread devastation of a major conflict only an hour's drive from my home in central Israel.

Ahead of my arrival at Nahal Oz, a friend in the news industry had given me the phone number of a man named Itay Maoz. He was a farmer in his early fifties who had stayed in Nahal Oz that summer despite the heavy bombardment, and he was willing to give me a guided tour of the place. Most of the residents had been evacuated to other parts of Israel because of the war with Hamas, so when I met Itay—a bald man with a soft smile—and he began showing me around, I found myself walking through a ghost town.

Nahal Oz has agricultural lands that literally touch the Gaza border fence and, ever since the community's creation, taking care of those fields has been an abiding commitment for the people living here: the land is plowed all the way up to the edge, the last furrow lying just meters away from Gaza. These fields are usually a beautiful sight, but when we first went out to them that day, I saw them in a different light: they were completely destroyed after the Israeli military had turned them into a parking lot for tanks. An orchard had been crushed by the military vehicles, water irrigation systems were badly damaged, and the countryside was littered with waste ranging from shell casings to discarded food wrappers.

Itay told me he wasn't angry at the soldiers who had destroyed the fields. They didn't really have a choice, he explained. I was surprised to hear that he also felt no anger toward the people of Gaza, even in the midst of the fighting. "I'm obviously angry at Hamas for shooting at us, but I'm not angry at the average Palestinian living in Gaza," he explained. "They suffer from this war just as much as we do."

Personally, I shared Itay's sympathy for the civilians in Gaza—but I was an outside observer. Here, by contrast, was someone on the front lines who still showed empathy and compassion for the people on the literal "other side," even after weeks of continued bombardment of his community. I knew that Nahal Oz, like many communities along the Gaza border, had a strong left-wing, liberal political leaning and that residents of the border area are some of the strongest advocates of Israeli-Palestinian peace. Still, the calm tone in which Itay discussed his views of Gaza resonated with me and left a deep impression.

When I got back to Tel Aviv that evening, I couldn't stop talking about my visit to Nahal Oz and how struck I was by the beauty of the place and the strength of its people. I told Miri, then my girlfriend, how much my visit to the place had affected me, and I mentioned Nahal Oz in several media appearances in the last weeks of that summer's war.

But as the days went by, my work as a journalist led me in other directions. I forgot about Nahal Oz. And then, a terrible tragedy drew my attention back to this stretch of the Israeli-Gaza border.

In the days before Friday, August 22, 2014, families from Israeli communities near Gaza, like Nahal Oz, began returning home. They mistakenly thought, based on public messaging from the military, that the war was about to end. Rockets were still flying above, but diplomatic efforts led by Egypt seemed to be bearing fruit; people who had been away from their homes for two months could no longer resist the temptation to return.

But in the early afternoon hours of that Friday, a mortar landed inside Nahal Oz. It hit a parked car, and the debris flew into a nearby house, killing a four-year-old boy by the name of Daniel Tregerman. He had tried to reach his family's safe room when a siren sounded, but he'd stopped to help his younger sister. She and the rest of the family survived; Daniel did not.

Daniel Tregerman's death plunged the entire country into a state of grief. Israel lost dozens of soldiers in that war and also some civilians, but Daniel was the war's youngest Israeli victim. This beautiful boy, whose picture was published on the front page of every major Israeli newspaper, was also one of the war's last victims: four days after his death, a ceasefire was declared, and the war was truly over.

For Daniel's community, however, the pain and suffering ran even deeper—and didn't end when the fighting stopped.

Nahal Oz faced an existential crisis. Out of approximately one hundred families, more than fifteen had declared their intention to leave—most of them with young children. The main reason was Daniel's tragic death. "How can I explain to my child why his friend from daycare won't be able to come over to our house anymore?" one mother asked.

The founders of the community, who had come there as young Zionist idealists in the early 1950s and had since watched the place grow as they became grandparents, were afraid that their life's project would go to waste. "This was always a place full of children," one of them said in a television interview at the time. "We didn't come here to build a nursing home."

Nahal Oz is a kibbutz, a unique Israeli invention. The Hebrew word means "gathering," and it represents relatively small communities—usually between three hundred and one thousand people—who live a communal life based on socialist ideals. The first kibbutzim were created before Israel was established as a state; in fact, those who built the kibbutzim paved the way for the country's creation by building homes, cultivating agricultural lands, and drawing Israel's future borders with their tractors.

Originally, all the kibbutzim were strictly socialist—meaning that the community members all worked shoulder to shoulder, received similar salaries, and enjoyed identical living conditions. In the 1980s, however, most of Israel's 270 kibbutzim began a process of "privatization" as Israel itself shifted from its socialist origins toward a capitalist market economy. This was also true of Nahal Oz. In its early years, its members adhered to the principles of socialism. But by the time I visited it, the now-privatized kibbutz—while still a strong, unified community—was no longer a place where residents had to work in agriculture or where they couldn't own a car.

Now, in the fall of 2014, this specific kibbutz was fighting for its life. The departure of so many young families following the tragic death of Daniel Tregerman put the long-term survival of the community in doubt.

It was under these circumstances that I received a call one day from the national chairman of the Kibbutz Movement, an umbrella organization uniting Israel's kibbutzim. "I heard you speak about Nahal Oz during the war," he told me. "Just so you know, they need young people right now." Without explicitly saying so, he was suggesting that I consider moving to the community to strengthen it at its most difficult moment.

My first reaction was a firm no. My work as a journalist usually centers on Tel Aviv and Jerusalem; Miri had just begun her postuniversity career as a social worker. We were not yet married, but we had been together for several years and had plans for the future. Leaving our apartment in Tel Aviv for a kibbutz at the edge of the country sounded like a crazy idea. But over the next few days, my thoughts began to change from no to a curious *maybe?* And that's when I decided to share the idea with Miri.

Like the young idealists who founded the kibbutz, Miri and I were Zionists in the most basic sense. For us, two liberal, left-leaning Israeli Jews, Zionism meant only one thing: securing Israel's existence as a Jewish and democratic state. This had been the mainstream Zionist position for most of the twentieth century. While there have always been more nationalist and right-wing schools of Zionism, the kibbutz movement was mostly moderate in its view of the Israeli-Palestinian conflict, advocating for decades in favor of a compromise that would allow Jews and Arabs to share this land, with agreed-upon borders—borders that, of course, would have to be protected.

Miri and I both come from families that survived the Holocaust. My grandmother lost both of her parents at the age of thirteen, arriving in Israel as both a refugee and an orphan. Miri's grandparents survived the Nazi siege of Leningrad in 1941 and lived the rest of their lives, despite having successful careers, in fear of hunger. For us, the need to protect Israel's borders wasn't a reflection of modern politics around immigration, but simply a visceral understanding that without secure borders, the world's one and only Jewish country would be unsafe and the dark past of our people could perhaps repeat itself.

In Israel's early years, the country's leaders, such as then prime minister David Ben-Gurion, believed that civilian communities like Nahal Oz, located directly along the border, were a crucial part of the young nation's defense strategy. Military bases, the thinking went, could be easily relocated if the country's borders were redrawn, but civilian communities—with kindergartens, schools, clinics, and homes—were a more durable presence. This made them critical for Israel, a country surrounded by hostile neighbors—some of whom would have liked nothing more than to redraw the new Jewish state right out of existence.

Miri and I shared that view, although we believed that in the long run, the only way to ensure real security for Israel was to make peace with all

9

its neighbors—most importantly the Palestinian people, with whom our nation has been in conflict for decades and many of whom live, to this day, under an Israeli military occupation.

We both firmly believed that peace with the Palestinians would require ensuring that they had a state of their own, just like our Israel—a place where their own civilian communities, with their kindergartens, schools, clinics, and homes, could afford them a stable and enduring connection to the land that Israelis and Palestinians both cherish. Until there was a breakthrough on this front, however, communities like Nahal Oz had a vital role to play—and losing one in the aftermath of the war would mark a step backward, a step toward a less safe world for the Jewish people.

Yet a sense of patriotism wasn't the only thing that was causing me to warm to the idea of moving to Nahal Oz. Ever since we met, Miri had told me about her desire to leave the city one day and raise a family in a small community, ideally "a kibbutz surrounded by green fields, but not too far from Tel Aviv."

So, I asked her, how about moving to just such a kibbutz: a small community where everybody knows their neighbors, in a beautiful area only an hour away from the big city?

Miri liked the idea—but she wasn't sure that Nahal Oz was the right place for us. "There are something like twenty kibbutzim on the Gaza border," she told me. "Why should we move to the most dangerous one?" Still, she was intrigued enough to go see the place for herself.

On Friday, September 26—exactly a month after the end of the war— we took the one-hour drive from Tel Aviv to the border region. In the fields, tractors were already working to repair the damages caused by the tanks.

Inside the main gate of Nahal Oz, surrounded by a perimeter fence that looked sturdy but that, to our surprise, lacked any barbed wire or security cameras, we were greeted by Oshrit Sabag, an optimistic and energetic woman who was in charge of "demographic growth" at the kibbutz—basically, convincing new people to move in. She told us that several other families had also made inquiries about moving to Nahal Oz since the end of the war. "So we're not the only crazy people in this country?" I asked her. "It's the other way around," she replied with a smile.

"The crazy people are the ones living in Tel Aviv. Here you can find what everyone is looking for: community, peace of mind, space."

It didn't take us long to see exactly what she meant. During our visit, we glimpsed Nahal Oz at peace: a green haven with tall, leafy trees and abundant patches of long grass surrounding modest one-story houses. In all the gardens, flowers were blooming; the people we met were friendly and asked us where we had come from and what we were hoping to find there. By the time we left, Miri told me that she understood what had attracted me to the place.

Two months later, we moved to Nahal Oz. Our relocation happened to coincide with the Jewish holiday of Hanukkah. "A new couple has arrived in the kibbutz!" the community's Facebook page announced on the day we unpacked our belongings in our new home: a two-bedroom trailer surrounded by muddy soil and flanked by two tall trees. "Amir, 25, and Miri, 26, moved from Tel Aviv to Nahal Oz in search of a strong community, and because they believed this was the right place to come to after the events of the summer. . . . Happy Hanukkah, and welcome home!"

Indeed, Nahal Oz quickly felt like home for Miri and me. We made friends with other young couples who had moved from different parts of Israel, many of them for reasons similar to ours. Within a year and a half of our decision to move, the kibbutz had overcome the demographic loss it suffered after the war, and by the summer of 2016—when we held our wedding at the kibbutz pool, surrounded by four hundred guests—it seemed like Nahal Oz had turned a corner. The community was growing, even flourishing. New children were being born, new homes were being built. By 2018, there was a waiting list for new families wanting to join the kibbutz.

The trend of young families coming to Nahal Oz continued despite the fact that, once every few months, there was another round of fighting with Hamas in Gaza and we found ourselves under mortar fire. This didn't deter us from staying in the kibbutz, and didn't deter other families from joining. Those rounds of fighting usually lasted a week or two, and when they started, all the families temporarily relocated to other parts of the country. Some of our friends and neighbors compared it, jadedly, to going on vacation.

Unlike Miri and I, who chose to move to Nahal Oz, our girls Galia and Carmel—born in 2020 and 2022, respectively—simply knew it as their home, the place where they formed all of their first memories. They learned to walk there, as we walked with them to their daycare every morning, and then to run, when they hurried to buy popsicles at the kibbutz grocery store in the afternoon. They loved feeding the cows and getting kisses from the giant, gentle animals. We took them to see a field of white cotton right before it was picked and a field of purple cabbages when the vegetables first emerge from the ground. We were happy to raise them in Nahal Oz, despite the dangers of living on the border.

In the evening hours of October 6, 2023, we went with the girls to an important event: a dress rehearsal for the kibbutz's seventieth anniversary celebration, which was to take place the following night on the big lawn outside the pool. Galia and her kindergarten friends would dance on the main stage, in front of the entire community and hundreds of guests. A sense of excitement was in the air. We were proud to participate in this important milestone, marking seven decades since the founding of what had become, over the past few years, our community. We watched Galia dance on the stage and imagined her doing it the next evening before a warm, supportive crowd. It was wonderful.

The next morning, as we sheltered in the safe room, mortars falling around us, we assumed that this time would be like all the others. We had a procedure for these situations, and we were following it calmly as the explosions rumbled on and on. Whenever a round of violence breaks out, we quickly pack two small suitcases—clothes, diapers, toothbrushes, a few other personal items—and at the first moment of quiet, we bundle the kids into our car and leave the kibbutz, knowing that within ten days or so, a ceasefire will be announced and we'll be able to return home and get on with our lives.

While Miri chose clothes for the girls, I glanced at our neighborhood's text-messaging group. After spending several years in the kibbutz's "caravan neighborhood," in December 2022 we and most of our friends had moved to a new neighborhood at the northeastern edge of the community. Surrounded by trees and overlooking the fields, this neighborhood was made up of twelve large homes with high ceilings, thick windows, and wide porches. The construction was brand new and top quality. We loved living there and were very close with our neighbors in the eleven surrounding homes. Now, I sent a quick message to ask if everyone was OK.

"Did Israel assassinate some senior *mehabel* in Gaza overnight?" one of my neighbors asked, using the Hebrew word for terrorist. What else, she reasoned, could have caused this seemingly endless barrage of mortars and rockets—a stronger bombardment than any we'd experienced since moving to the kibbutz. Another neighbor joked that this was Hamas's response to the rehearsal the night before, which went on for many hours and probably irritated people in Gaza with all its noise.

"Well, I guess Galia won't be dancing tonight after all," I whispered to Miri, and we both laughed quietly so as not to wake the girls. "At least she got to enjoy the rehearsal."

At 6:45 A.M., one of the neighbors asked if anyone else had a problem with their electricity. As if on cue, we lost power, too. Everyone started writing that they were in the same situation. For the next few minutes, we exchanged messages about who had heard the incoming rocket alarm and who hadn't. "We didn't hear an alarm," I wrote at 6:58. "Miri just heard the whistle and we ran."

The text group remained quiet for a few minutes. Then Miri and I heard a chilling sound that made us exchange a frightened look: automatic gunfire.

At first, we heard it in the distance, from the fields. Still, it was unusual. In past rounds of fighting, our only concern had been to evade the mortars; we had never experienced a cross-border infiltration by Hamas. But that was exactly what this noise suggested. Moreover, while the mortars were continuing to fall around us, their pace was slowing now, which made me wonder: Is the bombardment ending because the people responsible for it are now entering our community?

I didn't have much time to indulge these questions. The gunfire was growing closer, sounding as if it was on the ring road surrounding the kibbutz—well within the perimeter fence of Nahal Oz. And then it was inside our neighborhood, right near the window of our house. We also heard shouting in Arabic and immediately understood what was going on.

Our worst nightmare was playing out: Israel's defensive line—the network of fences, cameras, and other security apparatuses that we had always believed would protect us from the army of terror on the other side of the border—had been breached. Hamas was coming for us.

At 7:10, one of our neighbors sent a message to the group: "Hamas has invaded the kibbutz." Another neighbor wrote: "There's gunfire in the neighborhood, they're here." A third replied: "Where's the army? How come nobody is coming?"

Inside our safe room, with the metal plate protecting the window, it was as dark as night and dead silent. Then, somewhere in the darkness, I heard our daughters stirring in their beds.

CHAPTER 2

PIONEERS

1953–1957

THE FIRST THING THEY SAW when they got off the bus was the yellow-ish, dusty soil. There were very few trees back then—no orchards, no gardens. There was also no border fence, but to their west, they could clearly see an Egyptian military post marking the international armistice line and, on a hill behind it, the first homes of Gaza City, at the time under the control of Egypt. They couldn't see the Mediterranean Sea, but when the wind blew from the west, it carried a salty scent, reminding them how close they were to the beaches of Gaza.

It was early October 1953, and a group of about sixty Israeli soldiers—nineteen-year-old men and women from different parts of the country—were standing on the site of what would become Nahal Oz. They were not the first arrivals, however: already there was a tiny military base, really just a handful of sheds scattered across a small plot of land. The base had been established in 1951 to protect the border and the Israeli communities that lay farther back from it, and now these teenagers had arrived on a strategic mission of their own: to turn that base into a civilian community, a new kibbutz.

The order had come straight from Moshe Dayan, Israel's most influential military general at the time. Dayan and David Ben-Gurion, Israel's first prime minister, shared the view that Israel's borders, and specifically the border with the Gaza Strip, needed more than military installations in order to be well and truly fortified. There had to be civilian life on the border—especially agriculture—before the region would be completely safe. A permanent population to detect and deter attacks and to convince the Arab world that the young, recently founded State of Israel was there to stay.

The military unit to which these young men and women belonged was called Nahal, an acronym representing the Hebrew words for "fighting pioneer youth." The sixty of them now climbing off the bus had joined the military at the age of eighteen, conscripted like most Jewish citizens, and they had received basic combat training. But then, instead of being sent to an army or air force base, they received their real mission: to start a new kibbutz. The chosen name, Nahal Oz, was a combination of the unit's name and the Hebrew word for strength. In Dayan's view, this new community would be the front line of the front line: a place so close to the border that the very fact of its presence would help protect all the communities behind it.

One of the soldiers piling off the bus was a nineteen-year-old named Yechiel Chlenov who had come from Tel Aviv. He was born before the State of Israel's founding, in what was then British Mandatory Palestine, to a family that was considered Zionist royalty: he'd been named after a grandfather who was an early leader of the Zionist movement, a grandfather whose name also graced streets all over the country. But that august legacy was rarely discussed at home. Yechiel was expected to find his own way to contribute to the newly established State of Israel, not to rest on the laurels of previous generations. This is what had brought him to Nahal Oz.

Yechiel had enlisted in the Nahal unit as part of a "seed group" of teenagers designated to go and live in the Negev, the vast desert area encompassing most of southern Israel. The soldiers knew from the start that their mission was to create a new kibbutz. They were excited about it and didn't give much thought to the dangers of life on the border. "We were young, had no kids, we just didn't think about the security risks," Yechiel recalled decades later.

When these unusual reinforcements arrived in the fall of 1953, the soldiers who had previously manned the small military post left for other missions and the nineteen-year-olds took over. The physical conditions were rough: they turned several sheds into their living quarters, sleeping four to a room. A larger shed was turned into the communal dining room, and two other sheds served as a clinic and a social club—which contained books, newspapers, and board games. "We barely had any time to enjoy it," Yechiel said. "We were too busy."

The toilets were located in a separate shed, as were the communal showers: one for the men, one for the women. When the winter rains arrived, the dusty soil turned to mud. The soldiers worked every day from dawn to dusk and at night had guard duty, which everyone had to perform, seven people at a time: four would sit in guard towers on the edges of the kibbutz, two others patrolled, and one provided support to the others. In Yechiel's words, "There was one shift that only the girls received, which was to fry potatoes in the kitchen during the night and deliver them to those on guard duty. When you got those fries in the middle of the night, still warm, it was the best thing in the world."

Their daily meals weren't as enjoyable. In the morning, it was bread bought from a bakery in the closest town, Netivot, located fifteen to twenty minutes away; vegetables from their own community garden, which they had planted in the northeastern corner of the kibbutz; and one kind of cheese. On certain days there was also half an egg per person—a ratio that the residents of Nahal Oz had to endure until they had installed their own chicken coop and could indulge in scrambled eggs. Lunch was mostly carbs—potatoes, rice—with the occasional protein of meat or fish. In the evening, there was a repeat of the morning meal, with the addition of tahini, a spread made of crushed sesame seeds and lemon. Dessert was mostly fruits or sometimes a cake baked in the kibbutz's small kitchen.

A few weeks after they took over, the teenagers held a ceremony to mark the founding of the new kibbutz. Dignitaries from the government and high-ranking military officers came, as did the soldiers' parents, who could see for the first time what their children had signed up for. Rachel Levi, one of the founders, remarked decades later that their parents "were shocked" by the living conditions. They wanted to give their children better food and clothes—but this was forbidden in a kibbutz, where everyone had to be equal. Instead, the parents grouped together and thought of ways they could collectively improve the situation.

One of the parents' first decisions was to give "the kids," as they called their frontier soldiers, some cultural life. The shed serving as a social club was soon upgraded with the arrival of a black piano, purchased collectively by the parents. Bringing it in was a challenge: there was no paved road to the kibbutz at the time, only a gravel path that met the closest road two miles to the east. The piano was driven to that point on a small truck and then transported the rest of the way on a tractor. In the evenings, after dinner and a quick shower, those who weren't on guard duty would gather around the instrument to play and sing together.

The teenagers were living the Zionist dream, but it came with a price. Only a month after their arrival, Nahal Oz lost its first member when Ya'akov "Tommy" Tuchman was shot to death by Egyptian soldiers while patrolling the border.

At the time, the demarcation line between Israel and Gaza was nothing more than a ditch dug along the armistice line that Israel and Egypt had agreed on in 1949 at the end of Israel's War of Independence.

During that war, which had broken out after the British decided to end their thirty-years-long colonial adventure in Palestine, the Israeli military fought simultaneously against the Palestinians—the native Arab population that lived in British Mandatory Palestine on the eve of the war—and the armies of several adjoining Arab states, including the Egyptian military. The result was an Israeli victory, which led to the establishment of temporary borders between Israel and neighboring Arab countries, including the border between Israel and Egyptian-controlled Gaza.

Any healthy person could easily hop over this border, and indeed, hundreds of Palestinians from Gaza tried to cross it on a daily basis, some of them in an attempt to reach homes or lands they had lost in the war, others in an attempt to carry out attacks against Israel. The responsibility to patrol "their" stretch of the border, directly outside the kibbutz, fell on the young members of Nahal Oz. Tommy, just twenty years old, had died while doing just this. The Egyptian soldiers who shot him managed to flee the scene before any responders arrived from the Israeli side.

Exchanges of fire like this weren't a rare occurrence along the border, which was still just a nonbinding armistice line regularly crisscrossed by bullets and raiding parties. But for the young people of Nahal Oz, the personal loss was shocking—and brought home just how dangerous the mission was that they had chosen for themselves. Still, despite pleas from some of their parents, all of the surviving members of the kibbutz stayed. "We had responsibility—not just toward the state, but toward each other," Yechiel recalled. "You couldn't just get up and leave your friends behind."

Ali Montar Hill is situated to the east of Salah al-Din Street—the most important north-to-south road inside the Gaza Strip. From the top of this hill, Nahal Oz is laid out in front of you like a detailed map. In the early 1950s, an Egyptian military base on this hill collected intelligence on a daily basis about the events on the other side of the border. The Egyptian soldiers documented the first sheds being placed in the fields to create the temporary Israeli military base; they witnessed the arrival of the young group of soldiers who turned it into a kibbutz; they saw the construction of new homes and the paving of a new road connecting the community to the rest of Israel. They watched and reported.

The Gaza Strip, which includes Gaza City and several smaller cities, towns, and villages nearby, was a place of pain and misery at the time, home to approximately three hundred thousand people, spread out from Gaza City in the north to Rafah in the south. It was an arbitrarily created region, the result of historical negotiations between two empires—and the capricious treatment extended to its inhabitants.

In 1906, the British and Ottoman Empires had decided to draw a straight line from Rafah to Taba, a city some 130 miles southeast, on the other side of the Sinai Peninsula. The two great powers agreed that this line would mark the border between what was then British-controlled Egypt and Ottoman Palestine. The Ottomans turned Gaza City, one of the largest cities on the Palestinian coast, into the de facto capital of a new region, eponymously called "Gaza." Decades later, this region would become the basis for the "Strip" that is nestled today between Israel and Egypt.

A decade after the British-Ottoman border agreement, the two empires collided in World War I, and the British military conquered Ottoman Palestine and added it to its trove of colonial territories. Its new possessions included Gaza City and the region around it. But although the Crown now controlled both sides of the former British-Ottoman border, the city of Rafah, approximately eighteen miles south of Gaza, remained a border town, separating the British territory of Palestine from Egypt.

The area around Gaza City was one of the last in British-controlled Palestine to experience the establishment of new Zionist communities during the three decades of British rule. One such community, a small kibbutz called Be'erot Yitzhak ("The wells of Isaac") was founded in 1943, on almost exactly the same parcel of land that later became Nahal Oz. This area, immediately to the east of Gaza City, was not home to any Palestinian communities at the time, although Bedouin tribes living farther east would often pass through there on their way to Gaza. Maps documenting the Palestinian presence in the area in the 1940s show a small Palestinian village located about four miles to the south of present-day Nahal Oz, and another one about two and half miles to the east of it, near where the Israeli communities of Be'eri and Shokeda, respectively, now stand.

In 1947, with the British finally heading for the exits after decades of fighting between Jews and Palestinians over the land that had hitherto been encompassed by British Mandatory Palestine, the UN offered a plan to divide it into two separate countries, one for the Jews and one for the Palestinians. The plan, had it been implemented, would have left the entire area around Gaza as part of the future Palestinian state, with the scattered Jewish kibbutzim in this area given the option of living as a minority population in a new state of Palestine or relocating to the new Jewish state, Israel, whose allotted territory lay to the north.

But while David Ben-Gurion, the leader of the Zionist movement at the time, accepted the plan, the Palestinian and wider Arab leadership rejected it for a variety of reasons. Some Arab leaders opposed the idea of a Jewish state in Palestine outright, while others had reservations about the specific borders of the partition plan, which left Israel with 55 percent of the land, despite the fact that, at the time, Jews comprised less than half of the population of British Mandatory Palestine. While Zionist leaders viewed the plan's allotment of land to Israel as a vital step toward securing a safe haven for the Jewish survivors of the Holocaust, which had ended only three years earlier, Palestinian leaders decried the plan as favoring the needs of potential Jewish immigrants over those of the area's native Palestinian population.

By the end of 1947, a full-blown war had broken out between the Zionists and the Palestinians; when Ben-Gurion announced in 1948 the official formation of the State of Israel, the armies of neighboring Arab countries joined the war, including those of Egypt, which was still technically occupied by Britain but which had gained a degree of autonomy in the early 1920s. Things looked desperate for the Zionist project. But despite Israel's small population—the new country was home to only six hundred thousand people at the time—the fighting ended in a decisive Israeli victory.

The war changed Gaza completely. As Israeli forces advanced south along the coastline and then into the Negev desert, they conquered Palestinian cities, towns, and villages that were home to hundreds of thousands of people. Many of these Palestinians fled to the Gaza region—some expelled by force, others leaving out of fear for their lives as the Israeli military advanced toward their communities. By the end of the war, in January 1949, the population of the Gaza region had more than tripled; home to fewer than one hundred thousand people on the eve of the war, the area contained approximately three hundred thousand by the end of the fighting. The majority of the people living there were now refugees. Among them were the residents of the two small villages located to the south and to the east of Nahal Oz.

In early January 1949, Israeli and Egyptian officers met to negotiate a new border between the two countries, reflecting the results of the war on the ground. This wasn't going to be a mutually accepted border leading to the announcement of a peace agreement but rather a temporary line of separation that would put an official end to the war—and which would be based on the locations of both countries' militaries on the last day of the fighting.

One thing was clear even before they began their discussions: Gaza City and its immediate surroundings—land that barely any Israeli soldier had set foot on during the war—would become part of a new, Egyptian-controlled "strip" along the Mediterranean. The northern edge of this strip included the villages of Beit Lahia and Beit Hanoun. To the south, it ran all the way to Rafah and the old British-Ottoman border. The sea served as a natural border in the west.

After two months of negotiations between Israel and Egypt, an eastern border was also agreed upon, giving the new "Gaza Strip" its final territorial dimensions: approximately twenty-four miles from north to south and seven miles from the sea to its easternmost point. Inside the Gaza Strip, an Egyptian military governor was given absolute authority, while the newly created UN agency for Palestinian refugees (United Nations Relief and Works Agency for Palestinian Refugees in the Near East) was tasked with running schools, clinics, and welfare services for the new residents. The task it faced was monumental: the unemployment rate in the new Strip was spiraling out of control.

Gaza City, the de facto capital of this new territory, became one of the most densely populated cities in the Middle East following the war. It was also one of the region's oldest, continuously inhabited cities, with the first signs of human life in the area dating back at least five thousand years. In the Hebrew Bible, it is mostly mentioned as an important city under the control of the Philistines, an ancient people whose presence in the region caused the Greeks to come up with the name "Palestine." The legendary Israeli ruler King David fought the Philistines in Gaza and eventually took the city. Later, it also fell to the Egyptians and the Persians. The most famous Christian saint affiliated with the city is Hilarion, who was born there in A.D. 291 and whose remains are still buried to the south of the city. By the Middle Ages, however, Gaza had become an overwhelmingly Arab-Muslim city, which it remains today.

Following the 1948 war, Gaza became something different: a city of refugees. Most of them came from areas that were only a short drive away from the new Gaza Strip, some even within walking distance. As French historian Jean-Pierre Filiu writes, "Their grave difficulty of overcoming the trauma of dispossession was exacerbated by the artificial nature of the lines of demarcation when the former dwellings and family lands of the refugees were so close at hand." Every day, hundreds of Palestinian refugees would try to cross the border into what was now Israel, looking to return to their old homes or cultivate what used to be their lands. Others tried to steal cows, sheep, and donkeys from the Israeli farmers now living there. They were turned away by Israeli soldiers, often with violence.

Among those attempting to cross the new border were also the *fed-ayeen*, armed men carrying guns, hand grenades, and other weapons and whose intentions weren't as noble: they came in looking to kill Israeli soldiers or citizens in the frontier communities. They were motivated partly by an ideological opposition to Israel—a country whose very existence they viewed as being predicated on the banishment of the Palestinian people from the new nation's land—and partly by a wish for revenge over the loss that their cause had suffered in the 1948 war. Some of them hoped to push back the new Israeli communities and, by doing so, open up an opportunity to win back some of the lands that had been lost with Israel's creation.

The newly created Israel-Gaza border, in short, knew very few days of peace. And yet in the coming years, new Israeli communities sprang up along it, and thousands of people moved to what today is often called the Gaza Envelope—the region of Israel that is within firing range of Gaza. As they did, the Israeli military also built up its presence along the border—and also began crossing it more often. Dayan tasked a young Israeli paratrooper by the name of Ariel Sharon with creating a special unit that could strike inside Gaza in order to deter Palestinian militants from attacking Israel. As Filiu describes the new reality, "a cycle of incursions and reprisals now got underway across the armistice line," costing hundreds of lives on both sides.

Tami Halevi arrived at Nahal Oz in the summer of 1955 along with sixteen other nineteen-year-old female soldiers. A bus dropped them off at the closest junction, and then a tractor towing a cart came to pick them up. The girls were dressed in their finest clothes, but the cart was covered in dust and mud. When they reached their new home, they were given ten minutes to put their few personal belongings in their rooms before gathering in the kibbutz dining hall. A modest dinner awaited them: bread, cheese, and salad. Then, each new arrival was assigned a work task for the next morning—and that was it. "Quite a welcome," Tami later recalled.

Tami had grown up in Nahariya, a seaside town in northern Israel that at the time was home to many wealthy Jews who had emigrated from

Germany. Her mother was one of the first practicing female doctors in British Mandatory Palestine, and Tami grew up just down the street from two of the richest families in the region, owners of large factories there. Still, her parents raised Tami to be tough: Nahariya was bombarded and besieged by Arab forces during the 1948 war, and as a teenager, she was recruited to salvage supplies that were dropped into the sea by Israeli planes.

She arrived at Nahal Oz as part of a second "seed group" that had been organized to populate the new kibbutz. The first group, that of Yechiel and his friends, were twenty-one-year-old veterans by then, and they looked to Tami like the most confident, knowledgeable people in the world. Like the first group from 1953, hers was also a mixture of young men and women, all of them soldiers on a mission to strengthen the new frontier kibbutz. But compared to their predecessors, they felt painfully green.

A lot had changed at Nahal Oz since its founding: several homes had been built, new agricultural equipment had been purchased, and a small dairy farm was under construction. "We arrived at an existing kibbutz," she noted—unlike the previous group, which had to start everything from scratch. On the night of their arrival, a baby was born in Nahal Oz—the third since 1953.

Getting married was a priority for many of the kibbutz members. They were young, fit, and tanned from long hours of work in the sun; perhaps more significantly, they were completely isolated from the rest of the world. There was one telephone in the entire community, used for urgent communications with the military, and no regular bus services. Mail usually arrived once a week. It didn't take long for couples to start forming under these conditions.

In the fields of Nahal Oz lay the remains of Be'erot Yitzhak, the earlier kibbutz that had been formed in 1943 but that was later destroyed by the Egyptian military during the 1948 war. The surviving residents of that community had decided to rebuild it in central Israel, leaving only a water tower and a few half-standing homes as memorials to their ambitions. Young couples from Nahal Oz turned these ruins into a sort of lover's lane; Yechiel remembered one time when a few of the men went to conduct a shooting training exercise next to the deserted buildings, only to realize they had interrupted a new couple who'd been making out there.

For those living in kibbutzim like Nahal Oz, one incentive for getting married, even at the early age of twenty-one, was housing: married couples received their own rooms, and would be the first to move into "real" homes when those were constructed. But there were new challenges when newborns became part of the community: a daycare and kindergarten had to be built, and more important, so did a "children's home" where the little ones went to sleep every night. Up until the 1970s, children in most kibbutzim did not sleep in the same room as their parents but rather in a joint space with their peers, under the supervision of an adult caretaker.

Roi Rutberg and Amira Glickson were one of the first couples in Nahal Oz to get married and have a baby—a son. Roi was the community's security chief, responsible for all communications with the military. In case of an emergency in or around the kibbutz, he was the first responder. He had a horse on which he patrolled the fields each morning. Amira later described him as a "Greek idol," strong and tanned, often walking around without a shirt and with a comb tucked in the back pocket of his jeans.

The Egyptians overlooking the kibbutz from Ali Montar Hill knew Roi Rutberg by name. They followed his daily routines and often saw him driving away Palestinians who tried to cross the border into the fields. Roi often went about this alone, just one man on his horse. To his neighbors and friends in Nahal Oz, he was a living hero. To the Egyptian soldiers on the other side, he was a symbol—and, soon, a target.

April 29, 1956, was supposed to be a day of celebration at Nahal Oz. Four weddings were planned that day, part of a local tradition that began two years earlier whereby single weddings were dispensed with in favor of one big joyous event. Hundreds of guests were expected to arrive by bus from all over Israel. One of the couples sent an invitation to Moshe Dayan and was delighted to receive a letter from his office stating that the general—the man who had first conceived of Kibbutz Nahal Oz—would be honored to attend.

Preparations got underway in the early morning hours. Kibbutz members rehearsed a group dance while the couples tried on their wedding outfits. But soon, word began to spread that something terrible had happened. Tami Halevi recalled hearing whispers: "something about Roi's horse coming back without him." Within minutes, all of the festivities were canceled.

Over the next few hours, the details slowly emerged: Roi had gone out that morning to patrol the fields after learning that a group of Palestinians had crossed the border. The intruders were all civilians, but armed men were waiting for him on the other side of the ditch. They shot him to death and then dashed across the border and abducted his body, mutilating it along the way back to Gaza. The kibbutz called the military, which in turn contacted UN peacekeepers. By the early afternoon, the disfigured body had been returned. Instead of four weddings, Nahal Oz now had to plan a funeral.

The buses with the guests were all turned back at the kibbutz entrance and only the immediate relatives of the four couples were allowed to enter, shocked to learn of what had happened.

Dayan, however, did not cancel his visit. Decades later, Tami Halevi remembered the general's solemn arrival. "He gathered us together and said, 'There will be no party today, but don't cancel the religious ceremony. These couples need to get married.'" And so, while the entire community was grieving Roi's death, the four couples got dressed and drove with their families to a nearby town, where a rabbi quickly officiated their marriages. Dayan said farewell, but promised to return the next day for the funeral.

When Tommy Tuchman had died three years earlier, his parents asked to bury him close to them, in central Israel. But it was different with Roi. His family decided that he would be buried in the fields that he had died protecting. That meant an area near the kibbutz had to be designated as a cemetery. The community chose a small hill overlooking Gaza.

Dayan arrived for the funeral, as did hundreds of people from all over Israel. As Roi was laid to rest, the general read a speech he had written overnight. Its title, "The Gates of Gaza," was taken from the biblical story of Samson, the Israelite warrior who was strong enough to lift the heavy gates of the ancient Philistine city of Gaza and carry them on his shoulders after the Philistines living there, foresworn enemies of ancient Israel, had tried to trap him inside the city.

"Early yesterday morning, Roi was murdered," Dayan began. "The quiet of the spring morning dazzled him, and he did not see those waiting in ambush at the edge of the furrow."

Then came the most controversial part of the eulogy: "Let us not cast the blame on the murderers," Dayan told the crowd. "Why should we question their burning hatred for us? For eight years, they have been sitting in the refugee camps in Gaza, and before their eyes, we have been transforming the lands and the villages, where they and their fathers dwelt, into our estate."

Dayan's words represented a rare recognition by an Israeli leader of the Palestinian *Nakba*, or "catastrophe"—the mass displacement of civilians during the 1948 Arab-Israeli War, when approximately seven hundred thousand Palestinians had become refugees. Dayan spoke openly about their loss and trauma and the bitter frustration with which they viewed from their refugee camps the creation of new communities like Nahal Oz.

This recognition of Palestinian suffering, however, did not turn the speech into an appeal for peace. Quite the opposite: Dayan offered a pessimistic view of the future awaiting Nahal Oz:

It is not among the Arabs in Gaza, but in our own midst that we must seek Roi's blood. How did we shut our eyes and refuse to look squarely at our fate and see, in all its brutality, the destiny of our generation? Have we forgotten that this group of young people dwelling at Nahal Oz is bearing the heavy gates of Gaza on its shoulders?

Beyond the furrow of the border, a sea of hatred and desire for revenge is swelling, awaiting the day when serenity will dull our path. . . . This is the fate of our generation. This is our life's choice: to be prepared and armed, strong and determined, lest the sword be stricken from our fist and our lives cut down.

The young Roi who left Tel Aviv to build his home at the gates of Gaza, to be a wall for us, was blinded by the light in his heart and he did not see the flash of the sword. The yearning for peace deafened his ears and he did not hear the voice of murder waiting in ambush. The gates of Gaza weighed too heavily on his shoulders, and overcame him.

The moment Dayan finished speaking, his speech passed into legend. It was printed by several newspapers the following day, and the general was asked to read it aloud on national radio. Pundits praised it as historic and powerful, while teachers in schools across the country encouraged their students to read it. The broadcast version, however, omitted the first, explosive paragraph recognizing the Nakba and the tragedy of the Palestinian refugees. It has been rumored that Ben-Gurion himself asked Dayan to cut those sentences from the radio version.

In Nahal Oz, not everyone liked the speech. Some of the young kibbutzniks found it too dark. They wanted to believe that one day, maybe in the distant future, there would be peace between their community and the communities in Gaza.

Tami's boyfriend, Tzvika, a close friend of Roi's, replaced him as the kibbutz security coordinator. The couple got married several months later. This time, Dayan was not invited.

———

In October of that year, Israel started another war with Egypt, invading its southern neighbor's territory in coordination with France and the United Kingdom but against the wishes of the United States. The Brits and the French wanted to win control over the Suez Canal, one of the most important shipping corridors in the world, and wrest it away from Egypt. Israel, meanwhile, wanted to enlarge its territory and put an end to the cross-border attacks from Gaza, both by Egyptian soldiers and Palestinian militants.

The Suez War was short and decisive: by mid-November 1956, the Gaza Strip and Sinai Peninsula were both under Israeli occupation. Ben-Gurion declared in the Israeli parliament the formation of "the Third Kingdom of Israel." The UN, meanwhile, was accusing Israel of killing hundreds of civilians in different parts of the Strip and of committing a "massacre" in the southern city of Rafah.

David Ben-Gurion, first prime minister of the State of Israel (seated at the right-hand corner on a chair), is seen here conversing with the young residents of Nahal Oz; General Moshe Dayan (with an eyepatch on his left eye) is located in the middle of the image, seated among the members of the kibbutz—including Yechiel Chlenov, seated in the center of the group, with blond hair and glasses.

For the growing community of Nahal Oz, the war came as a surprise—and, at least for some, as an opportunity. "A few men from the kibbutz went to Gaza and brought back things they took from homes there," Tami Halevi recalled. "Most of us didn't go. The situation was dangerous; it was still a war zone." The looting made headlines in the Israeli and international media, drawing strong criticism against the kibbutzniks who participated in it. It also created an internal crisis for the community: at least two of the founding members left the kibbutz in protest and never returned.

In March 1957, Ben-Gurion and Dayan arrived together at Nahal Oz. They wanted to update the young kibbutzniks holding the frontier of their upcoming decision to accede to US demands and hand Gaza back to Egypt. It was an incredible scene: the prime minister himself arriving at a remote kibbutz, in which the oldest resident was only twenty-four years old, to share his geostrategic rationale for withdrawing from Gaza. He later also wrote a four-page letter to the community, in which he explained how much Israel needed US support, and also took credit for securing an important diplomatic achievement related to freedom of navigation in international waters for Israel-bound vessels, as part of his compromise with President Eisenhower. Most of the community, despite some reservations, accepted his explanation.

Ben-Gurion also used the occasion to scold the Nahal Oz community for the looting from Gaza. "He told us that he loved us, but if we didn't give back everything we took from Gaza, he would order the Israeli military to surround us and lay siege to the kibbutz," Yechiel Chlenov recalled. They told him that everything had already been returned a few days after the war, which wasn't exactly true: a rare drilling machine remained in the kibbutz, after the the majority of the residents insisted on keeping it.

Ben-Gurion claimed that he wasn't worried about the security repercussions of the withdrawal from the Gaza Strip. The Egyptian government, he said, had learned its lesson after the war and was likely to use brutal violence to clamp down on the Palestinian militants in Gaza whose attacks on Israel were one of the reasons the country had joined the offensive against Egypt. History proved him right: the next decade, from 1957 to 1967, was the quietest ever along the Israel-Gaza border, with no casualties in Nahal Oz.

CHAPTER 3

"THE MILITARY IS AWARE"

OCTOBER 7, 2023

WE DIDN'T REALIZE JUST HOW serious our predicament was until we heard shots being fired into our house. Everything that had happened up to that point—that heavy barrage of mortars, the panicked messages from our neighbors, even the sound of approaching gunfire—was unusual and alarming, but it hadn't caused us to fear for our lives. That changed in an instant when we heard the first bullets smashing through our living room window.

Miri and I were familiar with the sound of gunfire. Like the vast majority of Israel's Jewish citizens, we had both served in the military, something we were required by law to do at age eighteen. We had no combat experience—I served in a technological intelligence unit, and Miri taught immigrant soldiers about Jewish culture as part of the education corps—but we were required to do basic training, which included shooting an M16 assault rifle. During our years in Nahal Oz, there were, from time to time, military exercises in the region that included live fire. But we didn't own firearms and it had been years since we had discharged one ourselves. We certainly had never heard a bullet cracking through a window and hitting a wall inside a sealed house—let alone *our* house. But that's exactly what we were now hearing.

The sound was intense, almost deafening. There was one bullet, and then another. Two seconds of silence—and then three other bullets followed. We heard glass shattering, but we had no way of knowing how much of it had broken, and exactly which window of our house had been hit. From the safe room, unable to see anything, we couldn't even tell if the noise was an indication that the terrorists were now inside the house or if they were still outside, shooting in.

The shouting was also much closer now: no longer coming from a remote part of the neighborhood, but rather from a very short distance away. One of the terrorists, probably a midlevel Hamas field commander, was standing right outside our window and shouting orders to the others. I had learned some Arabic during my military service almost two decades earlier, and I had retained enough to understand: he was instructing them to search for ways to get into one of the houses—presumably ours. As he did, explosions continued reverberating through our neighborhood, signaling that Hamas was keeping up its mortar attacks, albeit at a slower pace than during the opening barrage, despite the fact that its fighters were now inside the kibbutz. It was strange of our attackers to subject themselves to this sort of friendly fire, but we had no time to ponder the decision; the bottom line of it all was that we, and our two daughters, were now in grave danger not from the mortars but rather from the men on the ground.

Our home in the new neighborhood of the kibbutz, like all the others there, was built out of relatively strong materials. The walls were all a mixture of cement and plaster; the windows were thick and designed to block shrapnel in case a rocket fell near them; the interior blinds were the electric kind and, in our case, had been completely rolled down before we had gone to bed the night before. The home's two doors—one at the front, the other at the back—were both locked. Still, we had no illusions about our situation: if these armed terrorists tried hard enough, they'd probably find a way to get in.

The real question was whether they'd be able to break into the safe room. Like others on the kibbutz, ours had a door handle that was, theoretically, lockable. But these rooms were built with one kind of threat in mind: rockets and mortars. The idea behind the safe rooms is that if the entire family gets into the room, shuts the door, and closes the metal plate covering the window, they will be safe from shrapnel even if the home suffers a direct hit. The door and metal plate are supposed to block even the smallest pieces of shrapnel.

But a ground invasion by Hamas terrorists? The metal plate on the window was probably strong enough to block their bullets, but would the safe room door stand up to that kind of assault? We had no way of knowing.

Miri and I were separately but simultaneously gripped by a cold realization: we were in mortal and immediate danger. Without knowing whether the terrorists were inside the house or right outside of it, we clearly understood that any noise we made would increase their determination to break into the safe room and find us. We also realized that if they were right outside the window, as it sounded, then the terrorists had already seen the baby stroller standing on our front porch—yet they were continuing their assault on our home, regardless. In other words, we had to assume that nothing would stop them from murdering all four of us if they had the opportunity. The only other option—that they'd try to kidnap us and drag us back with them into Gaza—was just as terrifying.

And so, our first and most urgent mission was to calm the girls. They were both awake now, as we could hear from the rustling of their bedsheets. Carmel was the first one to sit up in the dark and ask, with a sleepy smile that I could hear in her little voice, if she could go out and play. Galia yawned and said that today was Saturday and her daycare was closed. The gunshots had clearly woken them up, but they didn't ask about the loud noises at first. They couldn't see our faces in the dark or tell how worried we were.

Miri and I exchanged two quick sentences in English, to avoid having the children understand us. We both agreed that we had to stay as composed and calm as we could, no matter what happened. We couldn't afford one of our daughters, not to mention both, starting to cry. But could we really expect two young children, one just a toddler, to remain silent after waking up to such a situation?

Saturday morning was usually their favorite time of the week. Galia, our firstborn, liked to sleep late, while her younger sister Carmel would get up around 7:00 A.M. and ask me to take her for a walk around the kibbutz. Galia would use that opportunity to run to our bed and cuddle with Miri for another hour. How could we tell them that this morning there would be none of that and also no breakfast, no bathroom, and no television? How do you present such a situation to a pair of just-awoken, highly energetic toddlers without making them cry?

Miri started with a very simple explanation. "Girls, I'm really sorry," she said in a soft, quiet voice. "There are loud noises outside, and it's too dangerous to leave the room. So we have to stay here and be very, very quiet." She repeated the last part twice. "But if you want, you can continue sleeping a little longer," she added. To our astonishment, that's what they initially chose to do.

Galia always enjoyed sleeping late, so that was less of a surprise. Her younger sister was the one I was really worried about. We had dubbed her "the Energizer Bunny" because of her seemingly inexhaustible energy. The idea of keeping her calm, let alone silent, seemed ludicrous.

But Miri's words, and especially the tone of her voice, had a soothing effect on both of our daughters. The darkness in the room probably also helped. And so, while the gunfire and the shouting continued, our little girls put their heads on their pillows and closed their eyes again.

———————

When we had moved to Nahal Oz in late 2014, the scariest word in the world for us was "tunnel." In the early 2000s, Hamas had begun an ambitious project of digging passageways deep underground in different parts of the Gaza Strip and using them to carry out attacks against Israel. At first, in the years when Israel still controlled the territory, these attacks were aimed at Israeli military positions inside the Gaza Strip. Usually, the method involved filling one end of a tunnel with explosives and then blowing them up from the other end. The Israel Defense Forces (IDF), our nation's military, struggled to find a solution to this devastating tactic, and Israeli soldiers in Gaza constantly worried about an explosion erupting directly beneath their feet.

Later, in 2006, a cross-border tunnel was used to abduct an Israeli soldier from a position near the border and take him into Gaza. That tactic was used by Hamas on a massive scale during the 2014 war, as more than thirty tunnels were dug into Israeli territory. Most were detected by Israeli intelligence, but several were used for attacks on Israeli military bases, costing the lives of more than ten IDF soldiers.

The Palestinians who dug these tunnels didn't invent anything new: the use of tunnels has long been a preferred military strategy of fighters in the region due to the soft, loose subsoil, which is easy to dig into. When Alexander the Great tried to conquer Gaza City in the year 332 B.C.E., he expressed frustration with the local population's smart use of tunnels to break his siege and conduct counterattacks on his soldiers. It took him more than one hundred days to finally take control.

Hamas's tunnels were much more sophisticated, of course: they were dug with modern construction tools and featured electricity (often powered by generators), ventilation systems, and water lines. Some of the tunnels were wide enough to allow the passage of vehicles through them. Yet despite all of this, they were also very hard for the Israeli army to detect from aboveground. In this way, Hamas managed to penetrate the border right under Israel's nose.

The border itself had changed a lot over the years: the initial ditch from the 1950s had turned into a fence and later an electric fence and a high wall, both monitored by smart cameras and defended by remotely operated machine guns. But even after Israel thought it had secured the border aboveground, the underground tunnels remained a serious threat.

The Israeli military admitted that it wouldn't be able to discover each and every tunnel dug by Hamas, and for that reason, Nahal Oz and neighboring kibbutzim received an important security boost: in every community, a small group of highly trained combat soldiers was placed as a "guarding force" against a potential Hamas infiltration. For these soldiers, the assignment was a dream come true. Instead of conducting night raids in Palestinian towns or standing guard along the Lebanese border in an isolated watchtower, they were hosted generously by the kibbutz, enjoying delicious food, laundry services, and access to the community's swimming pool. For us, their presence was what allowed us to sleep at night and not worry about the digging noises and underground explosions, which we heard clearly from time to time.

But we knew that these soldiers were only part of the solution to the threat posed by Hamas. The government had also decided to invest billions of dollars in a different kind of defensive measure: an underground wall between Israel and Gaza that went as deep as 160 feet and was supposed to put an end, once and for all, to the tunnel threat.

The underground wall was completed in 2021 and led to major changes in Israel's military deployment along the border. Believing that the tunnels were no longer a threat and that the border—with its underground wall, electronic fence, and technological equipment—was practically impenetrable, the government and army gradually removed the soldiers from our area and sent them on other missions. On the morning of October 7, 2023, there were approximately twenty-five Israeli combat battalions in the West Bank and under four—fewer than six hundred soldiers—along the border with Gaza.

We, the residents of the Gaza border region, trusted the government and the military's assessment, tacitly demonstrated by the removal of troops from the border, that due to the completion of the underground wall, there was no chance we would wake up one morning and find Hamas terrorists outside our home. This trust is what made it possible for us to stay and raise our children there. Yes, we accepted certain risks that Israelis who don't live right on the border never had to take: we were within the immediate range of Hamas's arsenal of mortars and rockets, without the protection of the Iron Dome missile defense system. But that was never enough to overcome, in our view, the many great qualities of living in Nahal Oz: the beauty of the place, the joy of going out into the open fields, and the strong social connections that we enjoyed with our beloved friends and neighbors.

The underground wall, it transpired, was Israel's Maginot Line. Hamas didn't need to break through it, as some experts assumed it would try to do eventually. Instead, in the early hours of October 7, under the cover of the massive mortar attack, its fighters simply broke through the fences, aboveground, within plain view of the Israeli military. Approximately three thousand Hamas attackers stormed the border simultaneously at more than thirty different locations. They crushed the fence with bulldozers, blew up portions of it with explosive devices, and sent armed drones to destroy the security cameras and remotely operated machine guns along the border.

By the time we realized what a failure the underground wall project had turned out to be, it was too late. As one of our neighbors wrote that morning in a text message, "We need a miracle now."

———————

While Miri convinced the girls to get a little more sleep, I was whispering nonstop into my phone. The first person I called was my colleague Amos Harel, a veteran military correspondent and defense analyst for *Haaretz*, the Israeli newspaper where I've worked since 2016. Amos has covered wars, terror attacks, and everything in between for more than three decades. He is an incredibly knowledgeable and well-connected expert, but more important than that, he's a true friend.

Over the years, Amos had gotten used to receiving phone calls from me at weird hours to get his immediate take on whatever was happening, or about to happen, in our small corner of the country. "Call Amos Harel" was often Miri's first reaction to a mortar launch from Gaza or a headline in the news about a potential security situation. She usually wanted me to ask him one question: Should we pack our bags and leave the kibbutz, or is what just happened a single incident that won't grow into a larger confrontation?

This time, of course, there was no need to ask such questions. For one thing, it was clear that getting out of the kibbutz, or even just leaving our safe room, was going to be impossible for the foreseeable future. From the amount of sustained, varied noise we were hearing, including the shooting and the shouting, we could tell that Hamas was not just bombarding us from afar or conducting a small raid but rather had launched a much bigger, bolder invasion, something that had never happened before.

A few minutes before we'd heard the first shots being fired in the distance, Amos had warned me that this wasn't a standard mortar attack. "There's talk of a cross-border infiltration, be on alert," he texted me. Now, by the time I called him, I could only speak in a whisper.

"There are *mehablim*"—terrorists—"right outside my house," I said. "We're in the safe room."

Amos told me that he would update his contacts in the military, specifically in the Southern Command, about our situation. But he also warned me that what was happening in our kibbutz was happening simultaneously in many other places—including, ominously, local IDF outposts as well as the largest city in the border region. "They're in Sderot," he explained quickly, "in the kibbutzim, in some military bases. No matter what, don't leave the safe room."

In the first few minutes of the mortar attack, and despite the heavy barrage, Miri had done two things that now proved important. She had run to use the bathroom and then had returned to the safe room with several bottles of water. She'd thought that we might have to stay there for longer than usual due to the severity of Hamas's opening salvo. Now we had enough water to last us about half a day. But we had no food, and we also had no electricity, so we couldn't charge our phones—our only sources of light inside the safe room. The batteries could probably last until around noon. We also couldn't use the bathroom any longer, so we decided that the girls would both wear diapers when they woke up, while the two of us, if and when nature called, would relieve ourselves on towels and put them inside a plastic bag.

But these weren't our most pressing problems. We had to decide what to do once the girls woke up again, which I assumed would be in thirty to forty-five minutes at most. What would we tell them when they asked for food? What if they asked again to leave the room, to go out and play? What if they asked to watch *CoComelon* movies in the living room? We would have to say no, of course, but I worried about their reaction: Would they start crying and, by doing so, draw the terrorists' attention to our safe room?

Meanwhile, the messages in our neighborhood text group were getting worse by the minute. "I have mehablim inside my house," wrote one neighbor. "They came in white SUVs, dressed in uniform as if they're Israeli soldiers." I knew that this neighbor, who volunteered regularly in the Israeli police, had installed security cameras in his home and could probably see the terrorists from inside his safe room. His description of the attackers wearing military uniforms chilled me—and helped me internalize what Amos had told me earlier on the phone. This was not just a random attack by a terror cell that had somehow breached our neigh-borhood; rather, it was part of a larger, well-planned operation, one that, I feared, would not be over anytime soon.

The most difficult message to read was that of Sharon Fiorentino, a mother of three young daughters living across the street from us. Sharon's husband, Ilan, was the security chief for our community—a role similar to the one held by Roi Rutberg when the kibbutz was established. Ilan was the first one to go out and examine the situation when rockets or mortars started falling; he was the first one to update, and to receive updates from, the Israeli military; and, in the unlikely event of an assault like this, he was the first one to go out and fight.

On that morning, Ilan, thirty-eight, had received a phone call from a worried mother who lived on the other side of the kibbutz. Her twelve-year-old boy, she said, had gone for a morning jog and was caught in the middle of the fierce mortar attack. He was pinned down and afraid to make his way back home, she told Ilan, asking if he could somehow help. Ilan took his car and found the boy hiding along the road. He wanted to take the boy back home but realized the mortar fire was too heavy. So instead, he took him to his own house and told Sharon to take the boy with her to the safe room, where she had already barricaded herself with their eight-, five-, and three-year-old daughters. After making sure the boy was safe, Ilan turned around and went out again, taking his M16 rifle with him. By then, he had started receiving reports about the terrorist infiltration.

When Sharon heard the terrorists inside the neighborhood a few min-utes later, she realized what Ilan was up against. "I'm scared to death," she wrote to the neighborhood text group at 7:29 A.M., "and Ilan is out there fighting them."

One by one, neighbors wrote that the terrorists were entering their homes. I relayed to the group what Amos had told me. "The military is aware of our situation," I wrote at 7:40 A.M. "Stay locked in the safe rooms and wait. Don't open the door even if you hear someone speaking in Hebrew." This was out of fear that the terrorists would pretend to be Israeli soldiers in a bid to convince people to open their safe room doors. One of our neighbors replied: "Can't wait to hear Hebrew. So far, I'm only hearing Arabic."

When we first heard the rockets, I also sent a quick text message to my parents. They live just over an hour away, in Tel Aviv, and as I later learned, their day had started very differently from ours.

At 6:00 A.M., my mother and father had driven to the beach and gone for a morning swim, enjoying one of the last warm days of the year. While they were in the water, they noticed Israeli military planes overhead—an unusual sight on Saturdays, when government aircraft are usually grounded due to Jewish Sabbath laws.

My father Noam was a retired Israeli army general who spent more than three decades in uniform and once commanded IDF forces in Lebanon and the West Bank. He told my mother Gali, a retired high school principal, that what they were seeing was strange. "I wonder why those planes are in the sky right now," he said. Even so, my parents headed into the water.

Shortly afterward, the answer arrived when a barrage of rockets was launched from Gaza toward Tel Aviv. My parents heard the sirens from the water but decided not to hurry out. In Tel Aviv, unlike Nahal Oz, there is plenty of time to seek shelter once an incoming rocket alert goes off—approximately ninety seconds. In addition, the city and all of its suburbs are protected by the Iron Dome missile defense system. The government and the military still advise residents to seek shelter whenever the sirens go off, but if you're swimming in the sea, there's little you can do beyond hoping that the rocket won't fall directly onto you.

My parents kept swimming for another fifteen minutes or so, but as the sirens continued, they eventually decided that it would be smart to get out and check what was happening in our part of the country. At first, they sent a text message to our family chat, which also includes my younger brother (a combat doctor in the military) and his wife. "What's the situation in Nahal Oz?" my father asked at 6:45 A.M. "A lot of rockets," I replied. This was before we started hearing the gunshots and the terrorists' voices. "We're waiting for you here," my mother wrote, inviting us to come stay at their apartment once we were able to leave our safe room.

By 7:15 A.M., the situation had become much more dangerous, and I sent another message in the family chat, explaining that there were terrorists in our neighborhood firing into the house. "Mehablim infiltrated the kibbutz," I wrote. "We're under fire."

My father immediately called my cell phone. In a terse whisper, I told him that the girls were asleep and that we were all trying to stay silent, but that our house was under attack.

He asked if I could tell whether the terrorists were inside the house or firing at it from the outside. I said there was no way of knowing. He asked me if our dog, Pluto, an energetic black Labrador, was also with us in the safe room. I said that we didn't bring him inside with us, since he often got nervous when we'd shut the heavy door. "I think he's dead," I added, assuming the worst: we hadn't heard Pluto bark since the first gunshots had echoed inside the house.

My father said he was texting all of his contacts in the military. "Stay quiet," he advised before hanging up. "That's the most important thing you can do right now."

The girls woke up again shortly after 8:00 A.M. Gunshots could still clearly be heard outside, but the house itself sounded quiet to us. Inside the darkened room, I texted my father: "The girls are behaving really well, but I'm worried they'll lose patience soon and Hamas will hear us in here."

Carmel asked, again, if she could go out to play. Galia said she needed to use the bathroom. We explained to them, as calmly as we could, that it was still too dangerous to go outside and that it would be some time before we could leave the room. Again, they responded with incredible maturity—their quiet acquiescence surprising both me and Miri.

Even so, I suspected that we would only be able to keep the girls silent and calm for maybe another hour. I could only hope that the attack would be over by then. Help *had* to be coming soon.

Just a few minutes' drive from Kibbutz Nahal Oz is a midsized military base by the same name, typically manned by close to two hundred soldiers. *How long*, I thought, *will it take for those soldiers to get here and put an end to this siege?* "We'll be out of here soon," I told Miri, perhaps as much for my sake as for hers. "The military knows what's happening."

I had no idea how grim the situation was at the base at that exact moment. Even after Amos had warned me that our kibbutz was just one of many places attacked that morning, I didn't—couldn't—know the full picture.

One thing that did occur to me was that this Saturday was the Jewish holiday of Simchat Torah, the culmination of a monthlong period of Jewish holidays beginning with Rosh Hashanah, our version of New Year's. The holiday itself didn't mean much to Miri and me—we are not a very observant family—but I now realized that the base nearby was probably understaffed, as many of its soldiers had most likely been sent home to spend this festive weekend with their families. Fifty years earlier, almost to the day, Egypt and Syria had simultaneously attacked Israel during Yom Kippur, the Jewish day of atonement, surprising Israel and starting a war at a time when the majority of Israel's soldiers were at home with their families. Now, it seemed, Hamas had pulled the same move.

Still, even after realizing that the timing of the attack could influence the military's response, I had no way of knowing just how bad the situation actually was: that Hamas had sent approximately two hundred men into the base and had succeeded in capturing it by 8:30 A.M. Dozens of soldiers had died, including almost twenty female field observers, or "spotters"—intelligence soldiers tasked with following Israel's vast network of cameras along the border.

In the weeks leading up to October 7, we would later learn, these soldiers had warned that they'd seen worrying scenes through their cameras. Hamas, they'd reported to their commanders, was training for a major attack on the border communities. The spotters had reported that Hamas had constructed large-scale models of Israeli kibbutzim, which had then been stormed by heavily armed Hamas militants—clearly a dress rehearsal for an invasion. But their warnings were dismissed. On that morning, many of them lost their lives, knowing in their last moments that they had been right all along.

The massacre at the base had made our own situation even more dire. The soldiers there had been our best hope for a quick end to the invasion of our kibbutz, but now they were either dead or pinned down. Some of the survivors were fighting a desperate battle against the larger and better-armed invading force; the Hamas fighters had arrived with guns, hand grenades, rocket-propelled grenades (RPGs), and antitank missiles, while most of the IDF soldiers, having been caught by surprise, had only a sidearm and several magazines of ammunition at most. Other soldiers were simply hiding as best they could while sending out their own desperate pleas for help. In any case, with the base out of commission, there was no longer any chance of a large military force arriving quickly enough to save us from the immediate danger that we were in. Mercifully, perhaps, Miri and I remained unaware.

Another ten minutes passed, then another fifteen, and we were still stranded. To make matters worse, our cell phone connection was becoming unstable—probably because so many people in the kibbutz were trying to make calls and send messages at the same time. I tried to send a message to Avishay, one of my neighbors and a father of four young children, to see how they were all doing. The phone notified me, ominously, "no network detected."

Five minutes later, at approximately 8:30 A.M., the connection briefly returned and I got another call from my father. "Don't get out of the safe room, no matter what," he said. I could hear that he was speaking from inside a car and that it was in motion. "We're coming to get you out of there."

CHAPTER 4

NEIGHBORS

1967–1987

ARIE DOTAN, KNOWN TO EVERYONE on the kibbutz by his nickname, "Daum," came to Nahal Oz in May 1966 at age nineteen. Like the founders who had arrived a decade earlier, he was also part of a "seed group" from the Israeli army's Nahal unit, sent to support the growing border community. Now, though, his group of forty young men and women were entering a very different place. They joined a community of more than 150 people, with dozens of children running around. The old sheds had been replaced by real homes, the local dairy farm was selling vast quantities of milk to Israel's largest producer, and the security situation had been calm for several years.

Daum started working with the cows. It was hard, physical labor, often starting very early in the morning, but he enjoyed every minute of it. "For us, this was the dream: to live on a kibbutz, to work in agriculture, to settle the border area. I grew up in Tel Aviv, and my mother didn't like what I was doing at first. She used to ask me, 'Why did you have to go to this place on the border?' I told her that this was our mission."

A year after his group's arrival, Israel entered a tense period known as "the waiting days." It was the spring of 1967 and the clouds of war were once again gathering over the Middle East. From the northeast, Syria had been exchanging threats with Israel, and occasionally also military blows, due to an ongoing crisis regarding the control of water sources along their joint border. To the southeast, Jordan was blamed by Israel for attacks by Palestinian militant groups originating from its territory, while in the south, Egypt feuded with Israel over Israeli shipping rights in the Red Sea. Lebanon, to Israel's north, had fought against the fledgling Jewish state in 1948 and had since been used by militant groups as a launching pad for new attacks. In short, Israel didn't have even one peaceful border—and was preparing for a potential war on all fronts.

Beyond the tactical considerations of Syria, Jordan, and Egypt was a broader Arab goal: reversing the humiliation of 1948 and, if possible, seizing some of Israel's territory. Government-operated radio stations in Cairo and Damascus promised to erase Israel from the map and return its land to the Palestinian refugees. Meanwhile, the Israeli government led by Levi Eshkol, the country's third prime minister, was deliberating between initiating a preemptive strike and giving the United States an opportunity to resolve the situation through diplomacy.

Prime Minister Eshkol remembered how the Americans had forced Israel's hand after the Suez War in 1956, and against the advice of his own generals, he decided to act only after receiving a green light from the administration of President Lyndon B. Johnson. Specifically, Eshkol was determined not to repeat Ben-Gurion's mistake of acting behind President Eisenhower's back in coordination with the British and the French, which had eventually led to heavy American pressure for an Israeli withdrawal from Gaza and the Sinai Peninsula in 1957. Eshkol wanted to avoid such a scenario by closely coordinating Israel's actions with the White House.

His prudence would eventually pay off, but in the near term, it was costly for Eshkol—and for Israel's spirit. The premier's strategic patience was described by critics in the press as weakness and cowardice. For a few weeks that spring, Israel experienced an apocalyptic atmosphere. People dug shelters and stockpiled food, as memories of the Holocaust—scarcely two decades prior—stirred deep anxiety among much of the Israeli public.

Things were different at Nahal Oz. "We were too busy to worry about the war," Daum recalled. "When you spend your days in the mud with the cows and only have a few hours of rest, you fall asleep like a baby." Still, some security measures were taken to enhance the kibbutz's protection. More guns were brought to the armory, new guard shifts were added, and the military presence in the region was expanded.

Eventually, in June 1967, Israel struck first, attacking Egypt; Jordan and Syria came to their ally's defense. Other Arab countries, such as Iraq and Lebanon, joined in as well, although they ended up playing a relatively minor role in the fighting. This proved sensible, as Israel had enjoyed both the element of surprise as well as the support of the Johnson White House, which felt that it had exhausted its diplomatic options for averting a war. Within six days, the Israeli military had occupied vast swaths of Jordan, Egypt, and Syria, more than tripling the young country's land mass.

The most significant territorial addition was that of the area known today as the West Bank, stretching from the Jordan River to the foothills of the Judea and Samaria mountains. Just like the Gaza Strip, this area was an artificial creation dating back to the 1948 war between Israel and its Arab neighbors. When that war ended, the Kingdom of Jordan had been left in control of this region, ruling over both banks of the Jordan River—the eastern one, which was known before the war simply as "Jordan," and the western one, which had been part of British Mandatory Palestine and now became a separate part of the Kingdom of Jordan. To distinguish it from the "real" Jordan, the entire area was simply described as the West Bank of the river, even though some parts of it were closer to the Mediterranean coastline than to the Jordan River Valley. The name stuck with the region after Israel claimed it in 1967.

Another major conquest for Israel was the territory covering the eastern neighborhoods of Jerusalem. This, too, was a reversal of the post-1948 situation. At the end of that war, Jerusalem—a city of great religious and historical significance to Jews, Muslims, and Christians alike—had been left divided in two. The western parts of it were taken over by Israel and became the capital of the new country, while the eastern parts were left in the hands of Jordan—including the Old City, where the most important religious sites, such as the Western Wall, the Church of the Holy Sepulchre, and the Al-Aqsa Mosque, are all located. In the Six-Day War of June 1967, the city was "reunited," in the words of the Israeli government, and placed entirely under Israel's control.

Arie "Daum" Dotan had trained as a paratrooper before coming to Nahal Oz, and on the first day of the war, he had been summoned to

Jerusalem to fight against the Jordanian forces there. He was wounded shortly before his comrades entered the Old City. The religious dimension of the battle, however, did not excite him. As he later recalled, "I heard that we took back the Western Wall," a holy Jewish site that had previously been under Jordanian control, "but all I wanted was to get healthy enough to go back to the kibbutz and work in the cowshed."

During the war, Israel had also conquered several other areas: the Golan Heights, a strategically important mountain range in the northeast, had previously belonged to Syria. The Sinai Peninsula to the south fell to Israel now, too, for a second time; Israel had conquered the territory a decade before but then returned it to Egypt under American pressure.

Israeli troops also now returned to the Gaza Strip once again. One of the battalions that took over the Strip crossed the border right in front of Nahal Oz while Israeli planes flew over the kibbutz on their way to bomb Egypt.

It was a stunning victory that saw Israel turn, overnight, from a small country into a regional power. The apocalyptic public attitude was replaced by a sense of euphoria. If Israel could do all of this, what *couldn't* it do?

In Gaza, by contrast, the Six-Day War was viewed as the second disaster in under two decades. If the war of 1948—with the loss of land to Israel and the birth of the Palestinian refugee crisis—was called the *Nakba* (the catastrophe) in Palestinian historiography, then 1967 was the *Naksa* (the setback). The seizure of the Gaza Strip, East Jerusalem, and the West Bank meant that twenty years after Arab nations had rejected the UN Partition Plan for the land once known as British Mandatory Palestine, Israel now controlled that entire territory.

The United Nations estimated that approximately 40,000 people—more than one in ten Gazans—left the Strip after the Six-Day War. Most went to Egypt and Jordan. The 350,000 who remained now lived under Israeli military occupation. The same was true in the West Bank, which was then home to some 600,000 people. East Jerusalem, unlike the two other territories, was annexed to Israel, which meant that the

65,000 Palestinians living there received Israeli identity cards but not full citizenship.

A new, complex reality emerged in the lands controlled by Israel after the Six-Day War. The Palestinian population between the Jordan River and the Mediterranean was now divided into four subgroups, each living under a different kind of regime: Arab citizens of Israel, comprising about 20 percent of the country's population, were full citizens, with the right to vote and hold public office, although the majority of them suffered from various forms of official and societal discrimination; Palestinian residents of East Jerusalem, annexed to Israel, were residents of the Jewish state but not full citizens; and the Palestinians of the West Bank and Gaza Strip, each in their own separate geographical area, were subjects of an Israeli occupation administration, with very few rights or protections under Israeli law.

Moshe Dayan, by now Israel's defense minister, advocated for an "open border" relationship between Israel proper and the Gaza Strip. There was still no fence separating them, but new border crossings, connected to major roads, were nevertheless created, signaling that unlike the short-lived military occupation that had followed the Suez War, this time Israel had no intention of giving back the occupied territories. There was also no US pressure on it to do so: the Johnson administration had adopted a new policy, "Land for Peace," which allowed Israel to keep hold of the occupied lands until the Arab world was willing to sign peace accords with the Jewish state.

As this new reality sank in, Gazans were encouraged to seek work inside Israel. Meanwhile, Israelis—including the residents of Nahal Oz—began visiting the coastal enclave themselves.

"People went to the beach there and stopped in restaurants on the way back. We felt welcome in the beginning," Daum said. "I wasn't one of the first people to run over there, but eventually I started shopping in their markets." The prices were cheaper than anywhere in Israel, but that was only part of the story. For border community residents, something fundamental had changed: almost overnight, they had stopped living "in the middle of nowhere" and found out they were right next to a bustling metropolis. A bus line connecting Be'er Sheva, the largest city in southern

Israel, to Gaza passed through Nahal Oz several times a day, and residents of the kibbutz would often use it to go into the nearby city.

For tens of thousands of Gazans—especially those who had arrived in the territory as refugees two decades earlier—a similar process of revelation awaited as they discovered Israel, the country that had arisen from the ashes of the 1948 Arab-Israeli War. As a result of Dayan's open border policy, Israel was soon flooded with workers from Gaza. A low salary in Israel was still more than the average wage in the Strip. Palestinian day laborers crossed the border every morning to work in agriculture and construction. According to historian Sara Roy, salaries earned by Palestinian workers entering Israel represented only 2 percent of the gross national product of Gaza in 1968, but rose to 31 percent five years later and 44 percent by the mid-1980s. But statistics alone couldn't capture the impact of these visits on the Palestinians who crossed the border into Israel.

What these Palestinian workers saw when they entered Israel was a country that had become much richer than their own. In Dayan's 1956 eulogy for Roi Rutberg, he had evoked Arab refugees watching Israel's prosperity from their miserable camps in Gaza. Now, those refugees could see that prosperity up close, from their construction sites in Tel Aviv and other cities. Some of these guest workers experienced belittling and disrespectful treatment from Israeli employers—a reflection of the post-1967 high that led many Israelis to believe their country was invincible and that the Arab world at large, and certainly the Palestinians, were helpless against it.

In Nahal Oz, there was little awareness of the Palestinian perspective on this new reality—at least at first. Kibbutz member Ehud Doron, twenty-five at the time, recalled how "we felt like nothing could stop us. We thought very little of the people on the other side." It didn't take long, however, for that perception to change.

In the evening hours of May 21, 1968, almost a full year after the war, Ehud and six other men from the kibbutz were sent to the fields to put out a fire. They suspected it was intentional but had no time to investigate—they first had to douse the flames. Driving in a jeep that belonged to the kibbutz, they arrived at the area, extinguished the fire, and, after about an hour, started making their way back home. "We didn't realize that a trap had been set for us," Ehud wrote years later in an article describing the event.

On the way back, the jeep drove over a land mine. Two of the men inside—Moshe Ben-Hari, twenty-one, and Ze'ev Sagie, thirty—died from the blast. Several others, including Ehud, were wounded. The culprits were never caught, but there was no doubt in the kibbutz about who had laid the trap for their comrades.

The painful incident was, at the very least, a reminder that the defeat of the Arab armies in 1967 didn't mean that the Gazans themselves had given up their struggle against Israel. In the 1950s, it was the fedayeen who threatened Israeli border communities like Nahal Oz. In the years preceding the Six-Day War, the Gaza border had been mostly quiet, but Palestinian groups still attacked Israel from elsewhere, infiltrating the country from Jordan and Syria. Now, in the aftermath of the war and with the birth of the Israeli occupation, the Gaza region was once again becoming a hotbed of resistance.

In some ways, the bitter defeat of the Six-Day War actually strengthened the militant factions in Gaza. After the war, Palestinians who had previously counted on their fellow Arabs in neighboring states to come to their rescue realized that they were on their own. In the words of historian Tareq Baconi, after the Six-Day War, "the small guerrilla factions that had commenced sporadic and ineffective operations against Israel before 1967 suddenly emerged as a powerful alternative to pan-Arabism"—the leading policy idea of Egyptian president Gamal Abdel Nasser's regime. The growing insurgency, Baconi added, "imbued the dispossessed and broken Palestinian refugees with agency, pride, and direction."

The most important Palestinian force at the time was Fatah, a nationalist organization led by Yasser Arafat, the Cairo-born son of a Gazan family. Fatah was a militant group that carried out attacks against Israeli communities after crossing the border from Jordan and Syria, and, at the same time, was also an influential player in Palestinian politics, essentially controlling the Palestine Liberation Organization (PLO), a separate body that was founded in 1964 as part of an attempt by several Arab governments to create a political-diplomatic organization representing the Palestinian struggle. Those governments, most notably the Egyptians, wanted to have activists and groups loyal to them leading the PLO—but Arafat, who was an independent actor, managed within several years to upend them and turn his Fatah into the PLO's most dominant faction.

Fatah's initial base of operations was in Jordan. But after 1970, when Jordanian king Hussein bin Talal blamed Arafat for trying to instigate a revolution in his country, the organization was violently kicked out of the kingdom, forcing its leadership to relocate to Lebanon. That country, bordering Israel to the north, had only played a minor role in the region's earlier wars, but by the mid-1970s, it had turned into a stronghold for operations against Israel, carried out by Fatah and allied Palestinian groups. In Gaza, meanwhile, Fatah was growing ever more popular among young people and university students, who were inspired by its calls to fight the Israeli occupation.

After local Fatah cells carried out attacks against Israeli soldiers and citizens, both inside Gaza and along the border, Israel responded with brutal force. In 1969, one of its fiercest generals, Ariel Sharon, was appointed head of the military's Southern Command, whose responsibilities included the Gaza Strip. In the mid-1950s, Sharon had been tasked by Dayan and Ben-Gurion with leading a series of daring operations inside Gaza in order to stop the fedayeen attacks, and he had earned a reputation as a ruthless officer. As a senior general fifteen years later, he gave a young commando officer by the name of Meir Dagan the task of "pacifying" Gaza by any means necessary.

Dagan used methods in Gaza that made Sharon's operations in the 1950s seem moderate by comparison. His commandos raided neighborhoods and villages on a weekly basis, killing and arresting hundreds of Palestinians. While the military said that the vast majority of those killed were terrorists, UN agencies and local organizations blamed these military raids for the deaths of dozens of civilians.

It took approximately two years for this brutal campaign to significantly reduce the number of attacks against Israel, but by 1972, Sharon's operations were being hailed in the Israeli media for their success. Still, Israelis' fear of terrorism remained potent. One of the most popular Israeli songs of the 1970s, "Drive Slowly" by the singer-songwriter Arik Einstein, included the lines: "I think we're getting near Gaza / Let's hope some grenade doesn't blow us to hell." For people in Nahal Oz, who continued to frequent Gaza's markets and beaches, this was more than just a pithy lyric.

When twenty-year-old Dani Rachamim arrived at Nahal Oz in 1975, the post-1967 euphoria had long been forgotten. It had been replaced by a sense of national grief and humiliation as a result of the Yom Kippur War of October 1973.

While the 1967 war had started with an Israeli preemptive strike, in 1973 Egypt and Syria managed to strike first, surprising Israel simultaneously from the south and the north on Yom Kippur, a day on which Israel completely shuts down for twenty-four hours. The Egyptians and Syrians failed to immediately recapture any of their lost territory, but the Israeli public was shocked by the deaths of more than two thousand Israeli soldiers during the three-week-long war and by the realization that Israel may have lost if it hadn't been for the US, which had swiftly provided tanks, artillery, bullets, and other military equipment to its Middle Eastern ally. The Nixon administration viewed the region as one arena in the global Cold War with the Soviet Union, its most prominent rival at the time, which had sided with the Arab armies attacking the Jewish state. The US, therefore, had a clear interest in helping save Israel, even without the political considerations related to the influence of Jewish American voters.

There were no wartime deaths in Nahal Oz, but the kibbutz movement at large paid a heavy price: despite composing only 2 percent of the country's total population at the time, kibbutz members made up almost 20 percent of the fallen soldiers in the war. Many of those who had died were young men who had been born on kibbutzim in the 1950s; their parents, who had themselves served in the military a generation earlier, were heartbroken by the fact that twenty-five years after Israel's foundation, such a heavy price was still required to secure the country's borders.

The overrepresentation of kibbutzniks among the dead was a source of pride for the kibbutzim and a testament to their unique contribution to Israel's security, but it also led to widespread anger in many of these communities, where people were beginning to doubt their government's claims that the war had been necessary and inevitable.

Egypt's new president, Anwar Sadat, had offered several times to negotiate with Israel before the war—and each time had been rebuffed. Sadat had been willing to discuss an unprecedented deal with Israel: withdrawal from the territories captured in 1967, in exchange for peace and mutual recognition. This was a dramatic reversal of the Arab position since 1947, which had been a complete rejection of Israel's right to exist. But Dayan, its all-powerful defense minister, famously proclaimed that for Israel, keeping the occupied territories was more important than securing peace. From Sadat's point of view, this left him no avenue other than war to win back territory and recover his nation's lost sense of pride. And although his campaign against Israel didn't lead to any immediate territorial gain, it clearly boosted Egyptian morale—at the expense of Israel's.

Israel's dismal public mood at the end of the Yom Kippur War extended to the leadership of Prime Minister Golda Meir, who had shared Dayan's rejectionist approach to Sadat's diplomatic gestures. For many young kibbutz members, the entire ordeal showed that the country's leadership was too eager to go to war and too hesitant in its pursuit of potential opportunities for peace. The question of whether the war could have been avoided by agreeing to territorial concessions to Egypt, and perhaps also to other Arab countries, was asked in countless communities.

Dani shared that sentiment. From a young age, he'd believed that Israel needed to make peace with its Arab neighbors, a belief that wasn't shared by many in Israel following the 1967 victory but that started to gain more support after Israel's poor performance in the 1973 war. For Dani, that experience was proof that Israel's leadership was arrogant and misguided. He thought that peace—with both the powerful Egyptian state and with the Palestinians in Gaza—was not just possible but also necessary.

"I grew up in a poor home and became a socialist at age eleven," Dani later explained—a conversion that he'd undergone after trying to go see a movie with friends and being turned away for lack of money. Dani's parents were Jewish immigrants who had come to Israel from Iraq in the early 1950s and settled in a working-class town north of Tel Aviv. At seventeen, he'd heard about a "seed group" of teenagers set to enlist in the Nahal unit and move to Nahal Oz. Without knowing anyone in the group, or anything about the kibbutz, he'd decided to join. Three years later, he was working in a chicken coop on the border with Gaza, and learning what it meant to be a kibbutznik.

"As a child, I often faced discrimination," Dani said. "Sometimes it was because I was poor and other times because I'm Mizrahi"—the Hebrew term for Jews of Middle Eastern or North African origin. After the state's founding, Israel's elites in politics, business, culture, and most other fields consisted mostly of Jews who were of European origin. But Israel was also home to hundreds of thousands of Jews who had lived in Middle Eastern countries prior to 1948, including Arab countries such as Morocco, Egypt, and Iraq. Most of them were expelled from those countries after Israel's creation and found refuge in the new Jewish state—yet at the same time, faced discrimination in their new country because of the color of their skin, the accent in which they spoke Hebrew, or the social and religious traditions they brought with them from their birth countries.

In the kibbutz, however, Dani felt something different. "The moment I arrived there, I felt accepted and respected. Most of the kibbutz members back then hailed from European countries, but for me, that was never an issue. There was one older member who was an Iraqi Jew, like my parents, and he looked out for me in the beginning. But most of the time that wasn't necessary. I felt very comfortable."

From early on, Dani was also a frequent visitor across the border. He found in Gaza City a fascinating maze of colorful and alluring markets, but there was also a political dimension to his visits there. "I wanted to know these people, understand their point of view, and hear their stories," he said. Dani's curiosity stemmed in part from the trauma of 1973, when Israeli hubris and disdain for "the Arabs" had led to disaster. In visits to Gaza's shops, Dani made friends and discussed politics, in conversations that were a mixture of Arabic, Hebrew, and English.

It was through these conversations that Dani became attuned to the Palestinian perspective on the 1948 war and the refugee crisis and also to the way many Palestinians viewed Israel's presence in Gaza: as a brutal and illegitimate occupation regime. It wasn't always easy for Dani to hear these sentiments, but he felt that it was important to understand them, all the same.

By the late 1970s, Dani had become active in Shalom Achshav (Peace Now), a movement of Israeli reservists who demanded that their government seek peace with the Arab world. These men, who had served in 1973 and knew the price of war, wanted their country to make a real effort at achieving peace after three decades of grinding, relentless violence. When Egyptian president Sadat made a historic visit to Israel in November 1977, members of the movement held a major protest in support of an Israeli-Egyptian agreement.

Ten months later, they got what they wanted. On September 17, 1978, Israel and Egypt signed a peace accord at America's famed presidential getaway, Camp David—a location that signaled the major investment of the United States in brokering a long-term solution to the conflict in the Middle East. Egypt got back the Sinai Peninsula, and Israel got its first-ever peace agreement with an Arab country in return. It was essentially the same deal that Sadat had hinted at prior to 1973, a fact that only underscored the terrible cost of the war. Still, Dani was ecstatic at the time: "It was history in the making. We were so happy to see it happen in front of our eyes."

But the agreement had an important caveat: Gaza wasn't included in the "land for peace" tradeoff. Egypt insisted on getting back the Sinai region, but not the coastal enclave to its north. Israel, meanwhile, had begun in the early 1970s to construct settlements for its citizens in Gaza. At the time, these settlements were home to only several hundred Israelis, but then prime minister Menachem Begin—Israel's first right-wing leader, who came from the ranks of the nationalist Likud Party—was determined to keep them in place. His party, which was a part of the Israeli opposition during the country's first three decades and only rose to power in 1977, believed in a vision of "Greater Israel" that included long-term Israeli control of both Gaza and the West Bank, itself home to thousands of settlers by that point.

The Egyptians were more than happy to leave Gaza to Begin, along with the hundreds of thousands of Palestinians living there. *Let them have it* was Sadat's approach. It's not that he wasn't interested in enlarging Egypt's territory; the issue was the population. Sadat viewed Gaza as one big headache, a poor place full of refugees, militants, and troublemakers. If the Israelis were so hell-bent on keeping it, he told his advisers, then they deserved it.

After the peace agreement was struck, Israel's construction of settlements in the occupied territories accelerated dramatically. By the mid-1980s, there were more than a dozen settlements throughout the Gaza Strip and, while only three thousand Israelis lived in them, French historian Jean-Pierre Filiu estimates that they took up about a quarter of the Strip's agricultural lands, in addition to a particularly large segment of its southern coastline. Some of these settlements were founded on territory taken from Palestinian farmers. The settlements became easy targets for Palestinian militants and required an ever-growing Israeli army presence to protect their residents. In the West Bank, the dynamic was even more pronounced: Israel constructed dozens of settlements there, and these had become home to tens of thousands of people, all of whom needed—and received—the protection of the Israeli military.

Palestinians watched as Israel's original vision of an "open border" with Gaza was replaced by something different: a growing system of checkpoints, military bases, and road closures inside the Strip. Friction with Israeli soldiers became a common source of frustration and humiliation for many Palestinians.

Dani, like most residents of Nahal Oz, opposed the settlements and saw them as an impediment to peace. "Nahal Oz was born as a frontline kibbutz, with the goal of protecting the border," he explained. "The settlements were built in order to erase the border and blur the distinction between Israel and Gaza. These were two totally different missions." It wasn't only a historical contrast but also a political one: kibbutzim like Nahal Oz had always been strongholds of the Israeli Labor Party, which had led the country during its first three decades; the settlements, on the other hand, had enjoyed the support of Labor right after the war but by the 1980s had become much more closely associated with Likud.

There was also a demographic divide between these two projects: Nahal Oz, like the vast majority of kibbutzim all over Israel, was a strictly secular community, whereas most Gaza settlements were inhabited by the Orthodox Jewish religious Zionists, a more right-leaning part of Israeli society. This religious-nationalist cohort, which today represents approximately 10 percent of Israel's population, is made up of everyone from liberal moderates to messianic extremists who believe that settling the entirety of Israel, inciting conflict with the Palestinians, and eventually kicking them off the land is all a prerequisite for the arrival of the Jewish Messiah, a holy figure who will bring about a new age for humanity. This latter group was always a minority within the broader spectrum of Israel's religious nationalists, but starting in the 1980s, it became a growing force among the settlers, challenging and weakening other, more moderate factions. For the Palestinians in Gaza, these distinctions between the different groups of settlers were almost meaningless, and the same was true for Dani and most Israeli opponents of the settlement movement.

At Dani's wedding in 1983 to Siobhan, an Irish girl who had come to Nahal Oz to volunteer in agricultural work and stayed when the pair fell in love, there were at least five Palestinian guests from Gaza, most of whom had become his friends while working in the kibbutz. "It felt totally natural for them to be there and dance with us," Dani recalled. "We were neighbors."

These neighbors on the other side of the fence were experiencing a political drama of their own, however—and the people of Nahal Oz were completely blind to it. Starting in the mid-1980s, the secular-nationalist groups that had led the Palestinian resistance since the 1960s, most notably Fatah and the PLO, were being challenged by a new rising force in Gaza: the Islamists.

Gaza has a rich Christian history dating back to the days of the Roman Empire, but for most of its modern history, it has been an overwhelmingly Muslim-majority society. The Muslim Brotherhood, an Islamist political organization originally established in Egypt in 1928 with a goal of imposing an Islamic regime in that country and others, had been active in Gaza as far back as the 1930s but was always in the shadow of secular-nationalist forces. Under the Israeli occupation, however, the

Islamists became increasingly popular—especially among younger generations of Palestinians.

For Israel's right-wing leaders, this wasn't necessarily regarded as a bad development. They saw Arafat and the PLO as Israel's archenemies, and not without reason: Fatah and other PLO factions were responsible for a long list of terror attacks against Israel over the years, including the hijacking of commercial airplanes, and the brutal murder of Israeli athletes at the 1972 Munich Olympics, to name a few. Arafat led a campaign of terror against Israel for more than two decades, at first from Jordan, later from Lebanon, and, after Israel's invasion of that country in 1982, from his new base in Tunisia.

The Islamists, for their part, kept their distance from armed resistance—at least at first. They had a long-term plan and a lot of patience. Their focus in the early years of the occupation was on *dawa'*, an Arabic word best translated as "an invitation to Islam." The Islamists offered the population of Gaza a network of education, health, and welfare services. All they asked in return was for people to "get closer" to Islam and adopt a more religious way of life. To Israeli politicians and military officers, this made the Islamists seem like an appealing alternative to the combative secular-nationalists of Fatah and the PLO.

And so, while Fatah was busy attacking Israel, the Islamists worked on their network of institutions, laser-focused on the battle for hearts and minds—sometimes with the encouragement and support of Israeli authorities, who were happy to help an alternative to the PLO gain popularity and credibility on the street. There were even meetings between senior Israeli officials and Islamist leaders, in which the needs of the civilian population in Gaza were discussed. The Islamists began raising large amounts of money outside of Gaza and funneling it into the Strip for their educational and social projects. Step by step, they took over mosques, schools, and universities, all under the watchful eyes of the Israeli occupiers.

The most important Islamist figure in Gaza was Sheikh Ahmed Yassin, a religious leader who was confined to a wheelchair since a childhood accident that had left him paralyzed. Yassin became a hero to many Gazans through patient construction of social, educational, and cultural institutions in Gaza, doing his utmost to avoid an all-out, open clash with

Israel, at least for the time being. Even when his followers became violent and took coercive steps such as shutting down movie theaters, Israeli security and intelligence officials looked on from the sidelines, thinking this "internal feud" was none of their business.

In the mid-1980s, a political difference was beginning to emerge between the Islamists and the secular-nationalists. To a certain degree, it was a mirror image of the political trends in Israel. Inside the PLO, just like in some segments of the Israeli left, there was growing support for negotiations on the basis of a "two-state solution," which meant dismantling most Israeli settlements in the West Bank and Gaza and creating a new Palestinian state in those two territories. This solution echoed the guiding principle of US policy in the region, "land for peace." Some PLO activists even held secret meetings with Israelis to discuss this formula.

The Israeli right completely rejected this idea, swearing to forever hold on to the West Bank and Gaza while constantly expanding the presence of settlements there. The Islamists were also vehemently opposed to it. Yassin saw "two states" as blasphemy. Unlike some PLO leaders who were beginning to seriously advocate for that solution, Yassin held a strictly religious worldview, which included no place for any recognition of Israel. To him, the only possible solution was the establishment of an Islamist regime over the entire land. He saw no distinction between Israeli settlements in the territories occupied after 1967 and the State of Israel in its pre-1967 borders. The Jews, in his vision, would face two choices once the Muslims had conquered the entire region: swear allegiance to the Islamist regime and accept their fate as second-class citizens in a new Palestine—or leave. Still, as long as the Islamists didn't engage in violent attacks on Israeli soldiers and citizens, they faced very little scrutiny from Israeli occupation authorities.

Yassin *was* facing pressure, however, from his supporters, who wanted him to end his decades-long policy of strategic patience. He had stuck to it after the Israeli-Egyptian peace agreement of 1978, which most Palestinians viewed as an Arab betrayal of their cause and advised his followers not to get carried away by emotion. "We'll only attack Israel at the right moment," he kept telling them.

Before long, they got their chance.

In Gaza, the year 1987 had been a relatively violent one right from the start. There were armed attacks against Israeli settlers and soldiers, and Israeli military operations meant to quash the growing resistance. Filiu, the French historian, ascribes this rising violence to the "growing pressure" felt by Palestinians in Gaza as a result of the expansion of settlements, which took over more land, more water resources, and more of the Strip's coastline, and which required an ever-growing military presence inside the region. Many Israeli and Palestinian pundits, however, viewed it as a result of the twenty-year mark of the Israeli occupation, and the coming-of-age of a new Palestinian generation that had lived under Israeli control for its entire lifetime—and which was unwilling to abide by it any longer.

Israel at the time had a national unity government, led by Likud's Yitzhak Shamir—a right-wing hard-liner who was forced by political circumstance to invite the left-wing Labor Party into his governing coalition. Shimon Peres, the foreign minister and a prominent figure in Labor, advocated for a peace plan that included a decreased Israeli presence in Gaza and the creation of an autonomous government representing the Palestinian population there. The plan made headlines and began to garner international support, but Shamir shot it down in early December.

A few days later, things in Gaza reached a boiling point.

On Friday December 6, an Israeli businessman who came to shop in Gaza City was stabbed to death in broad daylight near one of the markets. Two days later, four Palestinians returning from work in Israel died in a car accident involving an Israeli truck near the Jabalya refugee camp to the north of the city. The Israeli media reported the incident as an accident, but in Palestinian media, it was described as retribution for the stabbing attack. What wasn't up for debate was the response.

Thousands of Palestinians took to the streets of Gaza City and started clashing with Israeli soldiers. Similar confrontations spread to other cities in Gaza, such as Rafah and Khan Yunis, and from there to the West Bank and East Jerusalem. Within days, the events were being described as an intifada—Arabic for "uprising."

Israel's response was to crush the resistance with brutal force. Then defense minister Yitzhak Rabin had reportedly ordered soldiers to break the arms and feet of Palestinian protesters. But the army's brutality seemed to have the opposite effect this time.

Not only did the intifada continue, but it also began to assume a more violent nature: shooting and stabbing attacks became more frequent, and the protests, riots, and stone-throwing didn't abate. In fact, the young people of Gaza, who led the clashes, became heroes in the eyes of the wider Arab world, for their determined struggle against the much more powerful Israel. Nizar Qabani, a prominent Syrian poet, caught this sentiment in his poem "The Wrathful," part of a trilogy titled "The Children of the Stones":

Teach us, oh students of Gaza
To be men.
Because our men
Have turned into dough.

The PLO, from its exile in Tunisia—where the leadership had fled following Israel's invasion of its previous base in Lebanon—was caught unaware and struggled to connect itself to this outburst of resistance. But Yassin and the Islamists, whose operations were centered in Gaza, responded quickly. Within days, they announced the formation of a new organization called Hamas—the Arabic acronym for Islamic Resistance Movement. The group published a charter filled with antisemitic conspiracy theories, in which it advocated for Israel's destruction and replacement by an Islamic state with dominion over the entire area that had once been British Mandatory Palestine. This was Yassin's answer to the PLO's maneuvers toward dialogue and compromise with Israel.

The intifada turned Hamas into "a central force in the Palestinian arena," explains Suleiman al-Shafi, an Arab-Israeli journalist who covered Gaza for Israeli news outlets for decades. "The Israeli response, which included the use of massive military force, only further created a sense of injustice and frustration on the streets of Gaza, and helped make Hamas's ideology even more popular among the Palestinian public."

Yassin was arrested by Israel in 1989 after Hamas members kidnapped and murdered two Israeli soldiers. By then, his organization had become a serious threat in the eyes of Israeli security officials—although Israel's leaders still viewed Arafat and the PLO as the more dangerous actor in the Palestinian arena. On the Israeli left, however, the intifada strengthened the view that the occupation in Gaza and the West Bank was unsustainable and that talking to the PLO was the only way to end the violence. Hamas was viewed by many left-wingers as more extreme and dangerous than the PLO, and advocates of the two-state solution believed that negotiations with Arafat's secular-nationalists was the best way to weaken and sideline the Islamists.

Dani Rachamim was surprised by the intifada. Like most people in Nahal Oz, he never saw it coming. "I knew that the people I met in Gaza were living under a military regime, an occupation regime, and I wanted to change that. But I thought change would come through politics and negotiations, not through violence," he said. "When the riots started, we stopped going."

The uprising and the corresponding rise of Hamas also made it difficult for some Palestinians to continue working on the kibbutz. "One of our workers—a man I worked with for years in the chicken coop—told me that Hamas found out he was working at Nahal Oz and threatened to hurt his family," Dani recalled. "One day he stopped coming, and we never saw him again."

Dani also faced a personal dilemma. In 1988, he was called for reserve duty in the occupied West Bank. While there, he and his friends were sent one Saturday morning to a Palestinian village in order to "disperse a violent riot," in the words of their commander. When they arrived, they saw a group of children hanging Palestinian flags on streetlamps. The soldiers were ordered to make them stop. "I found myself aiming my gun at a child," Dani said. "I already had two children of my own at that point. I said to myself: 'OK, this is the last time I'm doing this. Enough.'"

Six months later, when he was called to his unit again, Dani refused to serve—one of dozens of Israeli reservists who had made a similar decision during the intifada. "I went to my base with books and clothes, ready to be sent to jail," he said. "My wife told me I was crazy." His battalion commander, however, told him that he wouldn't be jailed but would instead be asked to man a checkpoint on the border, without having to set foot on occupied land. "That's something I felt comfortable doing," he explained. "Protecting the border was something I always believed in. It wasn't that different from what we were doing at Nahal Oz."

CHAPTER 5

"THIS IS IT"

OCTOBER 7, 2023

IN THE EVENT OF A cross-border attack on our kibbutz, the emergency procedure was clear: the community's security team would fight the invaders until being reinforced by a rapid-response force from the nearby military base. The soldiers would reach the entrance of the kibbutz within minutes of the assault commencing, and they would be met there by a member of the local security team, who would guide them toward the attackers. At 7:15 A.M. on October 7, that's exactly what Nissan Dekalo was waiting to do.

Sitting in the driver's seat of the kibbutz's bulletproof Land Rover Defender, Nissan gripped a loaded pistol and watched the main gate. Next to him—and wielding Nissan's M16 rifle—was Beri Meirovitch, another member of the kibbutz security team. Amid the ongoing mortar explosions, they could hear gunshots in the distance, coming from inside the kibbutz.

Nissan had trained for this moment several times; he had memorized it by heart. They had to wait at the gate until the soldiers arrived. Except now, when the crisis was actually at hand, it didn't seem like anyone was coming.

———

Nissan, forty-five, was the kibbutz's deputy security chief. This wasn't his full-time job: by day, he worked as a security expert at one of Israel's largest energy companies. But after he, his wife Lee, and their two children

64

moved to the kibbutz in 2015, he had been appointed to this community position, for which he was paid approximately $250 a month. "It's a role with almost no benefits but a huge responsibility," he would reflect. "I was always very proud of doing it."

That morning, when the first barrage of mortars had hit the kibbutz at 6:30 A.M., Nissan's first call was to the kibbutz security chief: my neighbor, Ilan Fiorentino. The two were close friends, and even under these grim circumstances, they still felt relatively calm. "It started strong this time," Ilan told Nissan, expressing no sense of panic.

Following their usual protocol, Ilan asked Nissan to pick up the security team's armored vehicle—the Land Rover—which was parked not far from the Dekalo family's home, and then to proceed to Ilan's house. Usually, whenever mortars were launched toward the kibbutz, the two men's immediate mission was to survey the community in this vehicle, looking for homes that had been hit and people who might need help. In addition to his security expertise, Nissan was trained as a paramedic, and he could offer emergency treatment to anyone who was injured.

But on that morning, while Nissan was busy collecting his weapons and donning his ceramic-armored vest, he received a call from another kibbutz member. "Is it urgent?" Nissan asked. He was in a hurry to get to the vehicle and then to Ilan's house.

"I see *Hamasniks* crossing our fields," the man said, using the Hebrew word for Hamas members. "They're on motorcycles."

Nissan's thoughts immediately flashed to his own family: Lee was out of the country, visiting relatives for the weekend. Their children, a seventeen-year-old boy and fourteen-year-old girl, were in the safe room at home, still a little sleepy. Before the mortars had begun falling, his plan had been to spend the morning at home with the kids, making pancakes.

Now, Nissan returned to the safe room and ordered the kids to lock the door. "Don't open it for anyone," he instructed them. "Even if they speak Hebrew." Then he grabbed his M16 and pistol, locked the house, and ran to the armored vehicle.

As Nissan ran, he called Ilan again. This time, it took his friend a few rings to answer, which was unusual—Ilan always picked up the phone quickly, especially in times of crisis. But when he finally answered, the cause of the delay became clear.

"Nissan, I'm fighting here, don't come," Ilan said, whispering tersely into his phone. Nissan could hear gunfire in the background. Then the call ended abruptly.

Nissan faced a dilemma. He wanted to drive directly to Ilan's house and help him, disobeying his order, but he realized that Ilan had probably told him not to come for a reason. If Nissan arrived alone and encountered a large group of terrorists, they could kill him and take the armored vehicle, leaving the entire community unprotected.

Still, Nissan couldn't abandon his friend—so he decided to take a roundabout way to Ilan's house, driving through one of the kibbutz's residential neighborhoods instead of using the main road. This way, he hoped, the terrorists at least wouldn't spot him as he approached.

As he wove through the kibbutz's side streets, Nissan received a call from Beri, another member of the local security team. Their group consisted of a dozen residents, all of whom had regular day jobs but who had also volunteered to be the kibbutz's internal fighting force in cases of emergency. They all went through combat training several times a year and were primed to respond to different emergency scenarios, including the possibility of a Hamas terror cell infiltrating the kibbutz.

Beri asked Nissan what was going on and mentioned that Ilan wasn't answering his phone. Nissan updated him, and asked: Could Beri join him in the armored vehicle? Without hesitation, Beri agreed.

A minute later, Nissan was outside Beri's house in a part of the kibbutz that the terrorists hadn't yet reached. Beri said goodbye to his wife Roni and their four children, who were inside their safe room, and ran outside to join Nissan. When he jumped in, Nissan took off for Ilan's house—but not before handing Beri the M16, keeping the pistol for himself.

Like the vast majority of the community's residents, Beri had no guns at home. Then, as now, Israeli law prohibited most citizens from possessing firearms, unless they were trained and licensed to do so. Those same laws, however, had allowed any member of the Nahal Oz security team to keep one rifle at home for emergencies, and for many years, that had been the policy. But the rules changed in 2021, when the military had ordered almost all the members of the security team to place their guns in a central armory—a small building located behind a line of homes on the opposite side of the kibbutz from the main entrance.

The military had justified its order by pointing, ironically, toward Gaza. Due to the construction of the new security barrier, the Gaza border was no longer thought to be at risk of being infiltrated, leaving the military more worried about a different kind of risk: theft. Gangs and crime syndicates were stealing weapons from homes all over Israel, officers said; Nahal Oz's rifles would pose less of a threat if they were under lock and key. Nissan and Ilan were the only members of the team who would be allowed to keep their M16s at home; the others could have a pistol but nothing larger.

When Ilan had protested the decision, he was told that if a Hamas cell ever tried to enter the kibbutz, there would be a warning—one early enough so that everyone on the security team would have time to get to the armory and retrieve their weapons. But on the morning of October 7, as the terrorists entered the kibbutz, no early warning came; the members of the security team were all in their safe rooms with their families, sheltering since the first mortar barrage. The armory was a mile or less from most of their homes, but as the terrorists fanned out within the community, reaching it became impossible. Hamas had effectively disarmed the team before firing a single shot.

As he and Beri drove toward Ilan's house, Nissan kept trying to call his friend but got no answer. At the same time, Beri saw a message in the kibbutz's community-wide text group. It had been written by an elderly man, Yonatan "Yonchi" Brosh, who lived two houses behind ours.

"Shoshi is hurt," he wrote, referring to his seventy-five-year-old wife, one of the nicest people in the kibbutz and someone I saw every morning as I was taking my daughters to daycare. Yonchi was now pleading for someone to come and save her. The message was filled with typos, which was unusual for him—a sign of how frantic he must have been.

Beri and Nissan decided they had to go there and help the old couple. They drove through another residential area, still avoiding the main road. They parked the vehicle right outside of Yonchi and Shoshi's home, got out, and made their way to the door. But just as they were about to step inside, they saw dozens of AK-47 shell casings on the ground.

Nissan grabbed Beri and pulled him away. "There are Hamasniks sitting in there, waiting for us," he warned. "We can't handle them alone. If we die in this house, there'll be no one left to fight."

Turning back to the Land Rover, they decided to head for the kibbutz's main entrance. This, too, was protocol: Just a few months earlier, the local security team and the Israeli military's Southern Command had held a weeklong joint exercise simulating a Hamas attack on the kibbutz, although a much smaller one than what had materialized in Nahal Oz that morning. In the exercise, nearby military units had been able to rush to the entrance of Nahal Oz only a few minutes after the simulated attack had commenced. Nissan's role as deputy security chief was to meet them at the gate and direct them toward the terrorists. Now real bullets were flying, yet almost fifteen minutes since the first gunshots were heard in the kibbutz, the military was nowhere to be seen.

Unable to contact Ilan, Nissan and Beri were at least better aware now of the severity of the situation—and of the desperate need for military backup. Maybe, by getting to the gate, they could somehow hasten its arrival.

But when they got to the kibbutz's entrance, there was still no sign of any military presence. Nissan was about to give up and drive alone toward the new neighborhood to join Ilan. "I thought to myself, OK, this is it, I'm going to die," he recalled. "And once I reached that conclusion, I lost all my fear. I was willing to do anything."

Just as he was steeling himself to head back, a white Mazda appeared, seemingly out of nowhere, and careened to a stop right outside the gate. A man with a handgun jumped out and started running toward the kibbutz. The gate was closed, so the man climbed over it. "My first instinct was to shoot him," Nissan said later. "I was waiting for military jeeps full of soldiers, not a single person in a civilian car."

Assuming that this infiltrator was a terrorist trying to join his comrades inside the kibbutz, Nissan took aim with his own pistol. But just then, the man noticed him and raised his hands in the air. He shouted in Hebrew. It took Nissan another second to recognize him.

Kibbutz Nahal Oz, with Battle Sites Marked

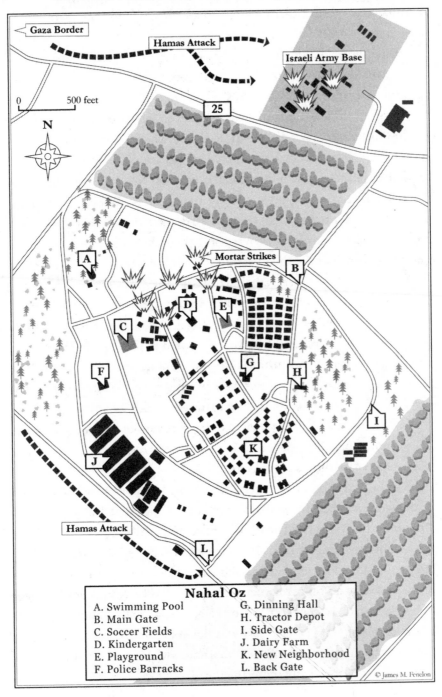

Gaza Border

Hamas Attack

Israeli Army Base

0   500 feet

N

25

Mortar Strikes

A
B
C
D
E
F
G
H
I
J
K
L

Hamas Attack

Nahal Oz

A. Swimming Pool
B. Main Gate
C. Soccer Fields
D. Kindergarten
E. Playground
F. Police Barracks
G. Dinning Hall
H. Tractor Depot
I. Side Gate
J. Dairy Farm
K. New Neighborhood
L. Back Gate

© James M. Fenelon

Three weeks earlier, the Israeli police had sent a team of ten elite troopers to Nahal Oz. Most of them were trained snipers, and they came to the kibbutz for a specific mission: to defend not only the community but also the entire border region.

In mid-September, Hamas had started organizing demonstrations near the border fence. Thousands of Gazans would march toward the fence, throw stones at it, and sometimes even get close enough to rattle it. This happened every day for more than a week. There were no direct attempts to cross the border, and on each occasion the military had successfully used tear gas to disperse the crowds. Nevertheless, the police sent a small team to the area, just in case armed terrorists tried to cross the border under the guise of the civilian demonstration. In retrospect, it is highly probable that Hamas was using these demonstrations to test the military's preparedness ahead of the October 7 attack.

Because of how close Nahal Oz was to the Gaza border, the police had asked the community to provide living quarters for this small team of fighters. The kibbutz offered them two trailers not far from the southern perimeter fence, caravans that had been used as soldiers' barracks back when there had been a constant military presence inside Nahal Oz. The fighters, all men in their twenties, slept inside the kibbutz at night and surveilled the border demonstrations from the fields during the day.

In the first days of October, the demonstrations suddenly stopped. But the police decided to leave the troopers in the region for just one more weekend, in case they were to be resumed.

On the morning of October 7, these ten troopers, just like the rest of us, were awoken by mortars exploding all around Nahal Oz; soon after, they, like us, started hearing gunfire. But while the vast majority of the kibbutz members barricaded ourselves inside our safe rooms, these ten men grabbed their weapons and rushed out toward the threat. Five of them, led by an officer named Amal, who hailed from a small village in northern Israel, went to fight in the area near the kibbutz's cowshed, where a cell of Hamas terrorists was holed up among the live animals; the other five ran toward our neighborhood, which was the first one the terrorists had reached after entering the kibbutz.

Ilan was the kibbutz's only point of contact with the troopers. Nissan had met them during their weeklong stay, but he had no way of getting in touch with them, and he wasn't even aware of their presence inside the kibbutz that morning; he thought that they had gone home for the weekend after successfully completing their mission, a reasonable assumption given that there had been no demonstration near the fence for several days. He certainly wasn't expecting one of them to roll up in a civilian car brandishing a handgun.

It was only when the man at the gate raised his hands that Nissan recognized him. It was Saul, the commander of the sniper team.

The resident of a town fifteen minutes to the east, Saul had rushed to Nahal Oz that morning after his deputy commander, who was staying in one of the trailers with the other troopers, had informed him of the attack on the kibbutz. Now, after climbing over the gate, spotting Nissan and Beri, and realizing that they weren't going to shoot him, Saul ran up to the Land Rover.

"I have a team fighting here," he told them, adding that some of the men had been injured and had barricaded themselves inside a house in the new neighborhood, sniping at terrorists through the windows. He had to get to them. Could Nissan and Beri take him?

Nissan gestured to Saul to climb into the armored vehicle, then gunned the engine and drove as fast as he could toward our part of the kibbutz, now using the main road. By then, he had given up any hope for reinforcements from the Israeli military. "I realized this was all we had," he said. But he was determined to make the most of it.

———

Saul's team of ten troopers had already been fighting in separate parts of the kibbutz for more than twenty minutes by the time he, Nissan, and Beri arrived in the new neighborhood, about two minutes after leaving the main gate. As they approached our row of houses, the trio saw an unbelievable scene. Our road was littered with bodies, and a handful of armed terrorists were running between the buildings, engaged in a pitched battle with some unseen enemy.

The Land Rover pulled to a stop, and from inside the vehicle, the sniper commander sprang into action. "Saul raised his weapon at one of the mehablim, shot him twice in the head, and, *boom*, I went deaf," Nissan said. "I got some of my hearing back a few minutes later, but not completely. Everything sounded as if I was in a dream."

From our safe room, I could hear the exchanges of gunfire but had no idea what exactly was happening. We couldn't know just how fierce of a battle was raging right outside our walls: That five of the troopers had run to our neighborhood after receiving a call from our neighbor, Ilan. That they had managed to kill most of the terrorists in the immediate area. But that they had also lost one of their own: Yakov Karsninski, a twenty-three-year-old officer from Jerusalem who had died after killing four terrorists and wounding a fifth along the road in front of our house. Yakov wasn't supposed to be in Nahal Oz that weekend; it was his turn to go home, but a friend from the same unit had asked him to switch weekends in order to attend a family event, and Yakov had agreed. He had led the team of troopers that ran to our neighborhood, thereby preventing the terrorists from breaking into our and our neighbors' houses, at least temporarily.

"Our guys were better fighters than theirs," Nissan observed later. "I saw with my own eyes how these ten guys had thwarted the plans of dozens of mehablim." But what the Hamas force lacked in quality, it made up for in a massive numerical advantage. Although the nine surviving troopers—who by now had all gathered in our neighborhood, after the team led by Amal had killed the Hamasniks in the cowshed and proceeded to join their comrades—could now count on backup from Saul, Nissan, and Beri, they were collectively facing a swarm of Hamas fighters, armed not only with Kalashnikovs (a type of assault rifle) but also with hand grenades, rocket-propelled grenades, and antitank missiles.

Nissan, Beri, and Saul remained in the armored vehicle, still searching for the rest of the troopers. As the Land Rover proceeded deeper into our neighborhood, they saw signs of a bloody battle in the home of Yonchi and Shoshi, two houses away from my family's, which Nissan and Beri had almost entered earlier. The police team had managed to kill all of the terrorists inside, but at a cost: several troopers had been injured and had been forced to evacuate to another nearby house. When Nissan, Beri, and Saul finally got there and joined the troopers inside, the first thing they saw was more blood. It was everywhere. "There was a wounded guy in every room," Nissan recalled—four wounded troopers in all. "We had to act fast."

First, they worked to save Yonchi, who was injured but alive. Shoshi was dead—killed at the very beginning of the attack when an AK-47 bullet had pierced the metal door of the couple's safe room. A second bullet had wounded her husband. Beri and Nissan, with the latter's certification as a paramedic, helped stabilize Yonchi; once he could be moved, they took him to a neighboring house and asked the couple there, both in their early seventies, to let him inside their safe room.

Next, they had to get the wounded troopers out of the kibbutz or else they would bleed to death. The defenders who were still standing couldn't risk parting with the Land Rover, but Saul told Nissan that his crew had two armored vehicles of their own, parked near their trailers. The problem was how to get there.

Nissan realized he had to take control of the situation. Ilan was still not answering his phone, and they hadn't seen him when they'd passed his home on their way to relieve Saul's troopers. By now, Nissan had to assume that his friend had been killed, like Yakov. If so, then counting the two of them and the other policemen who were now injured, there were only eight men inside the kibbutz with access to weapons and in a condition to keep fighting: Nissan, Beri, Saul, Amal, and four other troopers.

Knowing that they had to reach the other armored vehicles quickly, Nissan and Beri, together with two of the able-bodied police officers, opted to drive straight through the kibbutz to their barracks to retrieve at least one of them. "On the way, we saw apocalyptic scenes," Nissan said. "Hundreds of people were just running across our fields, looking for places to breach the kibbutz's perimeter fence. Dozens of motorcycles with armed men on them were heading east, toward our neighboring communities, and there was no Israeli military in sight."

When the four men reached the barracks, several Hamas fighters were already there, trying to set the place on fire. A quick battle ensued, but this time, it was the Israeli fighters who enjoyed the element of surprise.

Targeting the Hamasniks from inside the safety of their armored vehicle, they managed to kill most of them, but a few escaped and headed elsewhere in the kibbutz.

The two armored vehicles belonging to the police team hadn't been harmed by the terrorists; two of the troopers moved into one of them, while Nissan and Beri remained in their Land Rover. The small convoy then made its way back to the barricaded home where the wounded police officers waited.

It was now approximately 9:00 A.M. and the influx of Gazans entering the kibbutz was continuing at full pace. Alongside the Hamas fighters were dozens of Gazan civilians, some of them teenagers and even several who were younger children, who had come to loot Nahal Oz rather than to attack the kibbutz's residents—or so the defenders hoped.

"We put the wounded guys in their armored vehicle and I instructed one of them, who was well enough to drive, how to reach a point in the kibbutz fence that they'd be able to flatten," Nissan said. "They drove very fast, took down the portion of the fence, and then they were out."

The four injured police fighters eventually made it to the nearest hospital, about thirty minutes away. The rest of the crew was now left to fight the horde of terrorists entering the community—and to try to cope with the wave of ordinary Gazans accompanying them, noncombatants whom the defenders were trying not to hurt, yet any one of whom, for all they knew, could suddenly turn violent, too.

"We were just eight men, facing dozens of mehablim who were now spreading out to different parts of the community, joined by masses of Gazan civilians," Nissan said. "Someone in the military got in touch with me and said they were sending reinforcements. But I just nodded at that point. I knew we were on our own."

The entire crew climbed into the Land Rover, drove to the troopers' barracks, and retrieved the second armored vehicle, a type of SUV nicknamed "Wolf" in Israeli military jargon. Operating again as a convoy—Nissan and Beri in one car, Saul and his men in the other—they drove around the kibbutz, firing at any terrorist they saw, hoping that their vehicles would stand up to the seemingly endless stream of bullets being fired in their direction.

One of the police troopers in the second armored vehicle was a twenty-two-year-old named Ben, a US citizen who had immigrated to Israel three years earlier and enlisted in the military, hoping to join a special unit of the IDF; eventually, however, he was sent instead to the police, to join the snipers' unit that now found itself battling the terrorists inside Nahal Oz. That morning, as the mortar barrage began, he texted his dad, who was at home in Arizona, that he was inside a kibbutz on the border and that war had broken out.

Over the coming hours, as his son fought the terrorists in our kibbutz, Ben's father frantically tried to call him from the other side of the world, but Ben had no time to pick up the phone. From inside the armored vehicle, the only thing he saw was whatever was visible at any given moment through the scope on his M4 rifle.

"I was sure Israel no longer existed," Ben later recalled. "We kept asking for the military to come and help us, but nobody showed up." His thoughts grew darker by the minute. He feared that, while Hamas had attacked Israel from Gaza, Hezbollah, a powerful terror organization operating out of Lebanon, might also have opened up a second front along Israel's northern border. At one point during the fighting, Ben asked himself if the military's failure to reinforce Nahal Oz could be a sign that Iran was also now bombing Tel Aviv.

"I thought we had been forgotten at this small kibbutz," he said, "and that once we all finished our ammunition, we were simply going to die."

Inside our safe room, cell phone reception was erratic, and Miri and I could barely communicate with the outside world. Messages that we tried to send to people in the kibbutz in order to figure out what was going on were marked as "delivered" only ten minutes later. There was no internet, so we had no way to get updates from news websites about the general situation in the country. The girls were still quiet, playing silently with their dolls in the dark. Galia asked us for an apple; little Carmel asked for ice cream. Miri told them she was really sorry but we couldn't get either of those things for them right now.

After the first two hours, during which we heard nonstop gunfire outside our window, things became much quieter. By now, there were barely any mortars falling around us. As the hours passed, though, we continued to hear shouting in Arabic and there was still gunfire—sometimes close to our house, sometimes further away.

Our situation was dismal. But when I finally had cell phone reception again, a quick glance at my phone, which was quickly losing battery, made it clear that others in the kibbutz were facing even greater danger.

In one home, on the other edge of the community, the Idan family—father Tzachi and mother Gali, both forty-nine, and their children—had Hamas terrorists pounding on their safe room door. They told the family to open it, and when the Idans refused, the attackers began to force their way in.

Although the locking mechanism of the safe room door in some homes was strong enough that it couldn't be opened from the outside no matter what, with many others, that wasn't the case, as they had been designed to save anyone sheltering inside them from mortar and rocket attacks, not from terrorists with Kalashnikovs. Tzachi Idan knew that, in his home, the safe room lock wasn't capable of stopping a determined person on the other side from eventually opening it. But he held onto the handle with all his might, and a fight for the door ensued between him and the terrorists. They didn't just try to open it with their hands, though—they also shot at it, likely hoping that the blasts would kill Tzachi or at least force him away from the door.

After several minutes, in the midst of the fight over the door handle, one of the bullets penetrated the door and flew into the room. Tzachi yelled "Who's hurt?" and realized a second later that it was his eldest daughter, Ma'ayan—a teenage girl who worked in the kibbutz's daycare center and was beloved by the entire community.

Gali, Tzachi's wife, touched Ma'ayan in the dark and felt blood streaming from her head. She knew immediately: her daughter, who had celebrated her eighteenth birthday just four days earlier, was dead.

The terrorists gave the Idan family no time to grieve. As soon as they'd breached the door, they yelled at the survivors to move to the living room, ordering them to sit on the floor. While the children cried for their dead sister, one of the terrorists placed a phone with an active Facebook Live broadcast in front of them, documenting the horrific scene. The whole world could now see the helpless family in the hands of Hamas.

In the livestream, Gali and the children could be seen lying on the floor with Tzachi seated next to them, visibly in a state of shock. The children were weeping, and Gali, still in her pajamas, was trying to console them, fighting back her own tears.

At 11:28 A.M., a friend from outside the kibbutz, who had seen the unfathomable broadcast, posted an image from it on his social media account, tagging the official account of the Israeli police. "Send forces to Nahal Oz, to the Idan family!" he wrote. The post went viral and at one point, when I briefly got cell phone reception again, I received it from a colleague at the newspaper. I didn't watch the video, attempting to preserve battery in my phone, but the freeze-frame, which showed Gali's terrified look while a gun was being pointed at her children, told me everything I needed to know.

Knowing there was nothing we could do, I decided not to tell Miri, believing she was better off not knowing what was happening to other families when their safe room doors gave way.

The Idans were not the only family enduring such a nightmare. A similar scene was unfolding at the home of Dikla Arava, fifty-one, a teacher and parent counselor who had helped raise a generation of children in the kibbutz, and her partner Noam Elyakim, forty-six. They were being held hostage along with Dikla's seventeen-year-old son, Tomer, and Noam's two young daughters, Dafna, fifteen, and Ela, eight. Again, the terrorists opened a Facebook Live broadcast, during which it was possible to see that Noam was badly injured, bleeding from his foot, while Dikla was trying to calm their children. Soon afterward, the terrorists took Tomer and marched him at gunpoint to nearby houses. They ordered him to knock on safe room doors and beg the people inside to open up or else he would be killed.

In one of the homes that the terrorists brought Tomer to, they found a surprise. Micky, a kibbutz resident in his forties, had a pistol at home and was waiting for the mehablim inside his house. He managed to fire at several of Tomer's captors while taking cover behind a corner wall. After a lengthy "negotiation" during which Micky shot several more terrorists, the attackers threatened to fire an RPG into the safe room, which would have killed Micky's wife and daughter. He tricked them into thinking that he was about to surrender, promising to throw away his gun if they spared his family, but then immediately opened fire again and killed the Hamasnik who was holding the RPG. Eventually, after a lengthy stand-off, the attackers withdrew—perhaps deciding that this crazy kibbutznik had cost them too much blood, time, and ammunition.

Micky's family had been saved by his heroism, and by killing some of the terrorists and slowing down others, he had probably saved the lives of many of his neighbors, as well. Nevertheless, he felt powerless to do much more to help. Hearing the gunfire from neighboring homes, he knew that if he dared step outside, he'd be exposed and would face certain death. He sent urgent messages to the kibbutz WhatsApp group, begging for military forces to come to their row of houses and join him in fighting the Hamasniks.

Nearby, in a home that was often used to host visitors to the kibbutz, the terrorists found two American citizens: Judith Raanan, fifty-nine, and her teenage daughter Natalie from Evanston, Illinois. They were the daughter and granddaughter of Tamar Livyatan, an eighty-four-year-old kibbutz resident and the girlfriend of Yechiel Chlenov, one of the community's founders; they had come to visit Tamar and Yechicel at Nahal Oz for Tamar's eighty-fifth birthday. Instead of celebrating, they found themselves barricaded in the guest house's safe room for hours and eventually taken at gunpoint into the Idan family home, leaving behind their phones and computers. Judith informed the terrorists that she was a US citizen, and one of them was able to talk with her in English, promising not to hurt her and her daughter as long as they followed his orders.

The attackers also managed to break into the home of Omri Miran, forty-six, and his wife Lishay, thirty-eight. They were in their safe room with their daughters, two-year-old Roni and six-month-old Alma. Hearing the terrorists outside their door, Lishay sent heartbreaking messages to the kibbutz WhatsApp group, begging for help. Then, she and Omri heard Tomer, whom they knew well, crying from the other side of the door for them to open or else he would be shot to death in their hallway.

Omri, known throughout the community for his kindness and generosity toward others, took a deep breath and opened the door. The terrorists swept in and took the entire family to the Idan residence.

The Facebook Live video continued rolling, and the hundreds of people watching it now saw Lishay, holding little Alma in her hands, sitting on the floor next to Gali.

———————

It was now past noon, and still no military reinforcements had arrived at the kibbutz. Nissan, Beri, Saul, and the five fighters continued racing around the community, fighting Hamasniks and also shooting at any looters whom they saw entering residents' homes. The defenders' logic was that, once an intruder was inside a family's house, there was no way of knowing—no way of controlling—what that person could do to the people barricaded inside of it. Some of the looters seemed singularly focused on stealing cars, electronic devices, and anything else they could get their hands on. But others were actively aiding the terrorists' efforts to open safe room doors and kill or kidnap those hiding behind them. In the fog of war, it was difficult, if not outright impossible, to tell the difference.

Of the two vehicles that the eight-man crew originally had at their disposal, only one was still functional; the Land Rover had taken a direct hit from an RPG, killing its engine, so the entire group was now crammed inside the Wolf. They had lost count of how many people they had killed; however, waves of Gazans kept arriving, and the defenders' situation, already dire, was growing untenable. The surviving vehicle wasn't looking much better than the destroyed one. Bullets had cracked the front windshield, which was strong enough not to shatter completely but was now difficult to see through; another RPG had hit one of the front tires, slowing their progress considerably. On top of all that, they were almost out of water.

Beri was glued to his phone, trying to direct their small team to the various parts of the kibbutz where people were reporting the presence of terrorists. The problem was that these reports were arriving from almost every neighborhood, simultaneously.

Nissan thought the most important thing they could do was to constantly keep moving. "I wanted to fool the Hamasniks, make them think there were several armored vehicles operating inside the kibbutz, not just one," he explained. "I was hoping this might maybe scare them or cause them to make mistakes."

By 1:00 P.M., however, the relentless pace of the fighting was catching up with them. The crew in the armored vehicle was running out of bullets. The RPG had destroyed the vehicle's air-conditioning system, but for their own safety, its passengers couldn't open any of the windows—turning the SUV into an overheated death trap. Nissan and Beri were also worried for their own families. Nissan's home was in an area of the kibbutz that still had electricity and cell phone reception, so his children were constantly on the phone with Lee, their mother, overseas—but they had no idea if their father was still alive, and he had no way of knowing whether they were, either. Beri's wife, Roni, updated him periodically from their safe room, telling him that she and their children were scared but OK. As the hours passed, his fear for his loved ones, already crushing, became unbearable.

In our safe room, I was feeling the same sense of rising dread. More than six hours into the ordeal, things only seemed to be getting worse, with no end in sight. Carmel began wandering around the room, looking for something to do in the dark. Then she stepped on an object I couldn't see, fell to the floor, and, for the first time that morning, started crying.

I took our toddler in my arms, hugged her, and helped her calm down. She stayed nestled against me for a few minutes—and as she did, I noticed that she seemed sleepy. I put her in Galia's bed, where her sister was already resting, and the two quickly fell asleep together, almost hugging each other, exhausted from fear and hunger.

Once the girls were back asleep, Miri and I finally let down our guard. Up until that point, we had both taken pains to maintain our composure, knowing that any signs of distress from either one of us would make the girls even more scared than they already were. But now, all of our carefully restrained emotions came pouring out: the fear, the anger, the remorse.

Whispering lest we wake the girls, I told Miri that this was all my fault: it had been my idea to come and live here, and now our lives might be ending because of it. "I never should have brought us here," I said.

Miri tried to comfort me. She said that the decision to move to Nahal Oz was one that we had taken together. She said that she loved living in the kibbutz and raising our daughters here. "We both chose this place," she reminded me.

With nothing left to say, I told Miri how proud I was of her—as a mother, a partner, and a friend.

"I love you, I love our daughters, I love our life together," she replied. For all we knew, these could be the last words that we said to each other.

Then, for a brief moment, my cell reception returned. On my phone's screen, I saw a message from my mother.

CHAPTER 6

"THEY'LL NEVER FORGIVE THEMSELVES"

OCTOBER 7, 2023

THAT SAME SATURDAY MORNING, BAR and Lior Metzner, a couple in their thirties from central Israel, had left their home in the predawn darkness. At 3:00 A.M., they were already on the road, driving south along Route 232, a highway that runs parallel to the Israel-Gaza border. Their destination was the Re'im forest—a quiet expanse of pine and eucalyptus trees three miles east of the border fence, and about six miles south of Nahal Oz. They had left their kids, five and two years old, with Bar's parents for the weekend so that she and Lior could blow off some steam at an event that they'd been looking forward to for months: a music festival.

They arrived at the forest when it was still dark, parked their car at the edge of an improvised parking lot, and joined the party, which by this point was more than two thousand people strong. It was like a dream: in the waning days of Israel's long summer, while the weather was still warm, thousands of people had gathered to dance, unwind, and celebrate life in a natural setting only an hour's drive from Tel Aviv.

The fact that this celebration was taking place just a short distance from the Gaza Strip didn't seem to faze anyone: the preceding months had been mostly quiet along the border. When Bar and Lior arrived, the only blasts they heard came from the festival's massive speakers, which were pumping out techno music. The smell of marijuana—illegal in Israel but still prevalent at parties like this—wafted through the trees.

Then, at 6:30 A.M., everything changed.

Against the gentle pink light of the new day, a swarm of missiles suddenly filled the sky. Deafening explosions rocked the forest. The music stopped and people began screaming in panic.

At the exact moment that Miri and I were dashing to our safe room in the kibbutz six miles to the north, the Nova partygoers found themselves sprinting toward their own bomb shelters, several of which dotted the wooded area. Many were unable to reach them and simply had to throw themselves to the ground and cover their heads with their hands. As the barrage continued, it was clear that the party was over—but worse was still in store.

Instead of heading for one of the bomb shelters, Bar and Lior ran to their car. Lior had a bad feeling that something awful was about to happen—something worse, that is, than the deadly projectiles raining down from above. The large number of rockets flying overhead—and the fact that, as Lior could now plainly see, most of them were bypassing the Re'im area and heading toward large population centers—seemed unusual to him. This wasn't a "one-and-done" launch from Gaza, he realized. This was something different, something bigger. It was time for him and his wife to head home.

They reached their car unscathed and guided it safely out of the parking lot. At the exit, they encountered a police officer who told them to take a left turn, sending them back toward home along Route 232. They joined a procession of cars, all filled with other people fleeing the festival.

They drove north as the rockets continued flying over their heads. It was a frightening scene, but Lior was able to keep calm and focus on the road. His foot remained on the gas, his eyes were fixed on the cars ahead of him, and in his mind was only one thought: *I have to get us out of here.*

He couldn't tell exactly how many minutes had passed, or where exactly they had reached, when he first heard gunshots and realized that something terrible was happening—much worse than what he'd imagined when they first started driving away from the party. He anticipated a continuous barrage of rockets and feared that one of them would hit their car, but now he and Bar were hearing automatic gunfire ahead on the road. He kept driving and couldn't believe what he was now seeing in front of him—cars full of bullet holes and people jumping out of them, some looking injured, running for their lives.

Then, he saw the white pickup truck. Several armed men were standing on top of it, and they were aiming in his direction. His mind hadn't yet processed what exactly he was seeing—an improvised Hamas roadblock, located on a highway inside Israel—but he knew that he and his wife were now facing immediate, grave danger.

Lior yelled at Bar to put her head down, and he ducked, too—but continued driving, not daring to look up. One second passed and then another—Lior and Bar were still alive. Miraculously, they had made it past the SUV without hitting it or getting hit by bullets themselves. They raised their heads and saw an open road before them.

But one of the ambushers' bullets must have found its mark, because no sooner had Bar and Lior cleared the roadblock than their engine started to die. "All the lights in the car were blinking," Lior recalled, "and I realized we had to get out."

He pulled over to the side of the road, and the couple scrambled out of the car and quickly surveyed their surroundings. It was now approximately 7:30 A.M., and the full scope of Hamas's invasion of Israel was becoming clear. Bar and Lior, who had hardly ever visited the area before, were surrounded by an unfamiliar landscape of large agricultural plots that stretched off in all directions for as far as the eye could see. The couple could see the homes of an Israeli community in the distance—but cars and motorcycles with armed men, presumably more Hamas terrorists, seemed to be heading in that direction, which meant that Bar and Lior had no choice but to go the other way.

So they did the only thing they could: they abandoned their car and ran on foot into the surrounding fields. They couldn't tell how long they ran for, or in which direction exactly, but they knew they had to find someplace where they could hide. They saw no Israeli military presence anywhere.

"We kept running until we saw a ditch near one of the roads full of bushes and dry leaves," Lior recalled. "We lay on the ground and covered ourselves with the leaves." Bar tried to call the police, but to no avail: the emergency call center was flooded with appeals for help from all over the border region.

Bar recalled telling her husband, "This can't be real—we have two kids at home." The thoughts of their two little children continued to exert a powerful force—a reason to remain focused, to keep calm, to stay alive. Just then, the sound of gunshots and shouting in Arabic nearby ended any further possibility of conversation.

They had no water or food with them and had no idea of their exact location or of how much time had passed since they had abandoned their car. When would it be safe to emerge from their hiding place? Finally, they heard the wailing of an ambulance and decided to risk it.

Bar dashed out and waved down the ambulance, which was being escorted by an Israeli military Humvee. They had been saved—or so they thought.

"The soldiers took us into their vehicle, but instead of heading away from the border area, they suddenly stopped," Lior recalled. "They'd received a call from another unit that urgently needed their help, and they told us that they had to go. So they basically went back to the same spot where they'd picked us up, and dropped us off there."

Back in the ditch, Bar and Lior listened in horror as the gunfire grew louder and closer. In the distance, on the road that they were sheltering alongside, they could see cars that had been torched.

"And then—our guardian angel arrived," Bar said. "It was like a scene from a movie. A Jeep stopped next to us, and inside were a man and a woman about the same age as our parents. We had no idea who they were. But they told us to get in."

My parents had left their home in Tel Aviv at 7:30 A.M., roughly an hour after the rocket sirens had first sounded in their city. After their quiet morning at the beach had been shattered by the bombardment and by the news that we had terrorists outside our window, they had sped home, still wet and covered with sand, to regroup before heading in our direction—unsure of what, exactly, they would do but knowing that they had to do *something*.

Although he had retired from the military in 2014, my father Noam still had his uniform at home with his major general insignia clearly visible, but he was in such a hurry that he hadn't thought to put it on. Instead, he'd thrown on a pair of blue jeans and a black T-shirt. On the way out of the house, he'd taken his pistol and loaded it. Then he and my mother, who like him had hastily changed out of her bathing suit, had run outside to their gray Jeep Grand Cherokee.

My father had planned to drive alone toward Nahal Oz, but my mother Gali had insisted on joining him; she told him that, if she drove, he'd be free to text and call people in the military, in the hope that one of them would be able to send reinforcements to the kibbutz if they weren't already en route. At that point, they were still unaware of how large and efficient Hamas's surprise attack had been—or how badly the IDF was reeling.

While my mother navigated the Jeep through the maze of highways leading out of Tel Aviv, my father tried calling several senior generals who had served under his command in the past—including the army's chief of staff, the head of the Southern Command, and the commander of the Gaza regional division. None of them answered. So he texted instead, telling them that terrorists were inside Nahal Oz. One of them responded "I know," and that was it.

As they drove farther south and got closer to the border region, my parents noticed that their car was almost alone on the road. It was an ominous sign of what lay ahead.

Just north of the Strip, my mother took a left turn onto Highway 34 at Yad Mordechai junction, and my parents officially entered the Gaza border region. My father put down the phone and gripped his pistol, bracing himself for whatever they might find. Rockets were flying overhead toward central Israel, but the road before them was still clear.

Then, at the entrance to Sderot—the largest city in the border area, located some fifteen minutes from Nahal Oz—my parents ran into their first firefight of the morning.

A police cruiser was parked sideways in the middle of Highway 34, blocking both lanes. Several policemen were taking cover behind it, exchanging fire with distant opponents whom my parents could discern only by the bullets that were pocking the side of the police car.

One of the policemen saw my parents' Jeep approaching and waved them back with his hand. With no choice but to turn around, my mother pulled over on the side of the road. She was preparing to make a U-turn when suddenly a young man and woman appeared in front of them.

"We saw a couple dressed for a party, wearing clothes that you don't usually wear on a Saturday morning," my father later recalled. He and my mother hurriedly opened the doors and let them in. "They got into the Jeep and sat in the back. We asked where they'd come from and if they needed help. They were out of breath, but the woman said, 'They shot everyone. Everyone's dead.'" It was Bar and Lior.

With two unexpected passengers now in their Jeep, my parents turned around and drove away from Sderot and the shoot-out, heading toward the nearest city, Ashkelon, on the far side of Yad Mordechai junction, about twenty minutes north. As before, they were almost completely alone on the road.

As my mother drove, she and my father listened to Bar and Lior describe their ordeal. They told my parents how terrorists had descended on the festival and killed people in their cars as they'd tried to escape. My parents listened in disbelief and horror, finally understanding the depth of the disaster unfolding in the border area—and only growing more panicked about what was happening to us in Nahal Oz.

They drove the traumatized young couple toward safety, eventually dropping them next to a manned police car at the entrance to Ashkelon. Then my mother wheeled the Jeep around and headed back to the border area.

By this point, Miri and I no longer had regular cell phone coverage, so my father's messages to us were going unanswered. He tried to call some of our friends in the kibbutz, including Eitan and Dganit, a couple in their early sixties who had been our "adopted parents" since we'd moved to the community in 2014. Eitan, a carpenter and resident of Nahal Oz for over forty years, had told us after we joined the kibbutz that since we'd be living far away from our parents (at least, by Israeli standards), we should ask him for any kind of help we might need. Over the years, the relationship became so close that our own parents would call him "Grandpa Eitan" when they'd run into him while babysitting our daughters.

Eitan had lived through countless wars and security escalations during his four decades on the kibbutz, and he was usually nonchalant in times of crisis. But when my father called him that morning, he sounded different. There was fear in his voice.

Eitan explained that mehablim were going door to door inside the community and that Ilan, the security chief, was no longer answering his phone. He added that cell phone reception wasn't working properly in different parts of the kibbutz—particularly in the area near our home, which had also lost electricity, leaving us without the backup of Wi-Fi.

My father asked Eitan if there was any way to send reinforcements to our neighborhood. "What do you mean, reinforcements?" Eitan replied. "I don't think there's any military here."

With Eitan's words ringing in their ears, my parents resolved to try to get to Nahal Oz as quickly as possible by circumnavigating Sderot from the east, via a different road from the one on which they had run into the firefight earlier that morning. As they drove south, they managed to connect with us briefly over the phone and informed us that they were driving toward the kibbutz. They heard me whisper that there were gunshots outside our window but that the girls were still calm and quiet. Wanting to save battery and avoid making too much noise, I quickly ended the conversation. My parents were relieved to hear that we were alive but realized that our situation was still extremely dangerous.

As they proceeded south, my parents ran into an improvised police checkpoint on the eastern edge of Sderot. The officers wouldn't let them pass: everything beyond this point was a closed military zone, they explained. My father got out to talk to them and even produced a military ID card showing his rank, but the officers insisted. One of them, trying to calm him down, told my father that, as a retired general, he must know that "there's plenty of military forces here. They're taking care of it."

It was this last sentence, more than anything else, that convinced my parents they had to take matters into their own hands. By that point, it was after 9:00 A.M. and my father still hadn't heard back from any of his contacts in the military about the situation at Nahal Oz. His conversations with Eitan and me had left him extremely worried. One thing he knew for sure was that nobody was "taking care of it," as the policeman was claiming.

My father thanked the officers and climbed back into the passenger seat of the Jeep. Then, turning off the road, my mother drove straight into the surrounding fields, still heading southward, but simply bypassing the checkpoint from the west. They drove through the fields for several minutes, and then, once the coast was clear, they got back on the road.

At the southern edge of Sderot, just north of the junction where 232 and 34, the two main highways of the border region, cross each other, my parents encountered a second checkpoint. This time, they simply drove through it. The police officers aimed their guns at the Jeep, but my mother opened the window and shouted, "We're Israeli, our family is stranded in Nahal Oz. If you want, you can shoot us." The officers put down their weapons, and my mother sped past.

They were now at the Sha'ar Hanegev junction, where Highways 232 and 34 intersected approximately eight miles from Nahal Oz. My mother took a left onto 232—the road that Bar and Lior had first taken in their attempt to escape the music festival—and then she stopped the Jeep in its tracks. She couldn't believe what she saw in front of her.

It was a biblical scene: The road was strewn with corpses. Not one or two, but dozens of dead bodies. Inside cars, outside cars, on the sides of the road, in the middle of it. Bodies of Israeli citizens—men and women—and bodies of armed men, some of them Israeli soldiers and policemen, some of them Hamas fighters. Most of the cars on the road were charred skeletons; some were overturned. Several were still intact, with their engines running but with no one behind the wheel.

My father had been a military man for most of his adult life. He began his career in the special forces, had fought in Israel's 1982 war in Lebanon, and later took part in secret operations behind enemy lines in multiple countries. He had lost friends, been injured, and watched people die before his eyes. Still, what he saw that morning was different. "I've never seen so much death in one place before," he later explained.

My mother turned off the Jeep's engine, and she and my father sat there for a moment, staring out at this hellish scene. My father wasn't sure if they could keep going: clearly the area was extremely dangerous, and proceeding meant that they could very well die on the road like the people whose bodies now lay before them. Again, he tried to call someone—anyone—in the military's high ranks, but he couldn't get through. Again, he tried to call and text us, but with no luck. He had given up on trying to call Eitan or others in the kibbutz—they were clearly unable to help from inside their safe rooms.

What to do? Keep moving forward and very possibly die? Or go back toward safety and leave us to our fates in Nahal Oz, hoping that the policeman at the checkpoint had been right and that the IDF had the situation in hand? A decision had to be made, one way or another.

Finally, my mother spoke. "What if I told you about a couple," she said, "who are less than ten kilometers from the home of their son and their two granddaughters, and can go and try to save their family—or they can stop and wait at the side of the road for someone else to do something?"

It was a rhetorical question. But my father answered it: "I'd say they have to go to their granddaughters, and they'll never forgive themselves if they don't."

And that was it. My mother turned on the engine and nosed the Jeep forward—more slowly now, as she had to steer the car between the bodies and burned-out vehicles strewn across the roadway. But she and my father had made their decision: there was no turning back now.

A few minutes later, my parents had to stop again, this time at the entrance to Kibbutz Mefalsim, which lay just off the eastern shoulder of Route 232, only about ten minutes north of Nahal Oz. Like our kibbutz, Mefalsim was a border community but a little more distant from Gaza. Yet here, unlike at Nahal Oz, the terrorists had failed to get past the gate.

Earlier that morning, members of the local security team at Mefalsim had heard that terrorists had entered Nahal Oz and Kfar Azza, communities that were located closer to the border than theirs. This advance warning gave the volunteers just enough time to grab their weapons and set up defensive positions at key locations along their kibbutz's perimeter fence. As a result, when Hamas fighters reached Mefalsim, they found a much harder target than the ones they had encountered at other, nearby kibbutzim.

By the time my mother stopped the Jeep outside its front gate, at approximately 10:30 A.M., Mefalsim's defenders had been fighting off Hamas attackers for more than two hours—and now, as my parents quickly discovered, they had driven right into the middle of that firefight. Thankfully, they had pulled up next to a bomb shelter on the opposite side of the road from the gated entrance to the kibbutz, and they managed to dash out of the vehicle and into the concrete structure without getting hurt.

For a long time—they couldn't tell exactly how long—my parents waited in the darkness of the bomb shelter, listening to the battle raging right outside, just feet away. At some point, when the shooting stopped, an Israeli soldier came over and asked them to leave. "It's too dangerous for you to stay here," he said. "There are still a lot of mehablim in the area."

In a coincidence that could happen only in a small country like Israel, where the cliché is that "everybody knows each other," the soldier recognized my mother as his former high school principal. Incredulous but still insistent, he told my parents that they had to move to a second bomb shelter located across the road, closer to the gate of the kibbutz, until there was a safer place for them to go to.

My mother and father went reluctantly; what they really wanted was to get back in their Jeep and keep driving to Nahal Oz. That feeling only grew stronger when they stepped inside the second bomb shelter and immediately stopped in disbelief.

The bomb shelter that the soldier had guided them to was full of dead bodies. Some of them were made up in the same way that Bar and Lior had been dressed: for a party. But whatever connections my parents drew in their minds, they couldn't know the whole story: How, earlier that morning, some of the people who had escaped the Nova music festival had reached the gates of Mefalsim and taken refuge inside this very bomb shelter. How Hamas terrorists had chased them to the entrance and thrown hand grenades after them into the shelter, which was essentially just a concrete box with an open, doorless entryway, built to offer protection from rocket fire, not from a terrorist standing right next to it; how the grenades had exploded while some of the people inside were on their phones with their family members, saying their last goodbyes.

Unable to linger in all that carnage, my parents crossed back over to the bomb shelter on other side of the road—yet at this moment, ironically, my father felt hope for the first time that day. For he and my mother now watched as three black, armored vehicles stopped in front of the kibbutz's gate and fighters in tactical gear jumped out. It was an Israeli special forces unit. My father approached them and asked for their help.

"The battle here is over," he told the commandos, "but my family is in Nahal Oz. There are mehablim in their kibbutz and no military presence. You have armored vehicles; it's ten minutes from here. Let me guide you to the place where the mehablim are."

This was a team of veteran, professional fighters, my father realized. All of them were men, the majority in their thirties and early forties. Some of them had recognized him, having previously served under his command in various units. They clearly wanted to go with him.

But their commander vetoed the idea. He was trying unsuccessfully to contact his own superiors for further instructions. His men had already fought one difficult battle that morning inside Sderot, where terrorists had entered the city's main police station, killing more than two dozen officers before barricading themselves inside. He had lost several commandos there. "We need to follow orders," he told my father. "I can't do this without getting authorization from my superiors."

What this midranking commander didn't know was that, at the regional army command center thirteen miles to the south, another fierce battle was taking place. Dozens of Hamas fighters had attacked the base that morning and, after overcoming the guards at the entrance, had managed to get into an office building containing sensitive communications equipment and intelligence materials. The commander of the base, a brigadier general, had barricaded himself and several soldiers inside a bunker within the compound and was trying to coordinate the military's response to the broader assault on the border communities while simultaneously monitoring Hamas's advance inside his own base. This was why the officer with whom my father was speaking at Mefalsim was having a hard time getting through to anyone: the chain of command was broken.

The regional command base had been mostly empty that morning due to the Jewish holiday of Simchat Torah, for which many soldiers here, as at the base near Nahal Oz, had taken leave—another sign of the Israeli intelligence agencies' failure to predict the Hamas attack. And not all of the people who were inside the base at the time of the attack had even been soldiers: a small group of civilians had managed to escape from the Nova music festival and reach the base in the early morning hours of October 7. The guards had let them inside, and they had taken shelter in the installation's living quarters, thinking they were safe. Soon, however, the now-familiar din of approaching gunfire brought the realization that even this place, the most important military post in the Gaza border region, was in danger of falling into Hamas's hands.

Luckily for the people sheltering inside the base, among its defenders that morning were several officers and soldiers from Israel's Bedouin community, an Arab-Muslim minority group that mostly lives in the southern parts of the country. Unlike most Arab-Muslim Israelis, who are exempt from military service for political reasons (many of them define themselves as Palestinian citizens of Israel and are not expected to go to war against their brethren), Bedouin men—who are less likely to self-identify as Palestinians—often enlist in the Israeli army and serve in combat roles. What this meant was that as Hamas had begun its attack on the base, the Palestinian fighters from Gaza found themselves fighting opposite Israeli soldiers who shared their religion—Islam—and spoke the same language as them—Arabic. These men would play a crucial role in the battle ahead.

The battle inside the base ultimately lasted for almost four hours. As the refugees from the Nova festival hid in total silence inside a locked room in the base's living quarters, the Bedouin soldiers gradually managed to kill most of the Hamas attackers. At one point, one of the soldiers—whose name can't be disclosed for security reasons—volunteered to deceive the assailants in order to slow their progress. He took off his uniform and, dressed in civilian clothes, pretended to be a member of Hamas, shouting in Arabic to win the trust of several of the attackers who were approaching the living quarters where the civilians were hiding. This soldier succeeded in diverting the Hamas fighters to another part of the base—one where they were exposed to Israeli fire. His comrades killed them all.

Ten other Hamas fighters entered a sports facility inside the base and hunkered down inside it, sniping through the windows at anyone who got close. One of the Bedouin officers, a lieutenant colonel named Mohammad, managed to communicate with the senior Israeli commanders inside the nearby bunker and coordinated an air force attack on the sports facility, killing the Hamas fighters inside. "I never imagined this was something I'd ever have to do," he confessed afterward. An Israeli television segment on the battle later described Mohammad, with only a touch of hyperbole, as "the first officer in Israeli history to order the aerial bombing of his own base."

At approximately 10:30 A.M., a special forces team managed to reach the regional command base and reinforce the Bedouin fighters. Yet the fight still lasted for another hour or so before the base was finally declared clear. Until roughly 11:30 A.M., as a result, any officers throughout the border area who tried to get in touch with the commanders at the base were left waiting for instructions: Where to go? What to do? How to respond to the chaos around them? The orders never came.

Knowing nothing of this debacle, the survivors who were still hiding in Israeli communities along the Gaza border couldn't comprehend why, so many hours into the assault, the IDF still hadn't reached their homes to save them. With nowhere else to turn, they had begun calling and texting journalists with urgent pleas for help.

Israel's leading television channels had been in emergency mode since the early morning hours, broadcasting live as they tried to make sense of events along the border. Reporters were soon receiving heartbreaking calls from people hiding in their safe rooms—people who, unlike us, still had cell reception. One reporter for Channel 12, Israel's most widely watched television station, almost broke down on air as he pleaded with the military to send forces to Kibbutz Be'eri—a community not far from us. "People are seeing mehablim driving through the kibbutz on motorcycles with guns in their hands," he said. "Someone, please, do something."

One of my colleagues at *Haaretz*, a police and crime reporter named Josh Breiner, tried to direct the police to specific locations where people were reporting an immediate threat to their lives. He was contacted by survivors from the Nova party who were hiding in the woods and waiting for someone to save them, while the terrorists continued their killing spree. He sent these survivors' locations directly to Israel's chief of police, who encouraged him to keep forwarding any information he had and promised that he would try to send forces to the scene.

Josh was aware of the difficult situation at my kibbutz, though I wasn't in contact with him directly at this point. "Nahal Oz. I'm afraid to write about what's probably happening there," he wrote on social media around noon. "Residents are reporting that the military is nowhere to be seen."

———————

Back at the front gate of Kibbutz Mefalsim, my parents had resorted to begging the special forces unit to take my father with them to Nahal Oz. Their commander was still trying, to no avail, to get concrete orders from his superiors.

Then one of the commandos, a man in his late thirties named Avi, approached my father and said, "I'll come with you." Avi, a veteran of Israel's elite Duvdevan unit, which is responsible for undercover operations in the West Bank, didn't know my father personally, but like some of his comrades that morning, he had served under his command earlier in his career. More importantly, Avi had decided that he couldn't keep standing there in front of the gate of Mefalsim, waiting for instructions, when there were terrorists wreaking havoc inside a kibbutz just a few minutes down the road. His commander tried to talk him out of it, but Avi insisted: he was going to Nahal Oz. Rather than trying to stop him, the officer let Avi leave.

Avi and my father headed toward my parents' Jeep alone. By now it was almost noon; my parents had spent more than an hour at Mefalsim and were growing frantic at having been stuck there for so long. But they both agreed that my mother should stay behind in the roadside bomb shelter and wait: she had no combat training and no battlefield experience before that morning; it was simply too dangerous for her to come on this next phase of the journey. From inside the shelter, she sent me a text message informing me that my father was getting closer.

The drive from Mefalsim to Nahal Oz takes about ten minutes under normal circumstances, but these were anything but. My father and Avi had no idea what they might encounter on the road ahead. The sounds of gunfire were still echoing across the area, and my father was also aware that the stretch of road they were about to enter was completely exposed to potential sniper fire from Gaza. Still, he had no hesitation: everything he had seen up until this point, from the rescue of Bar and Lior to the scores of dead bodies on the way to Mefalsim and outside its gate, convinced him that we were in grave danger. And his faith in the IDF, the military to which he'd devoted most of his life, was waning by the minute.

My father climbed behind the wheel of the Jeep; Avi got in next to him and thrust his M16 out of the passenger window. Without saying a word, they started driving southwest down Route 232.

The Jeep was the only car on the road. A military helicopter shuddered overhead, traveling in the direction of Gaza. Our kibbutz wasn't visible from the Jeep yet, but as they drove, my father and Avi began to see something else in the sky: a thick, black tower of smoke rising from the direction of Nahal Oz.

CHAPTER 7

DREAMERS

1992–2007

THE BUSES FROM GAZA CITY reached Nahal Oz in the early afternoon hours of Friday, August 25, 1994. They took a right turn just beyond the gate, drove along the kibbutz's perimeter fence, and stopped at an improvised parking lot at the western edge of the community, within sight of the border.

As they piled out of the buses, the travelers—dozens of Palestinian families, with children of all ages—were met by residents of the kibbutz handing out cotton candy and corn on the cob; for the adults, there was fruit grown by local farmers. Colorful kites skittered overhead, dancing above a large patch of green lawn.

Normally, this expanse served as the kibbutz's soccer field, but on this day, it had been converted into a local arts and crafts market, with stalls offering paintings, jewelry, ceramics, and hand-knitted scarves, all made by the residents of Israeli communities along the Gaza border. In the center of it all was a rectangular stage, decorated with a large banner of a dove spreading its wings.

This was the first-ever Nahal Oz Festival of Peace, organized in coordination with the recently established Palestinian Authority, a governmental body representing the Palestinian population. This new entity had been founded a few months earlier as part of a historic agreement between Israel and the Palestine Liberation Organization, the umbrella organization of Palestinian nationalist groups led by Yasser Arafat. Often called simply "the Authority" in Hebrew and Arabic or "the PA" in English, it now presided over large parts of the Gaza Strip, although its power was limited: the entirety of the Strip was still under Israeli military control, while the PA mostly managed civilian affairs inside Palestinian population centers. Nevertheless, the PA's very existence marked a major change in the political realities of the Israeli-Palestinian conflict. After decades of fighting, there was now a new Palestinian government that was cooperating and coexisting with Israel.

The PA's creation was part of a regional diplomatic effort toward peace—a push that had begun two years earlier with the election of Labor Party candidate Yitzhak Rabin as prime minister of Israel. Rabin had served as prime minister once before, for a single term in the 1970s. Perhaps more significantly, he was also a onetime defense minister and former general who had led the Israeli military to victory in the Six-Day War, and he was considered a hawk on security issues. One of the reasons for his victory in the June 1992 elections was the durability of the intifada, the Palestinian uprising against Israel, which voters saw as a failure of the outgoing prime minister Yitzhak Shamir, the leader of the right-wing, nationalist Likud Party. They wanted someone to restore stability, and they hoped that Rabin would succeed where his predecessor had failed.

Despite his record as a man of war, Rabin had promised during his election campaign to also seek opportunities for peace; the Labor Party had even run advertisements with his face and a centrist message, proclaiming, "No to the extremism of the right, no to the extremism of the left—yes to security and peace out of strength." Yet in the first months of his government, Rabin wasn't ready for diplomacy. He still had a security crisis to deal with.

Roughly half a year after Rabin assumed office, a Hamas cell kidnapped an Israeli policeman in central Israel, smuggled him by car into the West Bank, and murdered him. In response, Rabin ordered the military to arrest and deport to Lebanon 415 Hamas activists, among them Hamas's top officials in Gaza—although not the elderly Sheikh Ahmed Yassin, the movement's religious leader, who had been jailed in Israel since 1989. The United States and other Western allies of Israel denounced the deportations, but most Israelis supported them. These measures, extreme as they were, further cemented Rabin's standing as the right man to restore security to Israel.

But while, in a single blow, Israel's new prime minister had succeeded in weakening Hamas, he hadn't yet solved his country's larger strategic dilemma, which Rabin saw as an existential one: what to do about the millions of Palestinians living under Israeli military occupation.

When Rabin had led the Israeli military to its victory in 1967, the Palestinian population of the Gaza Strip, the West Bank, and East Jerusalem combined had been just over one million people. When he was sworn in as prime minister twenty-five years later, that population had more than doubled in size. These Palestinians, along with the approximately one million Arab citizens of Israel, comprised almost half of the population living under Israel's control; they were not Jewish, and a majority of them lacked basic civil rights.

Rabin feared that Israel would face growing international pressure and isolation unless it agreed to either end its control over the Palestinians or provide them with Israeli citizensip and equal rights, a step that would endanger its Jewish character and turn it into a country where half the population wasn't Jewish. Israel's economy back then relied heavily on foreign trade, while its military strength rested on strong ties with the United States and the European Union—the former providing Israel most of its weapons and the latter being the country's most important trade partner. Rabin was worried that if Israel failed to find a solution to the Palestinian problem, it would find itself isolated from its benefactors in the Western world, somewhat like apartheid-era South Africa. Surrounded as it was by powerful enemies such as Iran and Syria, this was a risk that Israel could not afford to take. Yet in order to avoid this scenario, Israel had to find a way to break through the diplomatic impasse with the Palestinians. And that would require Rabin to offer some uncomfortable concessions.

At first, Rabin tried to negotiate with local political leaders from the West Bank and East Jerusalem while continuing his predecessors' policy of avoiding any official contact with Arafat's PLO. Over the years, after all, Arafat had been responsible for deadly terror attacks in which hundreds of Israelis had died; Israel's official position was to reject any dialogue or compromise with him and his organization. But the local Palestinian leaders who Rabin *did* try to engage with lacked public support and thus legitimacy. So in early 1993, after exhausting his other diplomatic options, Rabin greenlit a once unthinkable idea: direct negotiations with Arafat.

The Palestinian leader, from his exile in Tunisia, was facing his own political crisis after making the near-fatal mistake of supporting Saddam Hussein's Iraqi regime during the 1990 Gulf War. This debacle had left the PLO isolated in the Arab world, which had mostly sided with the United States in its defense of Kuwait, the neighboring Arab state whose invasion by Iraq had sparked the conflict. Arafat was also worried about his organization's detachment from the intifada and the growing popularity among Palestinians of the Islamist platform of Hamas, which unlike his exiled PLO had become deeply embedded within Gazan society.

In short, Arafat, like Rabin, needed a game changer. And he found one in the prospect of negotiations with the new Center Left government in Israel.

There seemed, at least, to be something that they could agree on. Even before Rabin's election, the PLO had been warming to the idea of a two-state solution, breaking from its decades-old position that Israel should be destroyed and instead calling for the creation of a Palestinian homeland that would coexist with the Jewish state. This new nation would encompass the West Bank, East Jerusalem, and Gaza—areas with large, and largely oppressed, Palestinian populations living alongside tens of thousands of Israeli settlers and under the tight control of the Israeli military.

In Israel, meanwhile, and especially among the Left, the idea of a two-state solution was also gaining support, even though putting it into practice would mean ceding territory to the Palestinians and evacuating dozens of Israeli settlements from these relinquished lands. Rabin, for his part, remained opposed: he feared that an independent Palestinian state, with its own military, would pose a serious security risk to Israel. But he realized that he had to offer the Palestinians something resembling a state—perhaps an autonomous government with its own police force but lacking a real military that could threaten Israel. Without a concession like this, the Palestinian question would never be solved, and Israel's continued existence as a Jewish state would be jeopardized by the demographic realities on the ground.

In short, Israel and the PLO had common ground—and Arafat and Rabin now set about exploring it. Secret talks between Israel and the PLO began in early 1993, first in London and then in Oslo, Norway, where Israel was represented by a team of diplomats who reported directly to Shimon Peres, Israel's foreign minister. Rabin was at first skeptical of their chances for success, but by that summer, he had become convinced that an agreement was within reach.

Rabin was still not ready to accept a Palestinian state, and the negotiations fell far short of the PLO's demand for an independent nation in the West Bank and the Gaza Strip. Rabin did, however, agree to the creation of a Palestinian entity that would gradually gain control over parts of the West Bank and Gaza and be responsible for all aspects of civilian life there—from policing and trash collection to health care and education.

This new entity, which would become the Palestinian Authority, was to enjoy certain symbols of statehood: it would have a government, a parliament, and armed security services loyal to it. But it would not have military capabilities: no tanks, airplanes, or battalions of soldiers. Its sovereignty would be limited in other ways, as well: there would be no evacuation of any Israeli settlements in the West Bank or the Gaza Strip, only a tactical redeployment of Israeli soldiers, who would gradually withdraw from large Palestinian cities, making way for the PA's internal security forces to take control there.

This framework was much closer to Rabin's vision at the start of the negotiations—his desire for a Palestinian entity that would relieve Israel from stronger international pressure, but still fall short of a real state—than to Arafat's demand for a new nation encompassing the territories that Israel had occupied since 1967. Nevertheless, the agreement that Arafat and Rabin's representatives brokered that summer would soon unleash a political earthquake in Israel.

Arafat, despised by the majority of Israelis for his history of terrorism, was about to be handed control of parts of the Gaza Strip and the West Bank. In addition, Rabin accepted a five-year-long negotiating period between Israel and the PA, which both sides assumed would eventually lead to further Israeli concessions ahead of the signing of a broader peace agreement between them. Many pundits and experts believed that at the end of the road, the result would eventually be a Palestinian state, and that some Israeli settlements within its borders would have to be removed. Rabin did not say this out loud, but neither did he rule it out.

The Oslo Accords were formally signed on the White House lawn on September 13, 1993. President Bill Clinton presided over the ceremony; Rabin, Peres, and Arafat later won the Nobel Peace Prize for their parts in the agreement. The world rejoiced: for a brief moment, it seemed like the Gordian knot of the Middle East had been severed.

In July 1994, Arafat entered Gaza as a victor, returning to the city after decades in exile. Tens of thousands of people greeted him in the streets. In October of that year, Israel signed a separate peace treaty with Jordan, an achievement made possible by the progress that had been made on the Palestinian track. "We were so happy," recalled Dani Rachamim, the eternally optimistic peace activist and longtime resident of Nahal Oz. "Our dreams were coming true."

The August 1994 peace festival in the kibbutz was a celebration of this new reality. Dani walked around the event in disbelief, as Israeli children, among them his own kids, played alongside Gazan children, with Israeli and Palestinian flags flying behind them. Only six years earlier, he had been sent to chase children in the West Bank who were putting up their national flag on streetlights. Now that same flag was fluttering here, inside his own kibbutz, and no one seemed to care.

At sunset, as an orange glow radiated from the direction of Gaza City, the musical part of the evening began. A choir from Kfar Azza, a neighboring kibbutz to the north of Nahal Oz, sang songs of peace; next came a group of women from Gaza who put on a traditional, Bedouin-style dance. In a tent at the edge of the event, two Palestinian men brewed herbal tea on a small campfire, inviting everyone to enjoy a sip before heading home. Four decades after Moshe Dayan's dark speech in Nahal Oz, the older members of the kibbutz felt they had finally proven him wrong: peace with the people of Gaza was now within reach.

Carine Rachamim, Dani's daughter, was five years old at the time of the peace festival. Her only memory from it was that some of the Palestinian kids wore gray shirts that looked to her like soccer jerseys.

Born and raised in Nahal Oz, Carine had fallen in love with the game from a very young age, when her older brother would ask her to play goalkeeper as he practiced his striking skills. "We'd come back from school, have lunch together in the communal dining room, and then run out to play," she later recalled. "We would play outside all day, until it was dark. Our parents didn't know where we were and what exactly we were doing." She often played soccer with the boys, at first as goalie and then, as her talent became more apparent, taking on offensive roles as well. The boys had a hard time admitting just how good she was—and how much better she was than most of them. The fact that their soccer field was just half a mile from Gaza was never a concern. "We felt like we were growing up in the safest place in the world," Carine recalled.

The 1990s were an optimistic decade along the Gaza border. A documentary filmmaker who made a short movie about the kibbutz during those years taped an interview with Arie "Daum" Dotan, the longtime resident who had moved to the kibbutz as a nineteen-year-old in the mid-1960s, in the fields overlooking Gaza. "They're talking now about peace relations between two entities, maybe two countries," Daum is heard saying, as the camera tilts toward Gaza. "Life is easier now. We have trade relations. Nahal Oz has shifted from being a community of war to one of peace and coexistence."

This sentiment, however, wasn't shared by everyone. The Oslo Accords were popular among the peace-seeking kibbutzniks of Nahal Oz but faced great obstacles among other communities on both sides of the border.

Inside the Gaza Strip, Hamas was still seething after the 1992 deportations. Most of its leaders had returned to the Strip in 1994, the same year as the peace festival, determined to seek revenge on Israel—and on the new Palestinian Authority, whose treaty with the government in Jerusalem the Islamists considered nothing short of treason. By accepting the two-state formula, they claimed, the PLO had essentially given up on 78 percent of the territory of British Mandatory Palestine, which stretched from the Jordan River to the Mediterranean Sea, while agreeing to negotiate with Israel over the establishment of a future state on parts of the remaining 22 percent—the West Bank, the Gaza Strip, and East Jerusalem. Hamas maintained its original stance that Israel must be eradicated and replaced with an Islamist regime that would rule over the entire land.

On top of this ideological concession, the new PA had committed an even greater sin in the eyes of Hamas: "collaboration." In a strictly literal sense, the word was accurate—especially when applied to the PA's security forces. The Oslo Accords had led to the creation of new Palestinian security forces, loyal to Arafat, that were responsible for keeping law and order inside the Palestinian cities but that were also expected to work alongside the Israeli military to thwart terror attacks. Most of their funding arrived from the United States, and their coordination with Israel was a key requirement for the funds to be appropriated.

When Hamas began describing these forces as "collaborators" in its propaganda, however, it was using a loaded term—one that, in Palestinian nationalist jargon, was synonymous with treason. During the intifada years, Hamas had executed hundreds of Palestinians whom the organization accused of collaboration with Israel. Most of them were ordinary citizens who, according to Hamas, had provided intelligence to the Israeli military.

The responsibility for these murders, which often involved extreme and gruesome violence in order to shame the victims, was placed in the hands of Yihiya Sinwar, a young Hamas operative from southern Gaza. Now, by using the term "collaborators" to describe Arafat's security forces, Hamas was implying that they, too, should be murdered—even if, at the time, Hamas lacked the power to go after them.

Arafat initially expected Hamas to accept his leadership, and at one point even expressed hope that its fighters will join his security forces and turn from terrorists to policemen. But Hamas's ideological leaders, among them the jailed Shiekh Yassin, refused to give such an alliance their blessing. To the contrary, Yassin condemned Arafat for agreeing to recognize the State of Israel and for establishing diplomatic relations and security ties with it, despite receiving in return a limited, powerless autonomy. No

Israeli settlements had been removed from the Palestinian territories as a result of the Accords, and although Israeli soldiers had left the large Palestinian cities, they still surrounded them and could enter at will to conduct antiterror raids. The occupation, Hamas argued, was simply continuing under a different guise.

Many Palestinians agreed with this analysis. Hamas was joined in opposition to Oslo by Palestinian groups that ranged all the way to the leftist communists of the Popular Front for the Liberation of Palestine, on the other end of the political spectrum from the Islamists. They all told Arafat that Rabin would never truly agree to a Palestinian state, and that Israel would never give up any settlements—noting that, after the Accords had been signed, Israeli settlers continued to build new homes and neighborhoods in both the West Bank and the Gaza Strip.

Meanwhile, the Israeli opposition, led by a young Likud politician named Binyamin Netanyahu, was also loudly opposing the Oslo Accords. They warned that Arafat was deceiving Rabin and that he would never truly make peace with Israel. Arafat himself reinforced this line of thinking with his tendency to say one thing in English and the opposite in Arabic, a behavior that Israeli and American officials came to describe as "doublespeak," in the Orwellian tradition; the Palestinian leader would give a rosy speech in English about the importance of peace and days later would contradict himself by praising, in Arabic, the armed struggle against the Israeli occupation. Every time that Arafat gave the Israeli media an opportunity to highlight his duplicity, Rabin lost a few more supporters among the Israeli public.

But it wasn't just a war of words. Fatally polarizing public opinion among Israelis and Palestinians alike, and further undermining the Oslo agreement and the governments that had signed it, was a series of killings and reprisals that, almost overnight, made the recent vision of peace seem like a desert mirage—ironically, at a moment when peace was perhaps the closest it had been in decades.

One of the most devastating blows was the Hebron Massacre. On the morning of February 25, Baruch Goldstein, a Far Right Jewish extremist who had immigrated from Brooklyn to Israel and moved to an Israeli settlement next to the Palestinian city of Hebron, entered the city's most important mosque and opened fire on worshippers with an AK-47. Several men who had been praying in the mosque managed to kill him with a fire extinguisher but not before he'd caused terrible carnage: Goldstein—a member of Kach, a Far Right Jewish terror organization founded by the extremist rabbi Meir Kahane, which advocated for the mass expulsion of Palestinians from all the territories controlled by Israel—had murdered twenty-nine people and injured dozens of others.

Goldstein's attack in Hebron was the first mass-casualty terror attack after the signing of Oslo. It unleashed a violent chain of events whose reverberations were felt across this disputed land.

According to Islamic tradition, the death of a cherished family or community member is to be followed by a forty-day grieving period—and not coincidentally, exactly forty days after the massacre, a powerful bomb exploded in Afula, an Israeli city fifty-five miles north of Tel Aviv. Eight Israelis died in the blast, and more than a dozen were injured. This was Hamas's revenge for the massacre, and it was followed by a series of other deadly terror attacks that together claimed the lives of dozens of Israelis over the next several months.

Among both Israelis and Palestinians, public opinion was shifting against Oslo and the peace process as a result of the deadly violence. In Israel, many people became convinced that Arafat and the PA's newly established security forces weren't just failing to fight terrorism aimed at Israelis but were in fact turning a blind eye to Hamas's increasingly brutal methods. On the Palestinian side, the Hebron massacre, and Israel's military response to Hamas's revenge attacks, led to a similar sense of suspicion and disillusionment.

And the violence didn't stop. Throughout 1994 and 1995, Hamas and the Islamic Jihad, a smaller terror group funded and supported by Iran, began using a new tactic they had borrowed from other Islamist organizations in the Middle East: suicide bombings. These attacks usually involved one or two assailants, who would arrive at Israeli bus stops, malls, or busy markets wearing civilian clothes that hid an explosive belt glued to their bodies. They would place themselves in the middle of a crowd of people—sometimes by standing in the center of a bus, other times by joining a line to enter a store—and then blow themselves up by clicking a small button on their vest or in their pocket, ending their own lives along with those of anyone unlucky enough to be caught around them. The vast majority of the victims in these attacks were civilians.

A dark pattern was emerging. Just like Goldstein, who had stormed the mosque in Hebron knowing that he was likely to die, Hamas's suicide bombers were usually religious extremists who believed that their own deaths—to say nothing of the atrocities they were committing—were worth the payoff. Death would bring personal rewards, for one thing: a place in heaven and a joyful afterlife. But death was also a means to a grim end: a zero-sum future, one in which Israelis and Palestinians wouldn't have to share the contested land because one of them would have it all.

———————

By late 1995, the Oslo Accords were in trouble, and so was Yitzhak Rabin. Hamas's terror attacks had hurt the prime minister's hawkish image and destabilized his governing coalition. Rabin was angry at Arafat but still committed to the diplomatic process, hoping to see more countries in the region join Jordan and make peace with Israel. Yet his standing in the polls was plummeting, and at the same time, some of the protests against him were turning violent. Israel's internal security agency, the Shin Bet, was increasingly concerned about the possibility of a Far Right political assassination attempt on his life.

Rabin himself blamed Netanyahu, the young Israeli opposition leader, for inciting violence and exacerbating the country's social divisions. He urged his supporters to take to the streets and send a message that peace remained possible. On the night of Saturday, November 4, 1995, the Labor Party and Israeli peace organizations held a rally in front of the Tel Aviv town hall. More than one hundred thousand people attended, including a bus full of residents from Nahal Oz and neighboring kibbutzim along the Gaza border. Several days before the rally, Dani Rachamim had written an open letter to the community:

In 1992, a new government promised to start a peace process with the Palestinians, causing us to feel hope and excitement. And indeed, a change has come upon the land. The process is difficult, but our hopes are coming alive. Against the historic process led by this brave government, however, stands a right-wing political camp that is trying to stop it, using violence and spreading panic among the public. Any person who cares about the stability of our democratic system, and more than that, the future of our children, has a moral obligation to strengthen the government. We have an opportunity to do just that on Saturday evening.

Carine, six years old at the time, joined her father on the bus ride to Tel Aviv. She remembered the huge crowd in front of the town hall, larger than any gathering she had ever seen before. She didn't follow all the speeches, but she did listen to the prime minister deliver one of his most famous quotes: "I have always believed that the majority of the people want peace and are ready to take risks for peace. In coming here today, you demonstrate, together with many others who did not come, that the people truly desire peace and oppose violence. Violence erodes the basis of Israeli democracy. It must be condemned and isolated. This is not the way of the State of Israel."

As he walked off the stage, Rabin was approached by Yigal Amir, a law student and Far Right Jewish extremist who, like Goldstein, saw terror as a religious duty. The young man raised a pistol and fired three shots at the prime minister's back. Two bullets struck Rabin's upper body. He collapsed on the ground, a red splotch of blood emerging on his white shirt. The prime minister was rushed to a nearby hospital but was pronounced dead shortly after arrival.

Instead of being killed in the attack, as Goldstein had been (and as he himself had expected), Amir found himself arrested and sentenced to life in prison. He never expressed regret. His goal, he explained, had been to stop the Oslo process.

As Dani and Carine left the rally, they had no idea that Rabin had been shot—they had to hurry to reach the bus back home. It was only during the hour-long drive to Nahal Oz that they, and the rest of the people aboard, became aware of what had just happened. When a special newscast on the radio announced that the prime minister had died, Dani felt shock and disbelief; then, rage.

As the bus neared Nahal Oz, the initial commotion over the news gave way to deafening silence. Driving through the dark night, some people cried in their seats; others stared out the window in despair. Just days earlier, in his letter to the community, Dani had warned of potential violence, but he had never anticipated this. "I knew one thing," Dani said later. "My country was never going to be the same."

Half a year after Rabin's assassination, Israel held an election. Shimon Peres, who had succeeded the slain prime minister, faced off against Binyamin Netanyahu, the upstart right-wing Likud politician who had clashed with Rabin before his death. On election night, exit polls showed a tiny victory for Peres, but by the early morning hours, as the last ballots were being counted, Netanyahu had taken the lead. Eventually, he won by a margin of thirty thousand votes out of approximately three million cast.

Netanyahu had received a late-stage boost from an unlikely source: in the months before the election, Hamas had committed several deadly terror attacks that had shaken Israel to its core, murdering dozens of people in suicide bombings in Jerusalem, Ashkelon, and Tel Aviv, including one attack on the eve of the Jewish holiday of Purim in which most of the casualties were children and teenagers. Politically, the attacks had played into Netanyahu's hands, allowing him to present Peres as weak and ineffectual.

Netanyahu's opposition to the ongoing peace process had clearly played a role in his victory, too. Peres was deeply committed to Oslo and had planned to continue negotiations for a final-status agreement with Arafat if he had he won the election. Netanyahu, on the other hand, while stopping short of a promise to fully rescind Oslo, had made it clear that he would slow down the peace process and offer less to the Palestinian Authority than his rival. At a time when Hamas's suicide bombers were blowing up buses across Israel, Netanyahu's antagonistic approach had won over just enough of the public to tilt the result of the election.

After taking office, and under pressure from the Clinton administration, Netanyahu announced that he was formally committed to Oslo and met Arafat briefly at one of the border crossings between Israel and Gaza.

He went on to negotiate two interim agreements with the PA, increasing the amount of territory under Arafat's control.

American officials who worked with Netanyahu, however, expressed great frustration at his conduct and blamed him for delays and dishonesty in the negotiation room. Their criticisms turned out to be well founded: under Oslo's original terms, Israel and the PA were supposed to settle on a final-status agreement for the creation of a Palestinian state by May 1999—but Netanyahu had no intention of letting that happen and was slowing down the process however he could. Netanyahu gladly took credit for the delays, and in doing so, he hurt Arafat's public standing and strengthened his rivals, as ordinary Palestinians saw their dream of statehood getting further out of reach.

Netanyahu also made a move around this time that dramatically benefited Hamas in particular: he ordered the release of the organization's religious leader, Sheikh Ahmed Yassin, from prison.

The disabled sheikh, who had been arrested by Israel in 1989, was serving a life sentence for his role in Hamas's terror attacks. The original indictment against him included two counts of murder for his role in the kidnapping and killing of Israeli soldiers, but eventually his lawyers struck a plea deal. The murder charges against Yassin were dropped, but the elderly sheikh had to admit that in his capacity as a religious leader, he had greenlit several other murders and provided his followers with the theological permission to commit them.

Yassin was supposed to live out the rest of his days in prison, but in July 1997, after a deadly Hamas attack in Jerusalem, Netanyahu took an unlikely first step toward making the sheikh a free man: he ordered Israel's Mossad, the nation's equivalent of the CIA, to assassinate Khaled Mashal, the head of Hamas's political bureau, who was then living in Jordan, a country with which Israel had only three years earlier signed a peace agreement. It was a dangerous gamble; the Jordanians were not aware of the operation and, had they been notified in advance, would have never approved it. Netanyahu, however, bet big—and lost.

An Israeli hit squad followed Mashal's daily routines in Amman, the Jordanian capital, for several weeks. Finally, on September 25, an undercover agent "accidentally" bumped into the Hamas official in the street while holding an open soda can in his hand. The can was filled with a poisonous liquid developed in Israel ahead of the operation, and the agent spilled several drops of it on Mashal's ear. The Hamas leader, realizing what was happening, managed to get to a nearby hospital while his bodyguards chased after the Mossad agents and forced them into a fistfight in the middle of the street, pinning them down until Jordanian police arrived and arrested two of the Israelis. Another four who had been involved in the operation took shelter in the Israeli embassy.

Netanyahu sent Efraim Halevy, a senior Mossad officer, to an urgent meeting with King Hussein of Jordan, who had loathed the young prime minister even before the botched operation and who often expressed his nostalgia for Rabin, with whom he had forged a personal friendship while negotiating the 1994 peace agreement. Hussein told Netanyahu's spy chief that, if Mashal died in the hospital, Jordanian authorities would execute the captured Mossad operatives in retaliation.

While Mossad agents often risk their lives when conducting secret operations in foreign countries, the last time an Israeli agent was publicly put on trial and then executed was in the 1960s, when the spy Eli Cohen had been arrested, tortured, and hanged in Syria; the prospect of such a spectacle happening in Jordan, so shortly after the country had made peace with Israel, would have been crushing for the Israeli public—and politically devastating for Netanyahu. Trapped in a snare of his own making, he agreed to provide the Jordanians the antidote to the poison, and Mashal's life was saved.

The Jordanian king, however, still had a major problem on his hands: How could he let the Israeli agents—both those in police custody and their peers hiding in the embassy—return to Israel? The majority of Jordan's population is of Palestinian descent, and the king had faced strong criticism for his decision to make peace with Israel; releasing the Israeli agents after they tried to murder a Palestinian leader on Jordanian soil was only going to make matters worse.

After a daylong negotiation, the two sides arrived at a solution. Netanyahu agreed to release Yassin and dozens of other Palestinian prisoners from Israeli jails, provided that Hussein would allow the Mossad crew to leave Jordan. The king now had something to show his Palestinian citizens for the release of the Israeli hit squad, and Netanyahu had avoided the nightmare of his own assassins being paraded before the cameras and hanged. But he, and his country, would pay dearly for that decision.

Almost literally by accident, Hamas had scored a major victory against Israel. Its political leader, Mashal, who had a relatively low public profile before the failed assassination, became a hero overnight. But more significantly, Yassin returned to Gaza an even greater hero and began to assail Arafat, the PA, and the Oslo Accords, promoting instead Hamas's vision of an Islamist state with dominion over all of the land controlled by Israel.

As if he had not already given Hamas enough help, Netanyahu also canceled the planned extradition to Israel of Mussa Abu-Marzouk, the organization's chief fundraiser. Abu-Marzouk, an American citizen whose family had left Gaza when he was a young child, had helped Hamas raise tens of millions of dollars from Muslim communities around the world. He had been arrested by the United States in 1995 and Rabin's government had made a formal extradition request, explaining that the funds Abu-Marzouk had raised had been used to pay for numerous terror attacks against Israelis.

The Clinton administration had been preparing to send him to Israel, but Abu-Marzouk had filed a legal challenge against his extradition, and the US Department of Justice was fighting it in court. The Americans expressed optimism that the extradition would be approved, but in mid-1997, Netanyahu rescinded the request. His aides explained that he feared that a lengthy public trial for Abu-Marzouk in an Israeli courtroom would encourage Hamas to carry out more terror attacks. Israeli defense and intelligence officials criticized the decision and accused Netanyahu of cowardice. Netanyahu's U-turn came as a surprise to the Clinton administration, which decided to deport Abu-Marzouk to Jordan instead. Once there, he joined forces with Mashal and continued to raise millions for Hamas.

It was failures like these, combined with internal problems such as the corruption trial of his most important coalition partner, that led eventually to the fall of Netanyahu's government. In May 1999, Israel held another election in which Netanyahu was defeated by Ehud Barak, a retired general and the new leader of the Labor Party. Barak received 56 percent of the national vote, while Netanyahu got 44 percent. In Nahal Oz the result was much more lopsided: Barak received 211 votes in the kibbutz, Netanyahu just 5. In his victory speech, he promised "a new dawn" for Israel.

Barak had an ambitious plan: he wanted to finalize peace agreements with both Syria and the Palestinians during his first two years in office. In May 2000, a year after his election victory, he surprised Israel and the region by pulling all Israeli military forces out of Lebanon, ending a military adventure that had started eighteen years earlier with Begin's invasion of the country. But this was a unilateral move and thus relatively easy for Barak to execute.

When it came to negotiations with Israel's neighbors, the new prime minister found the going much tougher. The talks with Syria fell apart in early 2000. Likewise, negotiations with the PA ended in failure that summer, after the Camp David summit hosted by President Clinton concluded with no agreement.

Countless books, articles, and research papers have tried to explain the failure at Camp David, but the bottom line is that Barak's most generous proposal for the borders of a future Palestinian state fell short of Arafat's minimum demands. Clinton spent almost two weeks trying to find a middle ground that the two leaders, and the delegations surrounding them, could accept, to no avail. As Barak returned to Israel from the summit, Israeli intelligence warned him that Hamas and other terror groups wanted to use the occasion to intensify their attacks on Israel, perhaps with Arafat's blessing. At the same time, Barak's own coalition government was on the brink of collapse after its more right-wing elements had threatened to quit over the concessions he had offered at Camp David.

On the Palestinian side, frustration was also growing: seven years after the signing of the Oslo Accords, the Palestinian state that they had been promised was still nowhere to be seen. What's more, Barak's government, just like the Netanyahu and Rabin governments before it, had continued to expand Israeli settlements even while negotiating with the PA. Israeli forces still had de facto control of the Gaza Strip and the West Bank, and the number of Israeli settlers living in the two territories grew with each passing year. Hamas accused Arafat and the PLO of making a fatal mistake by choosing to negotiate diplomatically in the first place, and argued that it was time to return to the previous method: armed resistance.

Netanyahu, who after his election loss the previous year had announced that he was taking a break from politics, now saw Barak's fortunes collapsing and began to plot a political comeback, hoping for new elections in 2001. But Likud, Netanyahu's party, had already chosen another candidate.

Ariel Sharon, the retired general who decades earlier had "pacified" Gaza with brutal force, was by then seventy-two years old. He had been a politician for more than three decades but had never held the nation's highest office. As Barak's hold on power was slipping, the old war hero had secured the backing of the Likud Party to mount a challenge against him, recognizing that this was his own last chance to become prime minister. He had no intention of stepping aside for Netanyahu.

In September 2000, two months after Barak returned empty-handed from Camp David, Sharon made a public visit to the most sensitive religious site in the Middle East: the Temple Mount, known also by its Arabic name, Haram al-Sharif. Jews believe that this is where the ancient temple of King Solomon once stood and underneath it, "the holiest of holies," a spiritual junction connecting heaven and earth; Muslims believe that from this same site, the Prophet Mohammed had ascended to heaven, and as a result, one of the most important mosques in the world, the Al-Aqsa Mosque, has been located there for centuries. The site has been under Israeli control since the 1967 war, but as part of a special arrangement dating back decades, its day-to-day management is in the hands of the Waqf, a Muslim religious association, and Jews are allowed to visit it but not to pray there. Tensions around control of the site, and the two mosques situated on it, have led to outbreaks of violence between Muslims and Jews dating back to the 1920s—all of which helps explain the audacity of Sharon's visit, and the way in which it ended.

As Sharon went up to the Mount, surrounded by hundreds of police officers, Palestinian men began throwing stones and chairs at him. The police responded with batons and tear gas, soon followed by bullets.

Palestinian media presented the event as an Israeli assault on the holy mosque, and called on the public to take to the streets in order to thwart it. Over the coming days, in demonstrations and riots across Jerusalem, the West Bank, and Gaza, dozens of Israelis and Palestinians died. A new intifada had begun.

"For two weeks now, we have been in the eye of the storm." That was the first sentence in the weekly update sent to the residents of Nahal Oz by the kibbutz management—the local equivalent of a city council, chosen every two years by the members of the community. It was October 2000, and in the days after Sharon's visit to Temple Mount, the entire region had exploded. The letter expressed hope that things would soon calm down and that "the forces of peace will regroup and lead us to a better place." But for most people in the community, that dream was slipping further and further from reach. Their outlook only dimmed further when, several weeks later, a senior military commander visited the kibbutz and remarked that the new intifada, which was proving to be much more violent than the previous one, would probably last for months, if not years.

Israel held new elections in February 2001, and Ariel Sharon easily defeated Ehud Barak, earning 62 percent of the national vote. Nahal Oz had once again voted overwhelmingly for Barak, the loser in the election, but Sharon's victory wasn't seen by most kibbutz members as a disaster. The new prime minister was himself a resident of the Gaza border region: decades earlier, he had purchased a farm outside Sderot and built his home there. Sharon was a hawk on national security issues and a strong supporter of the settlements in the occupied territories, but over the years, he had also expressed his admiration for the achievements of the kibbutz movement, despite its affiliation with the more dovish Labor Party.

A weekly update sent by the Nahal Oz management roughly half a year later, in May 2001, featured a short article written a decade prior by Sharon. Its inclusion was an attempt to show "a different side" of the right-wing leader. The article was full of praise for Nahal Oz and other kibbutzim along the Gaza border, for their "determined standing in front of the gates of Gaza, the gates of terror." Sharon had ended the article by blasting politicians who wanted to decrease governmental support for agricultural communities, describing them as "people who have never planted a tree, never worked in the fields, never bent their backs in the vegetable garden." These words were music to the ears of Nahal Oz, a community earning most of its income from agricultural work—and from the subsidies that accompanied it.

The Israeli election system includes multiple parties, and prime ministers never govern alone; rather, they must form a coalition with several other parties in order to have a majority of the votes in the Knesset, the Israeli parliament. Unlike Netanyahu, who during his tenure as prime minister had chosen to construct a narrow, right-wing religious coalition, Sharon invited the Labor Party into a "unity coalition" of the two largest parties from the right and the left, focused on defeating the new intifada. But during his first year in power, the results were far from impressive: terror attacks continued throughout Israel, costing the lives of more than two hundred citizens and soldiers. The best that Sharon could do was promise Israelis a lengthy and difficult battle while attempting to offset the blame onto Arafat, whom he accused of not only turning a blind eye to terror attacks but also actively supporting them. The new administration in the US, led by George W. Bush, offered strong support for Sharon's "war on terror," especially after the September 11 attacks.

The deteriorating security situation had a personal impact on twelve-year-old Carine Rachamim, who was preparing to celebrate her bat mitzvah in the midst of the second intifada. Just as the Nahal soldiers who'd founded the kibbutz had dispensed with individual weddings in favor of a collective celebration, Nahal Oz had since developed a tradition of organizing one coming-of-age party each year for all the children who were reaching this milestone, instead of having each family organize its own celebration. Carine and her cohort, a group of ten boys and girls, were supposed to have theirs in July 2001.

The preparations for these bar and bat mitzvahs were underway months in advance, and the kibbutz was expecting approximately one thousand guests to gather on the main lawn in front of the community's dining hall. Carine had followed her older brother's bar mitzvah three years earlier with excitement, and she couldn't wait for her turn.

For her eleventh birthday, her parents had bought her a soccer jersey with the name and number of Haim Revivo, Israel's most famous player at the time; she was eager to know what she'd be getting this year. Soccer remained her biggest passion, even though her parents had enlisted her in an all-girls basketball team at a neighboring kibbutz. "I'd come back to Nahal Oz from basketball practice, run to the soccer field, and play with the boys until it was dark," she later recalled.

But in the spring of 2001, just months before the big event, everything came to a halt. For the first time since the beginning of the intifada, Hamas managed to fire a rocket toward Nahal Oz. It was an improvised device—pundits in the Israeli media described it at the time, dismissively, as a flying pipe with explosives attached to it. But when another rocket fell in Sderot a few days later, and then a third was launched toward Nahal Oz again, the flying pipes became a serious concern.

It wasn't a coincidence that these rockets—which Hamas nicknamed "Qassam" after a famous Palestinian religious leader from the 1930s—had been invented in Gaza: after the Oslo Accords, Israel had built a new border fence around the Gaza Strip, which—combined with the presence of Israeli military forces inside the Strip and along the border—made it very difficult for Hamas to send suicide bombers from Gaza into Israel. It was much easier for Hamas to dispatch them from the West Bank and East Jerusalem, which at the time had no fence separating them from Israel; yet Gaza, where Hamas had been born as an organization, remained the Islamists' more important base of operations, and the terror organization's leaders plotted ways to continue the fight against Israel from there.

That's where the improvised, homemade rockets came in. By producing a cross-border weapon that could be launched from inside Gaza to land in Israeli territory, Hamas had found a way to overcome the obstacle of the border fence. The organization also had acquired old mortars, which were smuggled into Gaza from Egypt, and added them to its arsenal. Suddenly, Israelis along the Gaza border had to worry about a new threat: death from the skies.

For residents of Nahal Oz, life changed almost overnight. The kibbutz had several old communal bomb shelters on its grounds dating back to the 1950s, when the Egyptian military would fire mortars toward the community. These shelters hadn't been used in decades, however. They were decaying after years of neglect and, in any case, didn't offer much protection from the new, albeit primitive, Hamas weapons, which were landing inside the kibbutz mere seconds after being launched from Gaza.

Sharon and his defense minister, the Labor Party's Binyamin Ben-Eliezer, visited the border region and promised to come up with a better option for its inhabitants. The government soon made good on its word by embarking on an ambitious project: building "safe rooms," above-ground bunkers made of strong, thick concrete, in every house in Nahal Oz and other Israeli communities that were within range of Hamas's rockets and mortars. In addition, new public bomb shelters were brought into the kibbutz and installed throughout its grounds. These new shelters were basically oblong concrete structures with a large opening that were easily accessible in case of an emergency, and, unlike the old shelters, they were clean, well maintained, and more strategically located in different parts of the kibbutz.

These measures made Nahal Oz safer, no doubt. Yet for people living elsewhere in Israel, the new safe rooms and bomb shelters only further highlighted the risks posed by Hamas's rockets and mortars. What residents of the border communities viewed as potentially lifesaving interventions by the Israeli government soon became the subject of constant, often hysterical news reports that shaped public opinion elsewhere in the country.

For Carine and her peers, the results of all this drama were painfully simple: a week before the big celebration, cancellations from friends and relatives began to arrive. *We really want to be there with you, but we're afraid of the rockets*, guests kept explaining. The young teenagers worried that their big day would turn out to be a major disappointment. To make things worse, only forty-eight hours before the celebration a mortar from Gaza fell inside the kibbutz, landing between two homes. No one was injured, but the attack just reinforced the sense of danger to the prospective guests—and of gloom inside the kibbutz.

In a desperate attempt to reverse the trend of cancellations, the kibbutz decided to bring national attention to the story. A television crew from Israel's most popular news show was invited to Nahal Oz, and the birthday kids, including Carine, shared their fears that no one would celebrate their bar and bat mitzvahs with them. "My mom said that some of our guests won't come. I hope they change their minds," said Itai, a classmate of Carine's. Shir, a twelve-year-old girl, added that the mortars and rockets "make a big *boom*, but don't really do much damage." Carine was filmed in the back of the group, smiling.

The next day, hundreds of guests from all over Israel arrived at the kibbutz. Not everyone who had been invited was there, but the turnout was large enough for Nahal Oz to declare victory and for the newly minted teenagers to enjoy their party. "The TV report probably helped," Carine said in retrospect. In the end, however, she didn't get any soccer-related presents—only things that people considered more "feminine." But nothing could deter her from her dream: to become a professional soccer player.

In early 2003, Ariel Sharon easily won reelection. After two terrible years that had seen hundreds of Israelis die in terror attacks, the country was starting to turn the page and restore safety to its streets. Nahal Oz was still being pummeled by mortars and Qassam rockets, but the new safe rooms and bomb shelters, together with a new rocket alarm system that sounded a siren as soon as a launch was detected in Gaza, provided a relative sense of security. All residents had to do was stay alert, hear the siren when it went off, and run to the nearest shelter. After dozens of incidents, people were getting used to it.

Sharon, however, was going through an evolution of his own—a personal and political transformation of which only his closest confidants were aware. During his second election campaign, he had still expressed his decades-old hawkish views, at one point announcing that Netzarim—a small settlement across the border from Nahal Oz, sitting directly next to Gaza City and requiring a massive Israeli military presence inside the Gaza Strip to protect its tiny population—was no different than Tel Aviv, Israel's largest and richest metropolis. Statements like this one helped Sharon maintain the support of religious right-wing voters, but a small group of aides was coming to understand that he no longer believed his own rhetoric.

A decade earlier, Rabin had greenlit the negotiations that ultimately resulted in the Oslo Accords out of fear that Israel was headed toward a choice between its Jewish majority and its democratic system of government. Now, Sharon was starting to reach a similar conclusion. His government had successfully extinguished the intifada through massive force and the construction of a new security barrier separating most of the West Bank from Israel, yet the occupied territories remained home to millions of Palestinians who weren't going anywhere. Israel had to decide what to do with them—lest the world make such decisions for it.

Unlike Rabin, Sharon had no faith in negotiations, certainly not with Arafat, a man he viewed as a terrorist who had never truly changed his ways. Sharon wasn't impressed with the Bush administration's solution, which was to sideline Arafat by pressuring the PA to create a new role: Palestinian prime minister. Arafat remained president of the PA, but from 2002 onward, the Americans pushed and eventually convinced him to appoint a more moderate figure to serve alongside him and manage the day-to-day affairs of the PA, turning Arafat into a more ceremonial figure than he had been before. The task was given to Mahmoud Abbas, Arafat's diplomatic hand and a relatively moderate voice who had opposed the use of violence since the start of the intifada. Sharon agreed to work with Abbas but didn't think he was strong enough politically to negotiate a peace deal with Israel.

Without using the term, Sharon realized that Israel was drifting toward an apartheid-like future, which he dreaded less for moral reasons than pragmatic political ones. He feared that if Israel didn't present a bold plan to change the status quo of the occupation after Oslo's failure, world powers would try to impose a solution via the United Nations Security Council and the conditioning of military aid to Israel. One scenario that Sharon especially dreaded was an international consensus on the creation of a Palestinian state on the region's 1967 borders, a hypothetical outcome that Sharon considered a disaster from a security standpoint; an even worse option, in his view, would be a demand for Israel to give citizenship and equal rights to all the Palestinians living under its control, which would result in Jews becoming a minority in the world's one and only Jewish state.

To preemptively defend Israel against these threats, Sharon concocted a shocking plan: to unilaterally evacuate all Israeli settlements and military forces from the Gaza Strip and declare that Israel no longer controlled the territory or the 1.5 million Palestinians living there. Such a move, Sharon believed, would relieve diplomatic pressure on Israel and buy it precious time—perhaps measurable in decades—to decide what to do in the West Bank, which by then had become home to a large number of Israeli settlers.

These West Bank settlers, most of them right-wing ideologues, were a huge factor in Sharon's calculus. Their presence, numbering more than a quarter million in total, required a massive Israeli military presence throughout the area, given that the West Bank was also home to more than two million Palestinians, many of whom were deeply opposed to the Israeli occupation of their lands. In Gaza, by comparison, there were fewer than eight thousand settlers—surrounded by 1.5 million Palestinians. This demographic imbalance meant that, for the Israeli military, protecting this smaller group of settlers was just as much of a challenge as was guarding their peers in the West Bank, especially given the proximity of some Gaza settlements to the Strip's largest Palestinian population centers.

Sharon was determined, at that point, to keep most of the West Bank under Israeli control. He believed that the region, which overlooked Tel Aviv and Israel's populous seashore, was vital for the nation's security. The trick, in his mind, was to maintain Israeli dominance of the West Bank without paying a heavy price internationally. To achieve that goal, he was willing to abandon Gaza.

Sharon first hinted at his intentions in a December 2003 speech in which he blamed the PA for refusing to engage in serious peace talks and warned that if the Palestinians didn't change their ways, Israel would be forced to take unilateral measures and redraw its borders without their input. The word he used to describe his plan was *disengagement*.

The speech was a cynical move—Sharon himself had no interest in peace talks and was merely trying to pin the blame on the other side—but it was nevertheless historic. This was the first time he or any other prime minister had openly discussed the option of an Israeli unilateral withdrawal from parts of the occupied territories. No Israeli leader before Sharon, not even Rabin, had suggested unilaterally dismantling settlements or relinquishing parts of the occupied territories; to hear this from Sharon, considered at that point in his career one of the most right-wing prime ministers in his country's history, came as a shock to both Israelis and Palestinians. And yet, even then, few people realized just how far he was planning to go.

Two months after his seminal speech, on February 2, 2004, Sharon invited Yoel Marcus, a senior columnist for *Haaretz,*[*] to his official residence in Jerusalem. Marcus arrived at 9:30 A.M., and over a light breakfast, Sharon casually told him that later in the day, he was going to announce a plan to unilaterally evacuate seventeen settlements from Gaza, effectively ending Israel's military occupation of the Strip.

Marcus rushed to the *Haaretz* offices in Tel Aviv and caught the editor-in-chief in the hallway to fill him in on the shocking news. It was now past noon, and Sharon was supposed to unveil his plan at a 2:00 P.M. meeting of Likud lawmakers in the Knesset. Marcus was despondent: at the time, *Haaretz* still had a "print-first" approach to exclusive stories, meaning that reporters and columnists were expected to save their biggest scoops for the morning newspaper, while the *Haaretz* website was mostly updated with urgent breaking news, like car accidents and terror attacks. Now, however, Marcus had an enormous scoop—but it wouldn't last until the next day's newspaper.

The editor looked at his watch and told Marcus that, if they worked fast, they could get an article onto the website before the prime minister arrived at the Knesset. It was something they'd rarely done before, but the story was so big that it was worth a try.

Marcus dictated several paragraphs to the online news desk, and within minutes, the scoop became the top headline on the *Haaretz* website. From there, it reached the headlines of every other news website in the country, and dozens of news outlets around the world.

---

[*] I was not working for the newspaper at the time.

When Sharon arrived at his meeting, the Knesset members were waiting for him in disbelief, hoping that perhaps Marcus had gotten it wrong. But Sharon left no room for doubt. "The current vacuum, which is the Palestinians' fault, can't go on," he announced. "That's why I have decided, as part of my disengagement plan, to evacuate seventeen settlements, with all of their residents, from the Gaza Strip into Israel."

Sharon declared that the disengagement would take place in July 2005, giving the settlers a year and a half to voluntarily leave their homes and find new housing inside Israel, with the help of a special government agency set up to assist and compensate them. Many of the settlers in the Gaza Strip, however, decided to fight the decision, believing they could convince a majority of the Israeli public, and the Knesset, to oppose it. They began a massive campaign of demonstrations and door knocking across the country. But it was hopeless: Sharon's plan had been poll-tested even before he announced it, and the results were clear. After almost four decades of military presence in Gaza, most Israelis wanted to exit the coastal enclave and leave behind its Palestinian residents. Sharon's approach of withdrawing from Gaza unilaterally and shutting the door, without the air of conciliation or pacifism that had accompanied Oslo, managed to win support even among many right-wing voters.

In the months leading up to the disengagement, settlers from the Strip came to Nahal Oz several times, hoping that if they could persuade the kibbutzniks living on the border that Sharon's plan spelled trouble for them, perhaps the Labor Party would vote against it. They warned that the disengagement would make it much easier for Hamas to fire rockets and mortars into Israel. It was a desperate move, with almost zero chance of success: the overwhelming majority of Nahal Oz residents supported Sharon. They viewed his plan as a direct continuation of Rabin's efforts to broker peace with the Palestinians and a sign that the former leader's assassination a decade earlier had failed to change the course of history, after all. Members of the kibbutz and other border communities went so far as to participate in demonstrations in support of the disengagement. The settlers' gambit failed.

One of the only people in Nahal Oz who did have reservations about Sharon's plan was Carine's father, Dani Rachamim, who feared that the prime minister's insistence on acting unilaterally would backfire. The PA, now completely under Abbas's leadership after Arafat had passed away in November 2004, had tried several times to convince Sharon to officially hand over Gaza to Abbas. Dani thought that this sort of bilateral handoff would be a better move, since it would bolster the PA; he warned friends that by refusing to give the PA any role in the disengagement, Sharon was weakening the moderate Abbas and setting the stage for Hamas to take full credit for the Israeli withdrawal. If forced to choose between Sharon's plan or the continuation of the occupation, Dani knew he'd eventually side with Sharon; but he kept warning that there was a better way to get out of Gaza, with an agreement.

But voices like Dani's were drowned out that summer by the commotion that swept over Israel as the military evacuated Gaza and then destroyed all the settlements there. Abbas got no credit, whereas Hamas organized a massive rally days after Israel's last soldiers left and declared the disengagement a result of its own violent resistance to the occupation. For the settlers and, ironically, also for peace activists like Dani, it was a bitter vindication.

By September 2005, Nahal Oz was once again a border community. There were no longer any Israeli settlements or soldiers on the other side of the fence. Officially, the PA was in control of Gaza, but in reality Hamas—now under the command of a new generation of leaders who had been forged in the crucible of the second intifada—was growing more brazen and daring in the wake of the Israeli withdrawal. Yassin, the group's founder, had been assassinated by Israel in March 2004; Hamas's new leader in Gaza was a forty-four-year-old politician named Ismail Haniyeh, who had an ambitious plan for the future: to compete, and win, in the upcoming Palestinian election.

In the kibbutz, there was hope that Israel's withdrawal from Gaza would lead to a period of peace and stability in the Strip and the region more broadly. But Hamas had other plans. In the days and weeks after Sharon's disengagement, the organization continued to fire rockets and mortars at border communities. Sharon responded with aerial and artillery strikes on Gaza. Israel no longer occupied Gaza, but neither could it turn its back on the coastal enclave.

The rockets chased Carine everywhere she went. One fell next to her childhood home; another fell on the soccer field while she was playing with a friend. And then there was the time a rocket fell in the yard of her high school. She managed to snap a pixelated photo of it with the camera on her first cell phone.

The magical kibbutz where Carine had grown up was still her favorite place in the world, but five years of constant bombardment had taken a toll on Nahal Oz, and on the entire border region. "It became normal for me and my friends to sit outside and talk, and suddenly hear a siren and then a boom and realize we could have died if we hadn't run fast enough," she explained. "Looking back, there was nothing normal about it."

Carine had little time to worry about the security situation, however. She was too busy playing soccer. At age fifteen, she joined a professional team, becoming one of the youngest players in Israel's national women's league. Between practices and games, and the long trips to both, her schedule was always jam-packed. On many days, she'd come back home exhausted, take a shower, eat, and try to get some sleep ahead of the next day's workout.

But one thing did manage to distract her from her excruciating schedule—something she'd been grappling with for years but did her best to hide from everyone around her: she was attracted to women. She had first felt it as a young teenager but tried her best to repress her desires. By the time she'd entered high school, however, Carine could no longer hold it in. Ahead of her mandatory enlistment in the Israeli military at age eighteen, she had a secret relationship with another girl from the kibbutz, an affair that no one else knew about. It was her first real taste of love, and as often happens, it ended in heartbreak. But unlike most of her friends, Carine couldn't share the breakup's pain with her parents or siblings. She felt alone and helpless.

One of the first people to notice Carine's distress was Dikla Arava, a resident of the kibbutz who worked as a teacher and parent counselor. She was thirty-five years old at the time and had forged a strong connection with the kibbutz's high schoolers. Dikla had been raised in a religious community four miles to the east of Nahal Oz, but as a young woman, she had adopted a secular lifestyle, going on to marry a member of the kibbutz whom she'd met at the local pub. The couple eventually divorced, but Dikla stayed in Nahal Oz, where her children were born, and became a beloved figure in the community. For Carine and her peers, Dikla was more than a teacher; many of them saw her as the one adult they could trust with their most private thoughts and feelings.

"She noticed that I looked sad all the time and was crying more than usual," Carine recalled. One day, Dikla took her for a talk, and the truth finally came out. "I sat in front of her and just spilled everything." Dikla's response was exactly what Carine needed to hear. "She refused to make a big deal out of it. She spoke to me as if it was the most normal thing in the world. She listened to me, and she said, 'It's going to be OK. Don't worry.'"

After that conversation, Carine found the courage to tell her mother and eventually her entire family. Once they all knew the truth, and accepted her just as she was, Carine felt no fear anymore: "I didn't care what anyone else was going to say." The community, however, proved Dikla correct all over again. "People just said, 'OK, good for you,'" Carine remembered. "Nobody made a fuss about it."

Israeli society was rapidly changing. The first Pride parade in Tel Aviv, a decade earlier, had attracted just a few hundred participants; by the mid-2000s, however, the annual parade had become a massive event attended by over one hundred thousand people, with the mayor marching up front. Israeli celebrities began coming out of the closet, and even the new prime minister, Ehud Olmert, a centrist politician who replaced Sharon after the old soldier suffered a stroke and fell into a coma in January 2006, was the proud father of an openly lesbian daughter. In one of his first interviews in office, Olmert said that he wanted to turn Israel into "a country that people will enjoy living in." Supporting the LGBT community was part of that vision. But progress on this front, if transpired, didn't extend to others.

Ehud Olmert won Israel's 2006 election at the head of a new Center Right party called Kadima, Hebrew for "forward." He had campaigned on Sharon's legacy, promising to continue the disengagement by pulling out of certain areas of the West Bank and completing the task of unilaterally redrawing Israel's borders. His plans, however, soon ran into a major obstacle: just as Olmert began to publicly promote this plan, Hamas won a surprise victory in the Palestinian parliamentary election.

Mahmoud Abbas, the Palestinian president, had tried several times to cancel the 2006 election, fearing that Sharon's disengagement would help Hamas win a majority in the legislature of the Palestinian Authority. Going into the elections, Abbas's Fatah Party, a secular-nationalist organization that was committed to the Oslo Accords, held a majority in the Palestinian parliament, a dominance that further entrenched its control of the PA. But Hamas's claims that the Israeli withdrawal was a result of its armed resistance were loosening Fatah's hold on power, as was public anger over corruption, cronyism, and mismanagement at the senior levels of the PA.

Some of Abbas's top aides had concocted a secret plan to avoid Fatah's impending loss: they had asked Israeli officials to announce that Palestinians living in East Jerusalem, which Israel had annexed in 1967, wouldn't be allowed to vote in the parliamentary elections, since their neighborhoods were officially part of Israel. Once Israel made such an announcement, these aides said, Abbas would cancel the election altogether, accusing Israel of disenfranchising Palestinians in Jerusalem, while repeating the PA's official position that East Jerusalem should become the future capital of the state of Palestine.

The plot was seriously considered in the corridors of power in Jerusalem, but the administration of George W. Bush saw the Palestinian election as an important part of its "democracy promotion" agenda in the Middle East, and shot down the idea. The US insisted that the election take place on time and that Palestinians in East Jerusalem be allowed to participate in it, just like those in the West Bank and Gaza.

On Election Day, Fatah's top ranks expected a narrow loss—but the results were far more dramatic than anyone had expected and their reverberations, far-ranging. Hamas won seventy-four seats in the parliament; Fatah, just forty-five. Abbas was embarrassed by the results; the Bush administration was stunned; and the Israeli public cooled toward Olmert's disengagement plan. If this is what happened after Israel had left Gaza, people said, it would make no sense to now withdraw from the West Bank.

Abbas, the biggest loser of that election, was forced to accept Ismail Haniyeh, Hamas's young leader, as the new Palestinian prime minister, serving alongside him. The tables had turned: the position of prime minister had been invented by the Bush administration a few years earlier as a power-sharing device that would weaken Arafat and give moderates like Abbas a position of influence, but now the moderate Palestinian president found himself sharing power with Hamas.

Abbas was in an impossible situation. If he refused to accept Hamas's legitimate victory, he would effectively be deeming the election a farce, dealing a potentially fatal blow to Palestinian democracy and the prospect of future independence. On the other hand, if he accepted the results and brought Hamas into the Palestinian government, Israel would have to retaliate: even the moderate Olmert viewed Hamas as illegitimate, in light of the group's long history of terror attacks and blatantly antisemitic ideology.

Abbas tried at first to convince Hamas to change its ways by accepting the Oslo Accords and renouncing its hateful and conspiratorial charter from 1987. Haniyeh was willing to consider these steps, according to Shlomi Eldar, an Israeli reporter who interviewed him several times and wrote two books about Hamas. But Mashal, the group's exiled political leader, ruled out any form of compromise. In the battle between pragmatic governance and ideological zeal, the latter won the day. Hamas refused to budge.

Olmert's response was to begin a new policy of effectively placing Gaza, Hamas's stronghold, under siege. Israel no longer controlled the territory following the disengagement, but it still held the keys; aside from one border crossing with Egypt, all of Gaza's other points of entry and exit were connected to Israel, while the Israeli navy controlled the Strip's access to the Mediterranean. Olmert's government imposed severe restrictions on the movement of people and goods to and from Gaza; in addition, Olmert decided to withhold tax revenues that Israel collected from Palestinians in the West Bank and was supposed to transfer to the PA as part of the Oslo Accords. These funds, which had helped the PA pay salaries to its bureaucrats and security personnel in Gaza, suddenly stopped flowing after Hamas's victory.

The goal of these steps was to put pressure on Hamas—to bring it to a breaking point and force it to accept Abbas's demands. But the leaders of Hamas, emboldened by their win at the ballot box, refused to budge. As historian Tareq Baconi notes, they "interpreted the movement's victory as a resounding endorsement" of their fight against Israel. Mashal, according to Baconi, saw no conflict between Hamas's governing of Gaza and its continuation of terror attacks against Israel; Hamas had a mandate from the Palestinian people, Mashal felt, and he intended to "build a society of resistance" in the coastal enclave.

Under growing economic pressure from Israel, Hamas relied on the support of countries like Qatar, Iran, and Turkey and also on a vast network of underground tunnels that the organization had begun digging between the Gaza Strip and Egypt. The Egyptian government also viewed Hamas's takeover of Gaza negatively and often cooperated with Israel's attempted economic pressure. But the tunnels beneath the Rafah border crossing, some of which were dug after paying bribes to Egyptian officers so that they looked the other way, helped Hamas overcome that very same pressure. These tunnels were used for smuggling all sorts of goods into the region, and also massive amounts of weapons, from AK-47s to rockets and mortars.

The Israeli blockade, in other words, had backfired. Far from getting weaker, Hamas was gaining strength.

On June 25, 2006, the last hope for any kind of transformation within Hamas faded when the organization conducted a cross-border raid from Rafah into Israel, using an underground tunnel to avoid being detected by the military. A cell of Hamas fighters—mehablim, as Israelis had taken to calling them, a Hebrew word that could mean both "terrorist" and "saboteur"—killed two Israeli soldiers and kidnapped a third, a nineteen-year old tank gunner named Gilad Shalit.

Shalit was smuggled back into the Gaza Strip alive and held in a secret location while Hamas tried to coax Israel into a prisoner exchange—a deal in which it was bound to demand the release of hundreds of convicted terrorists. Rather than concede, Olmert ordered a large military assault on Gaza, which lasted several weeks and was slowed down by the breakout of a new war between Israel and Hezbollah, a powerful terror organization operating out of Lebanon. Almost four hundred Palestinians were killed by the Israeli military during the fighting.

Six months after he replaced Sharon, it was clear that Olmert's second disengagement plan—his publicly announced intention to pull out of parts of the West Bank—was dead. Hamas's election win, followed by the Shalit kidnapping and the war in Lebanon, had caused Israeli public opinion toward the Palestinian question to shift further to the right, forcing the Israeli government to abandon its plans for any more unilateral territorial withdrawals in the near future.

The final nail was hammered into the coffin in July 2007, a year after Shalit's abduction. That month, Hamas—which was largely unaffected by Israel's abortive operation inside Gaza—seized control of the Strip in a bloody coup d'état that the organization had planned for months amid growing frustration over its fruitless negotiations with Abbas. Haniyeh and Mashal, Hamas's top officials, had both sensed that the elderly PA president—far removed from Gaza in his office in Ramallah, the Authority's seat of government in the West Bank—had never truly accepted the previous year's election results. So they had decided to teach him a lesson.

The takeover of Gaza was brutal and cruel: PA officers and loyalists were tortured by Hamas militants, humiliated in the streets, and thrown to their death from rooftops. Thousands of them escaped into Israel, seeking refuge from the fury of the Islamists.

Thirteen years after the 1994 peace festival, the dream of peace was dead: Hamas was now firmly in control across the border, and the people of Nahal Oz once again found themselves shouldering the heavy gates of Gaza.

CHAPTER 8

"SABA WILL COME AND GET US OUT OF HERE"

OCTOBER 7, 2023

AROUND THE SAME TIME THAT my father and Avi were speeding down Route 232 in my parents' Grand Cherokee, another Jeep—a green Wrangler—was also racing toward the Gaza border. Inside of it were five IDF soldiers, helmets on their heads and rifles in their hands. They, too, were heading to Nahal Oz.

The soldiers' Wrangler wasn't bulletproof, which meant that it would offer no protection if they encountered an enemy along the way. And the odds of that happening were looking good: en route from their unit's base to our area, the soldiers in the Jeep had seen dozens of dead bodies on the road. But they didn't stop—didn't even slow down. They had a mission, an urgent one.

It was just past noon when they reached a road sign with our kibbutz's name on it and took a sharp right turn.

Afik Rosenthal, twenty, had woken up that morning at his parents' home in central Israel, approximately forty miles north of Gaza. He had gone to a party with friends the night before, enjoying a rare weekend at home, and he planned to sleep late and spend a quiet Saturday with his family before returning to his military base the following day.

Afik served as a combat paramedic in Maglan—an elite military unit that specializes in the use of advanced technological systems behind enemy lines. Most Israelis know very little about the work of this secretive unit, but thousands of young recruits attempt to join it every year. Only a few are accepted, and even then they must endure long months of exhausting training to officially become part of Maglan.

As a teenager, Afik dreamed of serving in a special unit within the IDF; he'd originally joined the paratroopers, but in the final year of his mandatory three-year service, he was transferred to Maglan. His father later said the day Afik made it into the special unit was "the happiest day of his life."

The sirens at 6:30 A.M. hadn't surprised the young commando. For several months before the Hamas attack, Afik had told his parents and friends that a major war would erupt in October. He didn't know exactly how it would happen or whether the war would start on the country's southern or northern border. But recent developments within Israel, he saw, signaled that a massive conflagration was on the horizon.

Israel had experienced unprecedented internal turmoil and tensions during 2023, after a religious right-wing coalition led by Binyamin Netanyahu had tried to pass highly controversial legislation weakening the judiciary and expanding the powers of the government. Hundreds of thousands of Israelis had taken to the streets in protest. In late March, Defense Minister Yoav Gallant—a member of Netanyahu's own Likud Party—warned in a televised speech that the social and political discord in Israel was becoming a national security threat. The country's enemies, he explained, could see that it was tearing itself apart, and its weakness could well be too great of a temptation for them to resist.

Afik wasn't a very political person. He believed that, ultimately, Israel's differing sides would have to compromise and find a way to stick together—perhaps as the result of the conflict that he sensed was coming. Now his premonition of violence, at least, had proven devastatingly accurate.

When the rockets began flying all over the country, Afik wasted no time. His parents—who had returned the night before from a vacation in Europe—and his sister, who also lived at home with them, watched him put on his uniform, grab his weapon, and call his friends in the unit. He also sent a short text message to a group of friends from high school, all of whom had heard his prediction for a war in October.

"Told you guys!" he wrote.

One of them replied, "Afik, you're a genius."

He left home as the sirens were still wailing. His parents took a picture of him on his way out, hugging his sister with a big smile on his face. Afik had enlisted in the military two years earlier in order to defend his country, and in addition to his combat training, he had also gotten certified as a paramedic in order to be able to save the lives of his friends in battle. Now, it seemed, he would have an opportunity to do both.

The Maglan unit's base was located about halfway between Afik's home and the Gaza border region; a friend who lived nearby gave him a ride. Once inside the base, Afik teamed up with Hen Bukhris, twenty-six, the deputy commander of Maglan, and Yiftah Yavetz, twenty-three, the unit's top intelligence officer. Other soldiers were arriving at the base, but the scene inside was one of chaos and confusion. Usually, Maglan commandos go into battle with antitank missiles, hand grenades, and other, more sophisticated kinds of military equipment; they drive in armored vehicles and use encrypted radio devices for communications. But assembling this sort of equipment took time—and on that morning, time was in precious short supply.

As Hamas breached Israel's defenses along the border, shocking and disturbing reports were starting to reach Hen, the deputy commander of Maglan, who found himself organizing the unit's immediate response. With the Gaza border regional command center already under attack, the chain of command had been broken, as my father had witnessed that morning when he tried to get forces to go from Kibbutz Mefalsim's entry gate to Nahal Oz. Young commanders like Hen had to make fateful decisions all by themselves, with time working against them.

Hen decided that the most urgent priority was to send as many Maglan fighters as he could toward the Gaza border to help the communities that were under attack there. They had no time to wait for specific orders or instructions, he realized; in fact, there wasn't even enough time to organize all of the fighters' regular battle equipment. He and Yiftah, his intelligence officer, were both seeing unbelievable images on their phones: photos of white pickup trucks full of armed terrorists driving through the streets of Sderot, the largest city in the border region. They also got push notifications from Israeli news outlets, describing the desperate cries for help coming from residents of kibbutzim along the border, who were hearing terrorists breaking into their homes as they cowered inside their safe rooms.

As officers and soldiers arrived at the base, Hen organized them into small fighting teams and sent them racing south in whatever vehicles were at hand. One group of fighters drove to Sderot; another went to Kibbutz Zikim, a beachside community at the northern edge of the Israel-Gaza border. Most of the unit, however, made its way to Kfar Azza, a kibbutz located three miles northeast of Nahal Oz.

As bad as our situation was that morning, our neighbors in Kfar Azza were going through even worse. The members of their local security team had rushed to their local armory when the Hamas attack began; however, the terrorists had gotten there at the same time, and a difficult battle ensued. Whereas in Nahal Oz a small police team had been fighting since 7:00 A.M., Kfar Azza—home to about eight hundred people—was left with almost no defenders by the late morning hours. The terrorists broke into homes and safe rooms, murdered dozens of residents, set homes on fire, and were in the process of kidnapping entire families and carrying them back into Gaza.

This kibbutz did, however, have one advantage over ours: it was located directly along Route 232 and was much easier for military forces to reach compared to the more remote and isolated Nahal Oz, which is connected to the main highway by a smaller road. That's why military reinforcements, including the first Maglan fighters, had arrived at Kfar Azza before noon, whereas in our community the eight-man crew led by Saul, the police commander, and Nissan, our deputy chief of security, was still fighting alone an hour later.

After sending as many soldiers as he could toward the border area, Hen told Yiftah that it was time for them to join the fight. The Wrangler wasn't the best vehicle to take into a war zone, but getting an armored vehicle would take time, whereas the Wrangler was immediately available. At this point, that was all that mattered.

Together with Afik and two other soldiers from the unit, Alon and Yonatan, the officers started heading southwest, in the general direction of the Gaza border, still not aware of where exactly they would be going. While Alon drove the vehicle, Hen and Yiftah used their personal cell phones to communicate with other officers, both in their unit and outside of it, to figure out where their help was most needed.

Through these phone calls and WhatsApp messages, the officers in the Jeep learned that IDF forces were already fighting Hamas terrorists in Sderot, Kfar Azza, Mefalsim, and other locations. Hen and Yiftah both noticed, however, that one community was missing from the list: Nahal Oz, the closest community to Gaza. The news media was already reporting that terrorists were inside the kibbutz as well as at the military base across the road from it. Urgent help was needed at Nahal Oz, but it seemed like no soldiers had gotten there yet.

So the five Maglan fighters decided to bypass Kfar Azza, which they knew that their comrades had already reached, and continue southwest toward Nahal Oz. As they were driving, Yiftah, the intelligence officer, managed to obtain the contact details for Ilan, my neighbor and the kibbutz's security chief. He tried calling, but there was no answer. So he texted: "Hi, this is Yiftah from Maglan. We're coming to the kibbutz." The message was sent at 12:02 P.M., but Yiftah's phone indicated that Ilan hadn't received it. They had no way of contacting anyone else in the community—and thus had no choice but to keep driving and hope that there was still someone left at Nahal Oz to save.

Yiftah had come down that morning from his home in Ramat Hasharon, an affluent town just north of Tel Aviv. His father, Gilad, had also been an officer in Maglan and had gone on to become a successful tech entrepreneur and the founder of one of Israel's largest solar energy companies. The night before, the family had come together at a restaurant to celebrate Gilad's birthday. He was born on October 7; however, it was easier to find a good table on Friday night, so they decided to go out a day early. Yiftah wrote his father a short letter, expressing how much he loved and admired him. The next morning, when Hamas's attack began, Yiftah drove south as fast as he could—but he called Gilad to let him know where he was heading and to say goodbye.

Now, after they had passed Kfar Azza, the five soldiers reached a roundabout. They could continue straight on Route 232 or take a sharp right turn onto Route 25, toward Nahal Oz. For many years, this road had been known as the Gaza–Be'er Sheva road because it had connected

Gaza with the largest city in southern Israel. Ever since Israel had sealed its border with Gaza, however, the once-famous artery had lost most of its traffic, becoming instead the only road leading to Nahal Oz and the nearby military base.

As the soldiers turned right toward Nahal Oz, their Wrangler was the only vehicle on the road. In front of them was a thirty-two-foot-tall concrete wall that blocked access to the "old" Route 25 and forced all traffic to continue onto a smaller, winding road that appeared on their left, surrounded by trees and orchards.

This smaller road had been paved more than a decade earlier, after Hamas, from inside Gaza, had fired antitank missiles at vehicles on Route 25. For several years, the two roads had existed next to each other, each serving a different function: the faster, wider Route 25 was preferred at times of relative calm, but whenever a security escalation was expected, the military placed roadblocks on it and instructed drivers to use the smaller, unnamed road running through the woods, explaining that the trees offered protection from cross-border fire. Eventually, after too many recurring closures, the larger road was permanently sealed off with the tall wall, and the smaller road became the only way to access the kibbutz and the base.

Hen examined the small, winding road and its wooded surroundings on a map and immediately decided that they needed an alternative: this road was sketchy to begin with, but there was a bend up ahead that offered a perfect place for an ambush.

So Hen decided to get off the paved road and continue on an even smaller road: a gravel way that bypassed it to the south. They drove on this gravel path alongside an avocado grove and then took a right turn and stopped in a wooded area from which they could see the paved road again, directly in front of them. They had bypassed the dangerous bend, which lay a short distance to their north, and were now only one and a half miles from the kibbutz.

Before they went any further, Hen, knowing that there had been reports of mehablim inside Nahal Oz, wanted to check one last time to see if any IDF reinforcements would be able to join his small group. He and Yiftah tried again to call other officers in their unit and in other parts of the military that had begun sending forces to the region.

Hen Bukhris, the deputy commander of Maglan (left), led his men to Nahal Oz after realizing that no other military force had reached the kibbutz. Afik Rosenthal (second from right) and Yiftah Yavetz (right corner), along with two other fighters, ran into the line of fire with him.

As they sat in the Wrangler waiting for answers, one of the commandos pulled out a cell phone and snapped a group photo. In the picture, Hen can be seen at the left-hand edge of the vehicle, smiling. Afik, two seats away from him, looks straight into the camera, appearing calm. Yiftah is in the other corner of the frame, opposite Hen, and seems more concerned than the others—perhaps a result of his one-sided communication with Ilan.

Several minutes passed, and it became clear that no reinforcements were coming. It was all up to them now, and they had to get going. But as they were preparing to turn back toward the road, Yiftah saw something moving between the trees. He took another look, and realized it was the ambush Hen had worried about, not far from where he had predicted it would be: a group of Hamasniks—approximately seven of them—hiding in the forest, in a position that overlooked the road to Nahal Oz from the south.

He shouted "Mehablim!"—and half a second later, the bullets started to fly.

My father and Avi were a few minutes behind the Maglan team, driving toward Nahal Oz in my parents' Jeep Grand Cherokee. Just like the five soldiers in the Wrangler, they also passed the gate of Kfar Azza on Route 232 and saw military vehicles at the entrance—a sight that gave my father hope that maybe some IDF forces had also reached Nahal Oz. Half a mile further, he and Avi reached the junction where Route 232 meets Route 25. They were about to take the same right turn toward Nahal Oz and saw the same tall wall, when suddenly, Avi said they had to stop.

An Israeli attack helicopter was flying above them. Avi and my father were both wearing civilian clothes, sitting in a civilian vehicle, Avi with a gun in his hand and my father with a pistol. The road to Nahal Oz, Avi reminded my father, could also be used to get directly to the Gaza border fence—which was completely breached. By that hour, shortly after noon, there were already preliminary reports of Hamas cells that, after attacking kibbutzim on the border, had returned to Gaza with Israeli hostages. Avi feared that from high in the sky, an air force pilot could mistake the two of them for terrorists driving west toward Gaza City and fire a missile at their car. The two of them agreed that they had to wait for a military vehicle to join them.

A few minutes passed. Finally, a large military SUV, clearly identifiable from its pale green exterior, approached. Inside of it were ten officers and soldiers from the paratroopers brigade, in which my father himself had served decades earlier. The senior officer in the SUV was a major named Roi, who had already fought earlier that day in Sderot and along Route 232; at one point, he had killed two terrorists who were firing at cars from a bridge overlooking the road, near the region's only train station. Roi didn't recognize my father, but when he and the other officers saw a vehicle with Israeli license plates and two armed men inside of it, they made a quick mental calculation and decided that they weren't a threat—probably saving my father's life.

Like my father and Avi, the paratroopers were heading to Nahal Oz. But they weren't going to the kibbutz; rather, their destination was the military base that lay next to our community. After fighting for hours in Sderot, Roi had wanted to head toward Kfar Azza with his men, in light of the disturbing reports emerging from that kibbutz about a massive assault by mehablim and a lack of military forces to repel them. But by the time he had arrived at the gate of that community, he had been told that other IDF forces were already fighting inside. An officer who was standing at the gate told him, however, that the Nahal Oz base was under attack and that the soldiers who were still alive were sending urgent distress signals. "They're being slaughtered there," the officer said. Roi told the driver in the SUV to turn around and get to the base as fast as possible. On their way, they had run into my father and Avi.

While my father later recalled asking Roi where they were heading and feeling relieved to hear him say "Nahal Oz," Roi remembered simply seeing two Israeli fighters heading in the same direction and hoping that they'd be of some help but not exchanging any words with them. But one thing is certain: the two vehicles—my father's Grand Cherokee and the paratroopers' SUV—were now both heading toward Nahal Oz, unaware of what they were about to find when they got there.

They took a left turn before the high wall, slipping onto the small side road. Unlike the Maglan crew a few minutes earlier, they decided to stick to the paved road and not bypass it from the south; in their hurry to reach Nahal Oz, they did not think about the possibility of an ambush waiting ahead.

All the same, my father was on high alert. He knew this was probably the most dangerous moment of the entire day so far: they were driving on a narrow road with trees on both sides, leaving them with very limited visibility. Gaza, and the breached border fence, were now just two miles away. The kibbutz, full of mehablim, was even closer.

Then they heard gunshots. The noise came not from the kibbutz or from Gaza, but from much closer—directly ahead of the convoy, just around a bend in the road. Unbeknownst to my father, this was almost the exact spot that Hen had wanted to avoid just minutes earlier, for fear of an ambush. Now, a battle was raging there, and my father, Avi, and the paratroopers had driven straight into it.

To the left of them, standing between two tall trees on the gravel path just off the paved road, was the Jeep Wrangler. It was pocked with bullet holes, its nose facing the new arrivals. To the left of the vehicle, approximately one hundred feet away and partly hidden by a dense patch of trees, was the ambush position, where at least five Hamasniks were sitting or kneeling on the ground. To the right of the Wrangler, taking cover behind the tires on the vehicle's driver's side, were the five Maglan commandos.

The terrorists had lost the element of surprise after Yiftah spotted them, but they still had a numerical advantage over the five soldiers and, in addition to that, were better equipped. Their AK-47 bullets were strong enough to pierce the doors of the Wrangler; they had hand grenades and RPGs; one of them carried a substantial medical kit, ready to assist his comrades in case they got injured. They were a formidable threat to the five lightly armed commandos sheltering behind the Jeep.

It took Avi and my father under a second to process the scene in front of them. From the road, they could see the entire battle: the Hamas ambush position inside the trees, the Wrangler, and the Israeli soldiers behind it. And almost as soon as they'd registered what was happening, they knew what they needed to do.

My father and Avi jumped out of the Grand Cherokee and ran toward the Wrangler, trying to get the vehicle between themselves and the Hamasniks as quickly as possible. Four of the paratroopers were right behind them, sprinting toward the Wrangler, while the others dispersed and took up positions in a rough half-circle around the Jeep, lying prone on the ground and opening fire toward the Hamas fighters.

My father was now crouched behind the midsection of the Wrangler, with two Maglan commandos to his right and three to his left. The men on his right began yelling at him for ammunition. The three men to his left were silent. He took another look at them and realized that they were dead.

Afik's body lay over Hen's, with his medic's kit in his hand; the young paramedic had died while trying to save his commander, who had been shot almost as soon as they had engaged the Hamas ambushers. Yiftah was next to them, also lifeless.

As my father was taking in this grisly scene, Avi and the four paratroopers who'd made it to the Wrangler maneuvered to the far side of

The Jeep Wrangler in which the small Maglan crew had arrived to the scene of the battle, as pictured outside Nahal Oz several days after the fighting. Of the five men inside of it, three had died and two were injured.

the three bodies. This left the five fighters partially exposed to incoming fire—but also gave them a better position to shoot back.

With no time to think, my father stripped the magazines of ammunition from the dead soldiers' vests and threw them to their two surviving comrades, Alon and Yonatan, who were wounded but still in the fight, and both still clamoring for ammunition. Then he grabbed Hen's M16, which had a Trijicon riflescope attached to it.

Early in my father's military career, when he was serving in one of Israel's top special forces units, he had made a name for himself as a sniper. In 1984, at age twenty-two, he killed a terrorist who was standing inside a bus full of dozens of Israeli hostages, bringing the man down with a single shot and without harming anyone around him. The "Trij" installed on Hen's gun just so happened to be one of my father's preferred riflescopes.

He checked Hen's pulse one more time and, after confirming that he was dead, took off Hen's helmet and secured it on his own head. Then, my father shouldered the M16, placed one eye on the scope, and rose quickly into a firing position. The retired general was now just another soldier; Alon, one of the wounded fighters, four decades younger than him, yelled at him to notice how the terrorsits were trying to attack them from their right side.

Spotting one of the Hamas fighters on the move, trying to reach the Wrangler from the right, my father fired one shot, killing the man. Then he moved the scope to the left and identified another Hamasnik hunkered down in the woods. He fired again, and saw the bullet hit the man's upper body, but wasn't sure if he had killed the fighter or merely wounded him.

Meanwhile, Avi and the paratroopers were also firing nonstop toward the ambushers, as were Alon and Yonatan. The noise was deafening, but their aim was to bring as much firepower to bear on the Hamas position as they could in order to force the mehablim out of their comfortable hiding spot.

The plan seemed to work: the Hamas ambush team, which had been on a mission to surprise the first Israeli force trying to reach Nahal Oz, had been surprised itself by the arrival of Avi, the paratroopers, and my father, and they now found themselves on the back foot.

As the minutes passed and the bullets flew, the gunfire from the ambush position gradually abated. Finally, silence fell over the forest.

The smell of blood and smoke lingered in the air. The forest floor was littered with shell casings—hundreds of them, a mixture of the M16 and M4 ammunition fired by the Israeli troops and the AK-47 ammo used by the Hamas fighters. In one spot, between two trees, a hand grenade thrown by a Hamas fighter had left a small crater.

The battle had lasted at least several minutes, possibly much longer; according to a log kept at the Maglan headquarters, the men may have

The Rescuers' Route to Nahal Oz

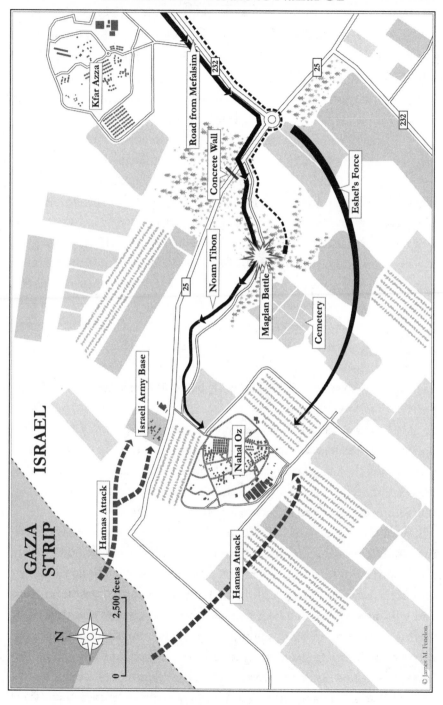

GAZA
STRIP

ISRAEL

N

0   2,500 feet

Hamas Attack

Israeli Army Base

Hamas Attack

Nahal Oz

Kfar Azza

Road from Mefalsim

232

25

232

Concrete Wall

Noam Tibon

25

Maglan Battle

Eshel's Force

Cemetery

© James M. Fenelon

fought the Hamas cell for almost half an hour. In the intensity of battle, the soldiers had all lost track of time. Earlier in the fighting, before my father and the paratroopers had pulled up, Alon, one of the Maglan men, had sent a voice memo to another officer in the unit: "Bukhris is dead, Yiftah and Afik are dead," he'd yelled. "You must get here immediately; we have just minutes left to live." His death had been averted, but the team's terrible losses were only just sinking in.

The ragtag crew of Israelis—Avi, the paratroopers, my father, and the two remaining Maglan commandos—had managed to kill most of the mehablim. But as they rose to their feet and scanned their surroundings, they saw one surviving Hamasnik running deeper into the woods. This was probably the second terrorist my father had fired at—the one he wasn't sure if he had killed or only wounded.

The injured Hamas fighter had run in the direction of the kibbutz, and the Israeli survivors were poised to pursue him—when one of the paratroopers, an officer, shouted that he'd been hit.

My father and another officer ran to him and saw blood pouring from a bullet hole in his stomach. It was clear that he had to be evacuated immediately; so, for that matter, did the two wounded Maglan commandos, Alon and Yonatan, who had both been hit by shrapnel in different parts of their lower bodies.

My father faced a painful decision. The road to Nahal Oz was now open. He hadn't heard from us in hours and had just seen firsthand how treacherous the situation around the kibbutz truly was. The battle along the road, moreover, had convinced him that it was very unlikely that any IDF reinforcements had already reached the community.

With the ambushers defeated, my father could simply get back inside the Grand Cherokee and speed toward the kibbutz. But could he really abandon the young paratrooper, not yet twenty-five, let alone the survivors of the brave Maglan team who had tried to reach the community first and who had paid such a heavy price? They had done everything right: getting off the main road, finding the Hamas ambushers before being fired on, and initiating a battle with them. But the Hamas cell had been better positioned inside the woods, while the commandos' Wrangler had been exposed and easier to target. By moving ahead, they had put their own lives on the line and saved the vehicles that came after them—those of my father and the paratroopers.

Saving these men, ultimately, would come down to my father, and the decision had to be made fast: Avi and the uninjured paratroopers wanted to chase after the wounded terrorist and ensure he wouldn't make his way into the kibbutz. What's more, Roi, the paratroopers' commander, feared that there could be more ambushers waiting ahead, so he wanted to proceed by foot through the woods—which would be safer for the soldiers but would take longer than if they charged ahead in their SUV. There was no time to spare: Roi—who by this point had recognized my father but had not had time to ask himself how a retired general had gotten mixed up in all this—told him that he needed to get the wounded men to the hospital so that the able-bodied fighters could continue on with the mission.

My father looked at the stricken officer and realized he had no choice: if the young man didn't get urgent medical care, he would die. He badly wanted to reach Nahal Oz, but he couldn't leave the officer there, bleeding to death on the road.

The paratroopers helped load their comrade into my father's Jeep, and the two wounded Maglan commandos joined him in the back. My father grabbed Hen's scoped rifle and climbed in alongside them, the dead commander's helmet still on his head. Then he started the engine and turned the vehicle back toward Mefalsim, while Avi and the others headed into the woods to find the missing terrorist—and perhaps more Hamasniks, if Roi's prediction proved accurate.

For the second time that day, my father was driving away from Nahal Oz. As he steered the Jeep back toward Route 232, he was gripped by fear—for several reasons. There was his ongoing fear for us, stranded in the safe room, unable to communicate with the outside world. But now he was also concerned for the wounded officer, whose name he learned was Yedidia and who was continuing to lose blood and was looking worse by the minute.

In addition, my father knew that the portion of Route 232 between Kfar Azza and Mefalsim, which he had traversed just an hour earlier with Avi by his side, was dangerously exposed to gunfire—and worse—from Gaza. Usually, whenever fighting broke out between Israel and Hamas, the police would immediately shut down this part of 232, for fear that

Hamas would fire antitank missiles from Gaza at cars driving on the highway. Now, my father was about to cross this stretch of road again, with three young soldiers in the back of his car—men whose lives were entirely in his hands.

So he did the only thing he could think of: he hit the gas, pushing the Grand Cherokee to speeds faster than any he'd ever dared. The four miles of highway between them and Mefalsim passed in a blur—and miraculously, minutes later, the Jeep was pulling to a stop unscathed in front of the bomb shelter where my father had left my mom just over an hour earlier.

My father got out of the vehicle and shouted for my mother to come out. She emerged from the bomb shelter glad to see him but also confused: he was now wearing a helmet and holding an M16 in his hand, two things he hadn't had with him when they last saw one another. There were blood stains on his jeans—clearly not his blood, but someone else's. And why had he returned so fast?

My father quickly explained what was going on: that there had been a fight on the road, that the way to Nahal Oz was now open, but that the three wounded soldiers in the Jeep needed urgent treatment, and that one of them was in critical condition.

My parents quickly agreed that my mother would take the wounded men to the hospital in the Jeep, while my father would head back to Nahal Oz—but how?

As my mother got into the Grand Cherokee, she told my father, "Talk to Yisrael." Then she sped off. For Yedidia in the back, time was running out.

My father looked around, trying to understand what she had meant. Then he saw a white Audi parked on the opposite side of the road. Behind the wheel was a familiar face. A sense of enormous relief swept over my dad. For the first time that day, he allowed himself to think that, just maybe, things were going to be OK.

Yisrael Ziv lived in a small Israeli community, an hour's drive from the Gaza border area. When the sirens began blaring that Saturday morning, he immediately realized that war had broken out between Israel and

Hamas. But it was only later that day, when he saw the television images of white pickup trucks full of terrorists driving through the center of Sderot, that he decided to leave his home and head down south to join the fighting.

Four months earlier, Yisrael had celebrated his sixty-sixth birthday. His military career had ended eighteen years prior, when he had left the Israel Defense Forces with the rank of major general. At one point, Yisrael had been my father's commander in the Paratroopers Brigade; now, like my dad, he had settled into retirement—but he still had an old uniform at home, just in case he ever happened to need it.

On the morning of October 7, the images from the border area convinced Yisrael that a disaster was unfolding and that the soldiers on the ground needed every bit of help they could get. So, like the old soldier he was, he put on his military garb, took up his pistol, and drove as fast as he could toward the border area.

Approaching the region from the east, Yisrael eventually reached the same landmarks that my parents had passed earlier that day: the city of Sderot, the junction of Routes 34 and 232, and then Kibbutz Mefalsim. He took part in a battle against a Hamas cell in the farmland surrounding that kibbutz; when that was over, a soldier told him there were civilians hiding in bomb shelters along the road in need of help.

Yisrael started methodically searching the shelters in the area, driving to each one, exiting the vehicle each time with his pistol in hand, ready for a close-range shoot-out. In many of the bomb shelters, he found nothing but dead bodies of Israelis who had tried to escape the Nova party and were massacred by Hamas inside the concrete structures.

But at one of the bomb shelters, after Yisrael had called out to anyone who might be hiding inside, he heard a familiar voice. He lowered the pistol and went inside. "Gali," he said upon recognizing my mother, "what the hell are you doing here?"

While my father and Avi had driven to Nahal Oz, waited for the paratroopers to join them, and then got swept up in the battle in the woods near our kibbutz, my mother had stayed inside the bomb shelter, still in the middle of an active war zone. She had seen more and more military vehicles on the road, which made her feel somewhat safer. But she still heard gunfire from the direction of the border, and inside the concrete structure, for all intents and purposes, she was alone in the world—that is, until Yisrael found her.

Relieved to see a familiar face, my mother briefed my dad's old commander on the situation, explaining that I, my wife, and our two children were stranded in our safe room in Nahal Oz; that she and my father had last spoken with us hours earlier; and that my father was on his way to the kibbutz.

After several minutes, Yisrael stepped out for a moment to speak with a group of soldiers nearby. Just then, my father's vehicle showed up in front of her.

As my mother rushed to get the three wounded men to the hospital, she told my father to speak to Yisrael. She didn't add his last name—there was no need. The second my father saw his old boss from the Paratroopers Brigade sitting inside his car, he knew: he had just found his ride back to Nahal Oz.

The dialogue between the two men was succinct. My father asked Yisrael if he could take him to the kibbutz and got two words in response: "Get in."

My dad warned his former commander that the situation was extremely dangerous and that he'd just returned from a battle where three soldiers had been killed and three others wounded. Yisrael simply stared at him and repeated the same sentence.

So my father got into Yisrael's Audi, still holding Hen's rifle, and the two men drove off, traveling again down the same dangerous stretch of Route 232, and then turning right toward Nahal Oz. By now, there was no longer much likelihood of an ambush on the road. Even so, my father stuck Hen's M16 out of the passenger window, just in case another surprise awaited them.

As they passed the site of the earlier battle, my father and Yisrael encountered the remaining paratroopers and Avi, who were still hunting for the wounded terrorist. Roi, the paratroopers' commander, was amazed to see my father and Yisrael pull up in the white Audi. Now there were *two* retired generals in front of him—and they were urging him to forget about this injured Hamasnik and instead move his men toward Nahal Oz, where there were Israelis under threat in both the kibbutz and the base situated right across the road from it.

"It's an honor to fight alongside the two of you," Roi told them, "but I'm the commander here."

My father and Yisrael insisted that it was wrong to focus on chasing a single enemy fighter—or even an entire cell, if indeed there were more Hamasniks hiding in the woods—when an entire community, and the base that was supposed to defend it, were under attack.

Roi took a moment to consider this—and he decided that the two retired officers were right. Their mission was to save as many Israeli lives as possible, not necessarily to kill every mehabel they encountered along the way. He ordered his men out of the woods and back onto their vehicle; within seconds, a new convoy—composed of the nine remaining paratroopers, Avi, Yisrael, and my father—was on the move.

The vehicles had to stop two minutes later at a small intersection, where Roi now faced another, even more agonizing dilemma. His original mission was to reinforce the soldiers at the Nahal Oz military base, which meant that he now should turn right; the front gate of the base was literally seconds away from where his vehicle sat. In that direction, Roi saw the same black pillar of smoke rising into the sky that my father and Avi had spotted an hour earlier from Route 232. It was now clear that it was coming from the base, not the kibbutz: after the assault by two hundred Hamas fighters had overwhelmed the smaller IDF force at the base earlier that morning, a slaughter had ensued, with more than sixty soldiers killed and ten more kidnapped and taken into Gaza. The base was now on fire, emitting a wave of heat that could be felt everywhere in the vicinity. The few soldiers who were still alive inside, hiding in their barracks, were begging for help; this was what had brought Roi and his men here in the first place.

But as a soldier, Roi's first and most important commitment, at all times, was to defend the lives of Israeli citizens. To fulfill that goal, he would have to turn left, not right; he would need to accompany my father, Yisrael, and Avi to the main gate of the kibbutz, which was just a minute away. Down the road in that direction, Roi could see an Israeli civilian vehicle: the white car in which Saul, the commander of the police force fighting inside the kibbutz, had arrived earlier that morning. Even at this distance, the car was now visibly disfigured by bullet holes. If a vehicle parked *outside* the community looked this bad, Roi thought to himself, what the hell was happening beyond the gate, in the homes of the families living there?

Half a mile separated the two places: the base and the kibbutz. Roi wished he could somehow go in both directions at once. There was no clear answer, and the pressure was overwhelming. The sight of the car, finally, made the decision for him.

I have to go to the kibbutz first, he told himself. *Our first priority is to save civilians.*

But no sooner had Roi made up his mind then he saw a large military convoy—approximately nine green Humvees—making its way through the fields to the south, driving toward the northeastern edge of the kibbutz's perimeter fence. This was the larger Maglan force that Hen and his men had spent several minutes waiting for before deciding to proceed on their own—and immediately running into the backside of the Hamas ambush. The reinforcements had now arrived, and they were clearly making their way toward the kibbutz.

Roi got out of the SUV and pointed out the convoy to my father. "I'm going to the base," he said. Then he ordered his soldiers to dismount and prepare to enter the burning military compound on foot; Avi planned to accompany them, seeing that a larger force was heading to the kibbutz. Now alone on the road, Yisrael guided the Audi to the left, leaving one crossroads behind—and heading toward another.

My father had driven down the small road leading to Kibbutz Nahal Oz—two lanes of paved asphalt, tucked between large plots of wheat— hundreds of times over the years, often with my mother by his side, first to see his son and daughter-in-law and then to visit his granddaughters. The cheerful yellow paint of the kibbutz's main gate had always been a welcome sight at the end of the hour-long drive from Tel Aviv. But now, as Yisrael steered them toward it, the atmosphere was tense. It was just after

1:00 P.M., more than five hours since my father had left home on his quest to rescue us. He had finally reached our community—but he had no idea what he would find inside.

They both agreed that it would be a mistake to try to enter the kibbutz through the main gate; it could have been booby-trapped by the terrorists. My father knew that there was a smaller side gate on the northeastern side of the kibbutz, used by agricultural workers to go out to the fields in the morning. This, he now realized, was the gate that the military convoy they'd spotted in the fields was also trying to reach.

Unbeknownst to my father and Yisrael, that larger Maglan force was now in touch with Nissan Dekalo, the kibbutz's deputy security chief, who had been battling terrorists nonstop inside the kibbutz since 7:00 A.M. Amid the ongoing fighting, Nissan had managed to not only direct the incoming force to the side gate, which he thought was the safest way for them to enter the community, but also to make sure it was open ahead of their expected arrival.

Meanwhile, a smaller Maglan force was also approaching the kibbutz from the north—bearing down on my father and Yisrael along the same road they had just traveled. This force had originally set out to help Alon and Yonatan, the two fighters injured earlier that day in the Hamas ambush; by the time it had arrived, however, my father had already evacuated them to safety, and so now, this small team of soldiers was also heading toward the kibbutz's side gate, only from the opposite direction as their comrades.

Seeing a military vehicle pull up behind them, my father got out of Yisrael's car to join the commandos who had begun piling out of it—but not before shaking his old commander's hand. Yisrael had heard that there were still young people in need of rescue in the area of the Nova music festival farther south, and he sensed that he could do more good there than at Nahal Oz. After a quick goodbye, he sped off.

My father and the small group of commandos ran east along the kibbutz's perimeter fence, bypassing the main gate. They arrived at the smaller entrance just as a complement of the larger group of Maglan reinforcements—several Humvees with more than forty soldiers in them—was rolling in. Avi, meanwhile, had also joined them, after the paratroopers whom he'd planned to accompany had been reinforced by more men from their own brigade, leading him to conclude that he could be more helpful in the kibbutz, after all. He had been slowed down due to an injury that he'd sustained earlier in the day, when he'd taken a piece of shrapnel in the hip while fighting terrorists in Sderot, but he was still determined to reach the kibbutz and help free it from Hamas.

My father introduced himself to the commander of the larger Maglan force, a twenty-seven-year-old major whose name, he learned, was Eshel. But there was no need; Eshel recognized him, with some apparent surprise at the sight of a retired general in the middle of this war zone. Quickly explaining what had brought him to the kibbutz, my father requested permission to join Eshel and his troops, hastening to add that he just wanted to help them clear the kibbutz from terrorists and reach his own family, not to challenge Eshel's authority. The major agreed, mentally reclassifying the retired general as simply another soldier on a day where every fighter counted. The fact that my father had been a frequent visitor to the kibbutz, and knew its terrain, was an added bonus in the eyes of the young officer.

Eshel, a resident of Tel Aviv, had almost been killed several times that day already. He had fought in the streets of Sderot, where he had rescued a group of elderly men from a synagogue that Hamas terrorists were targeting from a nearby rooftop. Later, his vehicle was attacked by ambushers along Route 232, and two officers who were fighting alongside him died before his eyes. One of his best friends, a fellow Maglan officer, had also been badly wounded, and Eshel had been forced to strip off the young man's clothes, all soaked in blood, so that his injuries could be treated. Had the Hamas fighters not made the fatal mistake of leaving their ambush position, after some twenty minutes of uninterrupted firing on the Israeli military vehicle before them, in order to try to capture the bodies of the officers who had been killed, Eshel would have run out of ammunition. But luckily for him, the Hamasniks had made a run for the vehicle—and he and three other soldiers managed to kill them at close range.

As if all of that wasn't bad enough, Eshel had also been on the phone with Hen Bukhris, trying to understand where to go next, when the

Maglan deputy commander had been hit by the first Hamas bullets of *that* ambush; Eshel heard the unspeakable sounds through his cell phone and realized that another friend from his unit had just died in battle.

It was that last conversation that had convinced Eshel of the urgent need to get to Nahal Oz—and to approach it from the fields and the banana orchards to the east of the kibbutz rather than along the same road that my father, Avi, and the paratroopers had taken: the road where Hen had been killed.

Now, Eshel's soldiers were entering the kibbutz through the side gate, and he was relieved to see a quiet scene in front of him: the commandos found themselves on a small hill overlooking an old, abandoned basketball court at the edge of the kibbutz, surrounded by tall pine trees. It was a place whose tranquility belied the terrible events unfolding a stone's throw away—events they could clearly hear, as bursts of gunfire echoed toward them from the heart of the kibbutz. But for Eshel, the most important thing was that this area was secluded and couldn't be seen from any of the kibbutz's neighborhoods. It was a place where he and his men could pause while he contemplated a map of the community, drawing up a battle plan for taking Nahal Oz back from the mehablim.

Just then, as if on cue, a battered armored vehicle pulled up. Inside were Nissan and the seven men who had been fighting alongside him practically since dawn.

Almost since he'd woken up that morning, Nissan had been hearing that soldiers were *on the way*, that the military was *almost there*, that it would take *just a few more minutes*. At some point, he'd stopped believing the officers on the other end of the phone. But when Eshel's force had been speeding through the surrounding fields toward Nahal Oz, and Nissan heard for the first time the name of a specific unit—Maglan *are on their way*—he regained a bit of hope. Now, the long-awaited reinforcements had finally arrived.

The little team standing before my father and the Maglan fighters was a sight to behold. Nissan and his partner from the local security team, Beri Meirovitch, together with Saul and the five other police troopers, had spent the past four hours crammed into a green Wolf SUV that looked like it had been to hell and back. The windshield was a mess of cracks

from the impact of countless bullets, and the engine was barely functioning thanks to a Hamas RPG. The men who spilled out of the rattletrap
were clearly exhausted, drenched in sweat after having all but run out
of water and being unable to open the SUV's windows even after the
air-conditioning had given out. One of the fighters had just passed out
inside the overheated vehicle, and was now brought back to consciousness by his comrades.

Nissan gave the Maglan commandos and my father a quick briefing
on the situation. My father was shocked as he absorbed what these seven
men had gone through over the six hours since the attacks had begun. If
the armed defenders of the kibbutz had it this bad, he thought, what had
his family been going through inside their safe room?

There were still approximately two dozen mehablim in the kibbutz,
Nissan said, and the residents were all locked inside their homes. He
warned that some homes, and safe rooms, had been broken into and that
there was no way of telling exactly how many families had been killed or
kidnapped. My father tried to push away any bad thoughts upon hearing
this; for all he knew, we were still alive and hiding. In the absence of any
evidence to the contrary, he had to hold out hope.

While the men were speaking, another force arrived, this one belonging to Givati, one of the largest fighting brigades of the Israeli military.
Like the Maglan commandos, these soldiers had all come straight from
their homes, with almost no time to prepare for the intense day of battle
awaiting them. One of their officers, a young man named Yehuda, had
driven almost four hours from his family's house in northeastern Israel.
Now, with the Givati troops' arrival, there were approximately seventy
Israeli fighters assembled on the eastern side of the kibbutz.

For the first time in hours, Nissan felt like he could breathe: at long
last, the cavalry was here. They finally had enough manpower to take
back Nahal Oz.

Eshel and Nissan wasted no time in putting their heads together to
formulate a plan of attack. They divided the kibbutz into four zones,
and the soldiers were organized into small teams that would comb and
clear these areas. The Maglan commandos would be responsible for two
areas, north and south of the old dining hall, which stood in the center

of the kibbutz—zones that included the new neighborhood, where our house was located. The Givati troops would go farther north, to the area around the community's kindergarten as well as to the homes near the community's swimming pool on the far northwestern edge of the compound.

Overall, there were more than 120 homes in the kibbutz that the soldiers would need to search. On top of that, there were more than a dozen public buildings—among them a grocery store, a clinic, a library, and a post office—where terrorists could potentially hide. The cowshed, the pool wardrobes, and other places also had to be thoroughly searched.

To ensure that none of these locations were overlooked, each IDF team that had been assigned to a specific area was further divided into two smaller teams consisting of approximately ten soldiers each. These smaller teams would each search approximately fifteen to twenty homes and buildings. There was no time to see if the math made sense and created an equal load for everyone; Nissan emphasized that mehablim were still on the loose inside the community. They had to start going.

My father asked to join the Maglan team that would eventually reach our house; their route would begin near the office of the kibbutz manager in the northeast, and then turn south, through the part of the community where our "adoptive parents," Eitan and Dganit, lived, before finally reaching our neighborhood.

As they combed the community, the soldiers would have two objectives: first, to kill any mehablim they saw and, second, to search each and every home for survivors of the terror attack. Under other circumstances, the soldiers might have tried to keep some of the terrorists alive so that they could be interrogated. But the situation they were now facing—Hamas fighters' conquest of an Israeli community and their ongoing attempts to murder or kidnap its inhabitants—was unprecedented. The Israeli soldiers had no professional Arabic-speaking interrogators with them and no place to keep detained terrorists under watch. They also had no illusions that the Hamas fighters who had carried out this unrelenting assault on a civilian community had any intention of being taken alive. Like so many of the terror attacks from years past, this one had all the hallmarks of a suicide mission, and the soldiers had to plan accordingly.

Although Nissan's briefing had made it amply clear that the soldiers needed to be on high alert, ready for a Hamasnik to be lurking around every corner, Eshel ordered them not to use their guns when entering the community's houses unless the soldiers had absolute confirmation that there was a terrorist inside. The risk of misidentifying a civilian and accidentally injuring or killing them was just too high. Eshel reminded his soldiers that they had come to save the people of the kibbutz, not to make them collateral casualties while searching for mehablim.

My father was particularly worried about friendly fire—for his own sake as well as for ours. Among a group of soldiers in uniform, he was a civilian wearing plain clothes. So, as the teams were preparing to move out, he asked if anyone had an extra uniform.

Having all come straight from home, none of the soldiers had any apparel beyond the shirts on their backs, quite literally. But one of them, who came from a religious family, found a solution: under his shirt he was wearing a green tzitzit—a Jewish ornamental garment that covers the upper body and has long fringes at its edges. My father, a secular man for whom religion was limited to the celebration of traditional holidays, had never worn a tzitzit in his life, but now he was happy to take it. The khaki-green piece of clothing looked like a dress on him. With Hen Bukhris's helmet still on his head, the fallen commando's M16 in his hands, and now the tzitzit on his shoulders, he cut a lonesome figure as he fell in with the Maglan commandos heading toward the southeastern corner of the kibbutz.

It was now approximately 2:00 P.M., but inside our safe room, Miri and I couldn't tell for sure what time it was. The batteries of both our phones had long since died, and in the pitch-dark, I could no longer see the dials on my watch. The only remaining sources of light were Carmel's glow-in-the-dark pacifiers. Two years earlier, as we'd been preparing for her arrival, Miri had the bright idea of buying pacifiers that shone in the dark so that we'd be able to find them more easily whenever the new baby lost one at night. Now, I thanked my wife for her foresight, and she replied drily that she'd never imagined these cheap things from Amazon would come in handy like this. Even under these grim circumstances, we could still make each other laugh.

The girls were awake again, which was bad news because they were clearly starting to lose patience. I couldn't blame them. They had behaved perfectly since rising that morning to the sound of gunfire. They had not eaten anything since the previous evening and were stuck in a dark room with no toys or other forms of entertainment, constantly being shushed by their parents. Miri and I were emotionally exhausted after the ordeal of the past eight hours, so it was a miracle that these two tiny children had kept their cool until now. But after waking up from their nap and finding themselves in the same situation, their frustration was unmistakable.

Miri and I both did our best to calm the girls down. Things were much quieter outside our home now, but still, every few minutes we heard shouting in Arabic. We knew that we remained in grave danger. It was imperative that the girls keep silent.

I had not heard anything from my parents after the message from my mother, around noon, that my father was getting closer to us. We couldn't tell what had happened since that message had been sent, but Miri and I were trying to stay optimistic. I believed that my father, a lifelong warrior, would win any face-to-face battle that he might find himself caught up in. I was mostly afraid that a rocket-propelled grenade or antitank missile would hit his vehicle on the road, depriving him of that chance.

I tried to repress the bad thoughts. We had an urgent mission in front of us: to convince the girls to stay calm. They were asking for food again and for toys to play with, two things we still couldn't give them.

I decided to make a promise to Carmel and Galia—and condition it on their behavior. Both of them were mature enough to understand the give-and-take dynamics of such a deal: *If you behave, you'll get to watch television after dinner* always worked on them. This time, though, the promise wasn't mine to keep, and I could only hope it wouldn't turn out to be a false one.

I took a deep breath and said, "Girls, if we all stay quiet, then Saba"—Hebrew for grandfather—"will come and get us out of here."

I repeated the terms of the deal twice, making sure they both understood it. I knew how much they loved their grandparents—particularly my father, who pampered and spoiled them at every opportunity.

Miri reinforced the message: "Saba is on his way to Nahal Oz," she explained. "He will come to our home and open the door for us. But if we want to see him, we have to be very quiet."

In the dark, I could almost hear the wheels turning inside their heads. Galia, in her sweet three-and-a-half-year-old voice, asked if grandma would also come; I replied that we'd first see grandpa but that later we'd get to see her, too.

Little Carmel giggled in joy, forcing us to immediately remind her that she needed to stay quiet. But on the whole, our gambit seemed to be working. The threat of one of the girls starting to cry or scream out of hunger, boredom, or fear was dissipating.

But how much longer could we keep them quiet with this promise? As if to underscore that question, just at this moment we heard the start of a gunfight in the distance—from the sound of it, in another area of the kibbutz to the north of our neighborhood.

Something was different, however. This wasn't the out-of-control shooting of the morning hours; now, there were shorter bursts of gunfire, often just a single shot, followed by another, then another.

"The military is here," I told Miri.

She'd had the same thought: "This doesn't sound like mehablim," she said. The gunfire was measured, precise: the kind you'd hear not from a mass-shooter but rather from a well-trained soldier firing on an enemy while also trying to avoid collateral damage. We could only hope that we were right.

———————

After leaving the grove on the eastern edge of the kibbutz, the second Maglan team—the one my father hadn't joined—had carefully made their way to the northeastern part of the kibbutz. There, they split into two subgroups; at a small junction in front of one of the kibbutz's oldest neighborhoods—several dense rows of single-story homes—one team turned left, and the other went right. The latter group of commandos were supposed to search seven rows of houses, each containing approximately six homes, starting with the buildings facing the old dining hall and going north until they reached the last row of homes, located directly next to the perimeter fence.

The plan of this ten-man team was to reach this farthest row of homes only after searching all the others before it, methodically clearing them of any mehablim who might be hiding inside. But only a few minutes into their search, the commandos realized that they might have to rethink their strategy.

In one of the first homes they reached, a woman named Hila Shefer, a nurse, opened the door of the safe room where she had been hiding with her children and told the commandos about the atrocities taking place several rows of houses behind hers.

Unlike our neighborhood, Hila's still had electricity and a more reliable cell phone signal—which meant that, from inside her safe room, she had been able to watch with horror as the terrorists sent out gruesome Facebook Live broadcasts from her neighbors' homes. One video showed the home of the Idan family and another the home of Noam Elyakim and his girlfriend, Dikla Arava, the kibbutz's longtime teacher and parent counselor. Neither house was far from Hila's, but Dikla and Noam's was closer.

Holding up her phone, Hila showed the Maglan soldiers the footage—now several hours old—of what had happened to the frightened family in that nearby house. They saw Noam, injured and badly bleeding as Dikla held Noam's youngest daughter, eight-year-old Ela, in her arms and Ela's older sister, fifteen-year-old Dafna, stared at the camera in desperation. They watched as the terrorists ordered Dikla's own child, her seventeen-year-old son Tomer, to get up, follow them outside, and knock on neighbors' doors to lure them out of their safe rooms.

These elite IDF soldiers, all of them twenty-one or twenty-two years old, were in the final weeks of their three-year mandatory military service. They were supposed to be discharged in November. But now, in Hila's living room, in front of a map of the kibbutz on which she was desperately showing them the location of Dikla and Noam's home, they found themselves facing the most dangerous and fateful moment of their entire service—perhaps their entire lives. The commandos had to make a quick yet impossible decision: Should they run ahead to the home where, they hoped, there were still living hostages in the hands of Hamas? Or should they continue with their methodical search of the entire neighborhood, house by house, row by row?

There was no right or wrong answer. Run ahead too fast and meha-blim hiding along the way could surprise and kill them. Continue going from home to home according to the plan and the hostages could be taken to Gaza—or worse, killed on the spot. Even an experienced commander would agonize over such a dilemma. Now, it was in the hands of these young soldiers—men who, had they been born in another country, would probably still be college students.

Without setting on a decision, the Maglan soldiers crept out of Hila's home and made for the next row of houses to the north. They intended to reconnoiter and investigate their options. But then, in an instant, the dilemma was solved for them—by the terrorists.

As the Maglan soldiers approached the home of the Dalal family, three Hamas gunmen opened fire from the windows. Further inside, the father of the family, David, a man in his late forties, was barricaded inside the home's safe room with his teenage son. David also had a teenage daughter, but she had crossed the kibbutz earlier that morning, after the mortar attack began but before the terrorists had entered the community, to go help her elderly grandparents. She was now sheltering with them in their safe room.

David had heard the terrorists enter his home shortly after 1:00 P.M., and began sending urgent distress signals to the kibbutz WhatsApp group. He could hear the Hamasniks walking around his living room and moving furniture to form barricades. Now he could hear them shooting through the kitchen windows at the Maglan team. And then he heard the same, characteristically disciplined return fire that we heard simultane-ously from half a mile away, in our own safe room.

David heard momentary quiet and then the sound of someone else entering his home. More silence, and then someone shouted, "Clean!"

Finally, there was a knock on the safe room door.

A young man on the other side of the door identified himself as an Israeli soldier. Like many people in Nahal Oz whose homes were searched that day by the Maglan and Givati soldiers, David at first refused to open up. The commandos, realizing that the man inside the safe room feared they were terrorists impersonating Israelis, began telling him about themselves—what unit they served in, what school they went to, what soccer club they were fans of. Eventually, they convinced him to open up. When he saw that they really were IDF servicemen, David wept.

Even more distraught was David's teenage son, who had spent the entire morning convinced he was about to be killed; now those pent-up emotions poured out of him. The commandos did their best to calm him down, telling him that he was a hero for surviving all day in the small safe room, surrounded by the sound of gunfire.

The Maglan soldiers had achieved both of their goals, in this home at least—but there was no time to rest on their laurels. They had to keep moving. They needed to get deeper into the neighborhood; they needed to reach the home of Dikla and Noam.

As they swept out of the Dalal home and maneuvered past more houses, the commandos braced themselves for another close-range encounter. But no more gunfire erupted from any of the windows they passed; the neighborhood was now quiet. Still, they realized that running ahead was just too dangerous; if more mehablim managed to surprise them at this point, the residents of this neighborhood could be slaughtered before the next fighting force arrived. They had to search every home— but do so as fast as humanly possible.

The rest of the search was indeed a quicker and easier ordeal. No other terrorists awaited them. When the soldiers finally reached the first house in the last row—the home of Noam and Dikla—they rushed toward the entrance with their fingers on the triggers of their guns, preparing for what could perhaps be the most important battle of their lives: a fight to release an entire family from the hands of the enemy.

When they reached the front door, however, they discovered that no one was there.

The commandos quickly searched the empty home, then stood there in disbelief, internalizing the meaning of what they were seeing.

The front door of Dikla and Noam's home was ajar. The windows were broken, and the floor was smeared with blood. Where, just hours earlier, Hamasniks had been pointing guns at an entire Israeli family, now the house stood empty.

There was only one way to interpret these terrible clues: the terrorists had kidnapped Dikla, Noam, and the girls and taken them back to Gaza.

In truth, this had happened before the Maglan force had even stepped foot in the kibbutz—yet the soldiers had no way of knowing this. They felt terrible, but had to keep moving. There were still four other homes to search in the last row.

Years earlier, Dikla had been the first adult in whom Carine Rachamim confided her love for women; the beloved teacher was the one who'd assured Carine that, despite her fears and anxieties, things would be OK—*she* would be OK. Now, however, no one could tell whether Dikla and eight-year-old Ela, whom she was last seen hugging in the terrorists' video broadcast, were going to be OK themselves—assuming they were even still alive.

———

On the other side of the kibbutz, the Maglan team that my father had joined was also making progress, walking from home to home and carefully checking everything along the way. My father advised the commandos to pay attention to every detail and to search not just the homes but also the surrounding gardens, storage sheds, even the cars parked out front. The worst thing that could happen, he warned, was for the group to declare a home clean—and then be surprised from the rear by a Hamasnik who'd been hiding in the bushes outside.

One of the first homes they'd reached was that of Eitan and Dganit, the couple in their sixties who'd "adopted" us after we moved to Nahal Oz in 2014—and whom my father had spoken to by phone earlier that morning, after he'd been unable to reach us. In the house across the street from theirs, an eighty-seven-year-old man named Haim had been murdered. After the Maglan team had found his body, my father grew worried about what he'd find behind Eitan and Dganit's front door. But for some reason, the same mehablim who'd shot Haim—a lifelong farmer who had immigrated to Israel from Argentina at age twenty—had skipped Eitan and Dganit's home. When the couple opened their safe room door, alive and unharmed, my father felt a surge of relief.

Eitan and Dganit knew my father fairly well, but it still took them a beat to recognize him. Standing before them was a tall, gun-toting man incongruously decked out in a helmet, blue jeans, and a tzitzit. Eitan—the man my parents jokingly called "grandpa" because he was so close to our daughters—identified my dad first.

"So, you made it," Eitan said.

From the backyard of the next home they searched, my father could, for the first time that day, see the green of our front door—in the distance, in a different neighborhood from the one they were still searching but nevertheless within sight. He calculated that it would take the team at least another thirty minutes to reach us, if not more. Still, based on every-thing he'd seen in the houses they'd checked until that point, he felt a dose of optimism. In most homes, the front door told most of the story—if it was locked and closed, the people inside were alive. If it was wide open or broken, there was a high likelihood that something bad had happened. Our door was shut, and it appeared to be intact.

As much as my father wanted to run ahead to our home and throw open the front door, he knew he was not a general now but a simple sol-dier, under the command of Eshel, the young Maglan major, who clearly did not need any distractions as he steadily navigated their team through this maze of houses and gardens. They all had to remain patient and focused: they had to assume that there were still terrorists inside the kib-butz and that they could be waiting around the next corner.

As the soldiers reached the new neighborhood, my father looked around in disbelief. There were bodies everywhere: in the road, in yards and driveways, inside houses. Most of them were dead mehablim, clad in green headbands bearing the Hamas insignia and tactical vests full of magazines. Most of them were bearded, and they all looked lean and in good physical shape. Many had died still holding their weapons. Seeing the quality of their guns and gear, my father was highly impressed—both with Hamas's evident preparation for the attack and with all the damage that the Israeli police team, together with Nissan and Beri, had managed to inflict on the invaders.

The commandos entered the first home in our neighborhood and found a family of three—two parents and a young boy—hiding in their safe room. The family's father asked the Maglan men to provide cover so he could go find some snacks for the boy, who had not eaten anything since the morning. They agreed and he ran to the kitchen, got whatever he could, and returned to the safe room. The soldiers instructed the family, like all the others they had found along the way, to remain locked inside their safe room and on alert. The kibbutz hadn't yet been declared clear, and they couldn't be too careful. *You're safe now, we're here*, the commandos told each family they liberated. *But don't leave the safe room just yet.*

———

Before this Maglan team started along their route, Eshel had been approached by Saul, the commander of the police team. He and his four remaining troopers, exhausted from hours of fighting, wanted to leave the kibbutz, knowing that it was now in the hands of the military; they were also worried about their injured friends who had been evacuated that morning, some of them heavily bleeding. But before they could leave, they had one last mission, Saul explained: they had to retrieve the body of Yakov, their comrade who had died on the road in front of our home.

In the course of their long odyssey, as they had battled waves of mehablim from inside the Wolf, the team had made sure to return to our area of the kibbutz every half-hour or so, to make sure that Yakov's body hadn't been taken into Gaza by terrorists or looters. Now, as the Maglan fighters and my father approached our neighborhood, they saw one dead Israeli fighter still on the ground where he had fallen, surrounded by a handful of dead Hamasniks. *What a hero*, my dad thought to himself. Minutes later, Saul and the police fighters arrived in their barely functioning armored vehicle and loaded Yakov's body into it. They were finally ready to leave Nahal Oz.

In front of our home, mere steps from the spot where Yakov's body lay, my father saw our two cars—a red Hyundai Kona and a smaller, gray Hyundai i20—completely destroyed by gunfire from the fighting along the road. The windows were broken, and bullets had perforated the doors and penetrated parts of the engine. Other cars in the neighborhood were in similar condition. The homes were also damaged—hit by hundreds of bullets and some of them, like ours, also scarred by hand grenades.

As he neared our house, my father quickly counted more than thirty bullet marks on its exterior. A dead terrorist was lying on our front porch, an RPG in his hand, the weapon pointed at the home of our next-door neighbors. Two other dead terrorists were blocking parts of the sidewalk directly in front of our door. Another had died next to our lemon tree, which we had planted months earlier in front of the window of the safe room—hoping that the girls would enjoy it as it grew taller outside their bedroom. Somehow, the tree was unscathed, but there were bullet holes in our garden chairs and in the empty baby stroller on our porch.

The devastation was breathtaking. But none of that mattered now.

My father pointed at our home and told the soldiers, "This is where my son lives." One of them came with him to the window of our safe room, which was still covered by the iron plate. My father stopped, took a deep breath, and hit the metal with his open hand.

Inside the darkened room, we heard a strong bang and then a familiar voice.

CHAPTER 9

VICTIMS

2009–2014

BINYAMIN NETANYAHU STOOD AT THE side of a busy road outside of Ashkelon, an Israeli city ten miles north of Gaza. It was February 3, 2009, a year and a half after Hamas's takeover of the Strip and a week before an Israeli election in which the former prime minister hoped to make a political comeback. A decade after losing power, and after several failed attempts to regain it, Netanyahu felt that, this time, the wind was finally at his back.

Two weeks earlier, Israel and Hamas had reached a temporary ceasefire after weeks of fighting that had culminated in an Israeli military offensive inside Gaza. The tensions that had led to this new spasm of violence could be traced back to 2006, when Hamas had used an attack tunnel to abduct Israeli soldier Gilad Shalit along the Gaza border, followed by an Israeli military incursion into Gaza and Hamas's seizure of the Strip in a bloody coup the next year. Israel had responded to those events by placing the Gaza Strip under an economic blockade, increasing its pressure over time in an attempt to break Hamas's hold on power; meanwhile the Islamist organization, now functioning as a de facto government, had bombarded Israeli communities along the border such as Nahal Oz; the organization had also improved the range of its rockets, eventually allowing them to reach cities farther away—cities such as Ashkelon, on whose outskirts Netanyahu now stood as cars whizzed past behind him.

In December 2008, just two months prior, Israel had decided that the threat along its southern border had become unacceptable and declared the commencement of another military operation inside Gaza, this one code-named "Cast Lead." It proved to be a brief and incredibly disproportionate conflict: more than one thousand Palestinians died in Gaza—Israel claimed that the majority were Hamas fighters, but human rights organizations estimated that at least half were civilians caught in harm's way—while Israel lost ten soldiers on the ground in Gaza and three civilians from Hamas rockets.

From a purely military perspective, Operation Cast Lead had resulted in a decisive Israeli victory. Yet among large segments of the Israeli public, there was a sense of disappointment—because by the time the fighting had ended, Hamas had not been removed from power, which was what most Israelis truly wanted. Hamas, meanwhile, declared victory, despite the heavy losses on the Palestinian side, claiming that its very ability to remain in power was a defeat for Israel.

The operation had begun auspiciously. Ehud Olmert, the prime minister, had announced four months earlier that he was planning to resign due to an ongoing corruption investigation against him, and by the time Cast Lead began, he had only several weeks left in office. At first, Olmert enjoyed wide international support for the operation—Hamas's constant bombardment of civilian communities along the border was seen by Israel's allies as a legitimate reason to go to war. But after three weeks of fighting, with hundreds of Gazan civilians killed, Israel was pressured to end the war without achieving what many Israelis had hoped to accomplish: the toppling of the Hamas regime in Gaza. Olmert realized that Israel's Western allies would not support the continuation of the war and agreed to a ceasefire in mid-January, exactly one month before Election Day.

With Olmert about to leave the political scene, Netanyahu emerged as the leading candidate to win the election scheduled for early February. His main opponent was Tzipi Livni, Israel's centrist foreign minister who was trying to become the country's second-ever female prime minister. But while the media coverage focused on the battle between those two, Netanyahu was more worried about a third politician who was gaining momentum in the polls and chipping away at his right-wing base: Avigdor Lieberman.

An immigrant from Moldova who began his political career as an aide to Netanyahu, Lieberman had since become the leader of a secular right-wing party that was challenging Likud, the party of his former boss. Upon throwing his hat in the ring for the 2009 election, Lieberman ran on a single, memorable promise: to "finish the job" in Gaza and take down Hamas. He derided as a national embarrassment the fact that the Islamists remained in power in the Strip despite the Israeli military's clear victory in Cast Lead, and many Israelis seemed to agree.

Netanyahu's team had watched with concern as Lieberman rose in the polls, fearing that he could attract Likud voters and then strike a deal with Livni to construct a governing coalition together, leaving Netanyahu once again out of power. As one of them later explained, "We had to stop the bleeding."

That's exactly what Netanyahu was trying to do on that day at the entrance to Ashkelon. Standing in front of the cameras, he put on a determined face and promised, "We won't stop. We won't back down. We will topple the Hamas regime in Gaza."

Netanyahu knew just how complicated and costly it would be for the Israeli military to complete that task. The price wouldn't be limited to the large number of soldiers who could potentially get killed or injured in battles against Hamas; any Israeli leader contemplating such an operation also had to consider the even larger number of Palestinian casualties that were sure to result from it—and the damage that their deaths would inevitably do to Israel's international standing. And then there was the question of what Israel would do with Gaza after the Islamists were removed from power—assuming that Israel did not want to go back to the pre-disengagement reality of a permanent occupation of the Strip, a scenario that would come with its own, ever-increasing price tag.

His advisers later said that he never meant to follow through on the promise. The most important thing at that stage, he felt, was to win the election.

And win the election Netanyahu did. A week later, he secured his victory at the ballot box. Suddenly, the politician colloquially known as "Bibi" was set to return to the office out of which Israelis had thrown him ten years earlier. Israel would never be the same.

Oshrit Sabag had moved to Nahal Oz in the early 2000s, when she was studying for her undergraduate degree at a college in the nearby town of Sderot. She had grown up in a city in central Israel, but this small kibbutz on the border immediately seemed like the best place in the world to her: "It was beautiful and green, the rent was cheap, and they allowed me to bring my dog with me," she recalled. "Back then, that was all I cared about."

The security issues weren't much of a concern to Oshrit—at least, not in the beginning. She often ignored the sirens indicating an incoming attack because "we didn't really have enough time to reach shelter, so there was no point. I didn't have children back then. I didn't have any real responsibility for anyone."

Things began to change in 2008. In April of that year, Hamas fired a major barrage at the kibbutz and, at the same time, sent a terror cell to a nearby terminal, situated along the border fence, through which Israel was transferring fuel to the Gaza Strip. Despite the fact that this terminal played a crucial role in supplying Gaza with energy, the terrorists murdered two workers there. At Nahal Oz, people were locked in their safe rooms, and many of them heard the gunfire to the west of the community. The terrorists didn't enter the kibbutz, or even get close to its perimeter fence, but their infiltration of the fuel terminal was a flashing warning sign. "After that day, I began to take things more seriously," Oshrit said.

Still, she had no doubts about continuing to live in Nahal Oz. By then, she had graduated, started working as a teacher, and married Gidi, a member of the kibbutz who managed the local dairy farm. During Operation Cast Lead, they stayed in the kibbutz even as Hamas fired hundreds of rockets and mortars at the community and even while most families were evacuated to other areas of Israel. Gidi had to take care of the cows, and Oshrit chose to stay close to him. She never believed that Israel would succeed in toppling Hamas during that war; indeed, she was almost amused by the politicians who promised to do so. "I'll believe it when I see it" was her response. She was happy, however, with the relative quiet that the community enjoyed in the months after the operation: the number of rocket launches from Gaza dropped by more than 90 percent. To her, this reality was as close as one could get to peace.

Meanwhile, in Jerusalem, Netanyahu was assembling his new government coalition and trying to show the Israeli public that he had learned some lessons from his previous term in office. Back then, he'd chosen to lead a narrow right-wing coalition with Likud and several religious parties, but they'd run into a direct confrontation with the United States and other key allies over the implementation of the Oslo Accords. Although Netanyahu once again invited other right-wingers, most notably Lieberman, into his coalition, he also surprised political pundits by offering the all-important role of defense minister to his former rival Ehud Barak, who had made his own political comeback to once again lead the Labor Party.

Netanyahu was counting on Barak to help him deal with a major challenge in Washington, DC: the rise of President Barack Obama, who had entered office a few weeks before Netanyahu. Obama wanted to make a serious push toward a two-state solution, finishing what the previous Democratic administration led by Bill Clinton had failed to achieve at Camp David in 2000. Netanyahu's hope was that Barak's presence at his side would help him soften the new president. Barak, for his part, believed he could influence Netanyahu from inside the coalition and guide him in a more moderate direction.

Facing pressure from Obama to enter talks with the Palestinian Authority and hoping to recruit the young American president into Israel's campaign to thwart Iran's nuclear ambitions, Netanyahu considered the situation in Gaza to be a relatively minor concern. Hamas was licking its wounds after Operation Cast Lead, and there was quiet along Israel's southern border in the aftermath of Olmert's short war. Netanyahu chose to devote his attention to what he considered more important problems.

But as the months went by, one thorny issue in Gaza continued to dominate the headlines: the fate of Gilad Shalit, the Israeli soldier abducted by Hamas in 2006. He was still being held in Gaza: exactly where, Israeli intelligence didn't know, but Hamas had provided proof on several occasions that he was still alive, although it was visibly clear that his health was seriously deteriorating. Olmert, on his way out, rejected Hamas's demands for the release of approximately one thousand Palestinian prisoners, many of them convicted terrorists, from Israeli jails in exchange for Shalit.

Israeli prisoner swaps with militant groups had always been lopsided affairs, with Israel agreeing to release large numbers of Palestinian prisoners for very few IDF soldiers in return. In 1985, Israel released 1,150 prisoners in exchange for three soldiers who had been held by a militant group in Lebanon. In 2004, Israel released 436 prisoners in order to free a retired army officer who had been kidnapped by Hezbollah. Hamas's demand to release a thousand prisoners for one soldier, however, set a new precedent—one that Olmert considered unacceptable. He chose instead to increase the economic pressure on Gaza, essentially placing the entire territory under siege from 2006 onward, in an attempt to force Hamas into accepting a more reasonable deal.

Netanyahu inherited Olmert's blockade of Gaza and continued it. But in 2011, the tactic became much less effective due to a political earthquake that rocked Egypt: the aging president Hosni Mubarak, a regional ally of Israel, resigned after massive demonstrations broke out as part of the series of revolts known as the Arab Spring. Mubarak's ouster opened the door for the Muslim Brotherhood—a global Islamist movement that Hamas had a close affiliation with—to run in, and win, Egypt's first-ever free and democratic election the following year.

From the start of the Israeli blockade, Hamas had relied on a network of tunnels beneath the border between Gaza and Egypt to overcome Israel's economic stranglehold on the Strip. Mubarak's government turned a blind eye to those tunnels, and Egyptian military officers reportedly accepted bribes in order to allow the underground trade to continue. But with the fall of Mubarak and the internal turmoil in Egypt, Hamas felt even more confident and increased its digging-and-smuggling industry, flooding Gaza with goods—and weapons.

Suleiman al-Shafi, an Arab-Israeli reporter who had covered Gaza since the late 1980s, explained in an interview for this book that the blockade hurt the lives of ordinary Palestinians but not necessarily those of Hamas's top leadership. "The people of Gaza became prisoners," he said. "Only very few could leave and return, there was no freedom of movement and severe restrictions on trade. This had a terrible impact on the entire society, and led to a sharp rise in levels of trauma, anxiety and depression." The impact on Hamas and its leadership, however, was negligible, and in his eyes, even advantageous: as Israel increased its economic pressure on the population, Hamas gained more power internally by controlling the underground smuggling operation, which became Gaza's only lifeline to the outside world.

The realization that the blockade was ineffective—that it wouldn't force Hamas to compromise, after all—left Israel with nothing but bad choices. With Shalit entering his fifth year in captivity, there was growing public pressure on Netanyahu and the Israeli government to do *something* to retrieve the soldier, who had become one of the country's most famous citizens, and to relieve the pain of his parents, who for more than a year had been sleeping in a tent in front of the prime minister's office. One option was to start another military operation against Hamas, but this time, as Netanyahu had promised before the election, to go all the way—forcing Hamas to choose between Shalit's release and the fall of its regime in Gaza. The other option was to accept Hamas's demands, the ones Olmert had rejected in 2008, and make a deal.

In 1996, ahead of his first run for office, Netanyahu published a book titled *Fighting Terrorism: How Democracies Can Defeat the International Terrorist Network*, in which he explained at length why Western governments should never negotiate with terror organizations and must strive to defeat them instead of compromising with them, which he argued would simply lead to more acts of terror down the road. According to the approach that he advocated for in his book, Netanyahu should have ordered a military operation to secure Shalit's release. But he was worried about the costs: the number of soldiers who would die in battle, the damage that Israel's reputation would suffer in the international arena, and also the responsibility that Israel would shoulder if its operation succeeded—for who would control Gaza if Hamas were actually removed from power? Not to mention the option that Shalit would be killed by his captors during the operation.

And so, ignoring his own advice, Netanyahu chose to compromise with Hamas. In the background was another consideration, more political in nature: Israel was rocked by massive demonstrations during the summer of 2011, as hundreds of thousands took to the streets to protest over the country's economic situation. The demonstrations were seen as a major risk to Netanyahu's hold on power; the Shalit deal diverted attention from them and focused public attention instead on the joyous return of the young soldier.

On October 18, 2011, there began the most one-sided prisoner swap in the history of the Israeli-Palestinian conflict. In return for Shalit, Israel agreed to release 1,027 Palestinian prisoners, many of whom had been convicted of murder for their part in gruesome terror attacks against Israeli citizens. As uneven of a deal as this was, however, the majority of the Israeli public supported it, and Shalit's return from Gaza became a televised national event. Lieberman was one of only three members of Netanyahu's government to vote against the deal, explaining that he did so "with a heavy heart" but felt compelled to oppose the prisoner swap due to the gains that it would confer on Hamas.

Indeed, the deal was a major coup for Hamas, arguably the organization's greatest ever achievement—especially in the political sense. Of the 1,027 prisoners released by Israel, many were members of Hamas, but some belonged to Fatah and other Palestinian factions. Approximately half of the prisoners released were residents of the West Bank—which meant that Hamas, from inside the besieged Gaza Strip, now took credit for obtaining the release of prisoners into the territory of its political rival, the Palestinian Authority.

PA president Mahmoud Abbas was left humiliated: he had spent the past two years negotiating with Netanyahu as part of Obama's two-state solution effort, but nothing had come of the talks. Hamas, meanwhile, had brought Israel to its knees by abducting a soldier and holding firm to the conditions that it had imposed on his release.

Hamas now found itself in an ideal situation: solidly in control of Gaza, enjoying the backing of the Muslim Brotherhood in Egypt, and gaining popularity among the Palestinian public due to the Shalit prisoner swap. Netanyahu had been elected based on his promise to topple the organization, but as he was entering the third year of his second term in office, Israelis found that Hamas was stronger than ever.

The year 2009 was the quietest along the Gaza border since Sharon's unilateral disengagement from the Strip four years earlier. Operation Cast

Lead had created a period of calm, one that would extend into 2010, with fewer than one hundred rocket launches into Israel and no casualties on the Israeli side.

By 2011, however, things were shifting in the opposite direction: the number of rocket launches more than tripled. One specific incident, right outside Nahal Oz, showed that Hamas was once again willing to risk war with Israel.

It happened on April 7, a Thursday afternoon, right before the Passover holiday. A yellow bus was bringing the children of Nahal Oz back to the kibbutz from their regional school, located eight miles northeast of the community. It was the same bus that, on a daily basis, took them to school in the morning and brought them back at the end of each day.

The driver entered the kibbutz and dropped dozens of children at the community's bus stop before turning around and heading out. He had only one passenger left aboard: Daniel Viflic, a sixteen-year-old boy from a city near Jerusalem who was visiting family in a neighboring community, where the bus driver was supposed to make his final stop.

As the school bus exited the kibbutz and drove onto Route 25, which connected Nahal Oz to the region's main highway, Route 232, a large blast suddenly rocked the bus, and fire enveloped it. "My entire body was filled with glass and shrapnel," the driver, a resident of a kibbutz thirteen miles to the east of Nahal Oz, later recalled. "I lost consciousness for two seconds and when I came round, I removed all the glass and looked at Daniel. I yelled to him, but he didn't answer me." A Hamas antitank missile had hit the bus, killing Viflic.

Inside Nahal Oz, the blast was heard clearly in every home. Had Hamas fired the missile two minutes earlier, the death toll would have probably been significantly higher and included many children from the kibbutz.

"This incident shook the community to the core," recalled Carine Rachamim. In her early twenties at the time, she had returned to the kibbutz after completing her compulsory two-year military service and was living out her dream of being a professional soccer player. She was already playing for one of the top teams in the Israeli women's league. Like everyone else in Nahal Oz, she used Route 25 on a daily basis, every time she left the kibbutz or returned to it. "It was scary," she said. "Every person in the community was asking themselves: How can I drive on this road again? How can I go to work? How can I send my kids to school?" Growing up under the threat of Hamas's mortars and rockets, Carine and others in her age group knew they were living in a dangerous place, but "until the bus incident, we didn't feel like our own lives were at risk."

As if to make the whole situation more frightening, the type of anti-tank missile that Hamas had used in the attack was laser-guided and thus highly accurate—leading to the grim conclusion that the terror group had deliberately targeted the school bus, intending to hurt anyone inside it. Nevertheless, a Hamas spokesman justified the attack as "self-defense to protect Palestinian civilians and citizens."

Oshrit Sabag, the teacher who had moved into the community a decade before the attack, also considered this a watershed moment. She now had a young daughter at home, and the security risks associated with life in the kibbutz suddenly looked different. "There was a community gathering immediately afterward and people demanded a new route into the kibbutz to replace Route 25," she recalled.

The military agreed that, under the current conditions, it would be impossible to protect cars on Route 25—so it created a new access road immediately to the south, onto which all the traffic to and from Nahal Oz was soon diverted. Running parallel to Route 25, this road, which did not have a name or a number, was a ribbon of asphalt running between two patches of forest to the east of Nahal Oz. This road was longer and more winding than Route 25, but the trees on both sides meant that it wasn't visible from Gaza. Twelve and a half years later, on that same road, my father would fight the Hamas team that had ambushed the first Maglan commandos trying to reach our kibbutz.

The members of the kibbutz were so distraught by the school bus attack that they missed another major development that happened the same day—one that would end up having an even greater influence on the future of their community: the first successful use of Israel's Iron Dome missile defense system.

Iron Dome—a complex network of computers and missile batteries invented in 2005 by Israeli engineer Danny Gold, developed under the

Olmert government, and finally made operational in 2011—had a mechanism that was difficult to build but easy to explain: the system would identify a rocket once it had been launched from Gaza, calculate its route in the sky, and then send an intercepting missile to destroy it before it could reach its target.

The US government participated in the project's development and funding. Several tests were conducted between 2008 and 2010, but the first successful use of the system happened hours after the attack on the school bus. Israel began bombing Hamas targets in Gaza in retaliation, and Hamas responded by launching rockets at nearby Ashkelon—only to watch them get intercepted in the sky before they could reach the city.

The next morning, Israel's most widely read newspaper, *Yedioth Ahronoth*, carried both stories on its front page. Above a shocking image of the destroyed school bus and a headline devoted to the sixteen-year-old boy who had been killed was a separate one declaring: "Unprecedented Success: Iron Dome Intercepted a Rocket over Ashkelon."

Iron Dome soon proved to be a game changer for Israel. Every time there was a round of fighting with Hamas—and there were several such occasions throughout 2012, usually lasting less than a week—the system improved its interception rate, at first blocking approximately 75 percent of the rockets launched from Gaza, but later improving that statistic to 85 percent. Hamas had developed, by then, long-range missiles that were able to reach as far north as Tel Aviv, forty-five miles from Gaza. But the vast majority of these missiles were shot down by Iron Dome and barely caused any damage.

The system, however, had one major downside: it couldn't offer protection to border communities like Nahal Oz, which were simply too close to Gaza. When a rocket or mortar was fired at Nahal Oz, it usually took only a few seconds to reach its target—not enough time for Iron Dome to calculate its route and send an interceptor. Hamas soon realized that, although firing at Tel Aviv was good for generating headlines, it would be smarter to concentrate as much firepower as possible on places like Nahal Oz, which had no aerial protection.

"We became the victims of Iron Dome's success," Oshrit later explained. "Everybody else could just go on with their lives. We couldn't."

In early 2013, Israel held another election, and Netanyahu won again—but this time, he found it much more difficult to assemble a coalition. Barak, his partner in the outgoing government, had retired from politics; the two missions that he had considered most urgent and which had led him to join Netanyahu in the first place—stopping Iran's nuclear program and making progress in negotiations with the Palestinians—both remained unfinished, and he blamed Netanyahu for the failures. Lieberman, despite his criticism of Netanyahu's policy toward Hamas, continued as his foreign minister, while Livni—who had held that role in Olmert's government, and who now led a new center-left party—joined Netanyahu's coalition as justice minister.

The biggest surprise of the election was the rise of two young politicians: Yair Lapid, a former journalist and TV presenter who founded a new centrist party; and Naftali Bennett, a tech entrepreneur who led a right-wing religious party but presented himself to the public as a moderate and pragmatic figure, not a hard-liner. After the election, the duo formed an unexpected political alliance and forced Netanyahu to offer both of them senior positions in his government.

In Nahal Oz, the new government was received with cautious optimism. It was still led by Netanyahu, who enjoyed almost no support within the kibbutz, but his new partners Livni and Lapid, who were more representative of the Israeli center-left, were very popular there. What's more, President Obama's new secretary of state, John Kerry, had renewed the administration's diplomatic push for a two-state solution, forcing Netanyahu and the PA's Mahmoud Abbas into a new round of negotiations. After so many disappointments, the peace-seeking residents of Nahal Oz still found reason for hope.

At first, such optimism seemed justified: 2013 was another relatively quiet year on the border. Hamas lost a powerful ally that July after a military coup in Egypt wrested control of the country from the Muslim Brotherhood. The general who took over, Abdel-Fattah al-Sissi, made clear that close coordination with Israel was a top priority for him, whereas his government viewed Hamas with suspicion due to its ties with the recently sidelined Muslim Brotherhood.

One country, however, seemed determined to help Hamas overcome its isolation: Qatar. A tiny kingdom located in the Persian Gulf region, Qatar sits on a massive reserve of oil and natural gas, and its government is also the owner of the popular Arabic news channel Al Jazeera. Ideologically, the state's leadership is aligned with the Muslim Brotherhood, and was therefore very supportive of its rule in Egypt under then president Mohamed Morsi. After the Brotherhood was ousted, the Qataris understood the implications for their Islamist comrades in Hamas—and pledged to send more than $400 million to the regime in Gaza.

Suddenly, the quiet on the Israel-Gaza border took on an ominous tone. Israel publicly criticized Qatar for supporting Hamas but didn't take any concrete steps to stop the money from entering Gaza. It could have, for example, asked US lawmakers to apply more pressure on Qatar, a country that relies on strong ties with the US for its national security and hosts one of the largest American military bases in the world on its soil. But instead of looking for ways to make Qatar pay a price for its support of Hamas, the Israeli government under Netanyahu did quite the opposite.

Netanyahu, who was mostly interested in maintaining quiet along the Gaza border, decided to adopt a totally different approach—one that was also supported by the top echelons of the Israeli military and intelligence community at the time. He began telling close aides and political confidants that Qatar's support for Hamas would end up serving Israel's security interests by averting a humanitarian crisis inside Gaza, while also giving Hamas an incentive to avoid another round of fighting with Israel: as long as there was calm on both sides of the border, the money would keep arriving, whereas if a war broke out, Qatar would face heightened international pressure to stop the funding.

For a while, Netanyahu's hands-off approach seemed to work: the border remained quiet, and Qatar took pride in funding the construction of new neighborhoods, schools, and hospitals in Gaza. But once the Qatari money entered Gaza, it was Hamas's to do with as it pleased. And although the organization now functioned as a de facto government inside the Strip, fixing the roads and running the schools, at its core it remained a militant group committed to fighting Israel.

By 2014, it had become an open secret that some of the money that Qatar was sending to Gaza was being used to fund the group's preparations for the next round of war with Israel. Aboveground, in warehouses and factories, Hamas was assembling new missiles and rockets. But the real drama was happening underground, deep below the homes of Gaza City, where Hamas was working 24-7 on a strategic surprise: a new, larger, and more sophisticated network of attack tunnels leading into Israeli territory.

———————

The peace talks led by John Kerry ended in failure in April 2014, and Israelis and Palestinians alike braced themselves for a new outbreak of violence, as usually happened when negotiations reached a dead end. But when it came, the escalation first happened not in Gaza but rather in the West Bank, where a small terror cell kidnapped three Israeli teenagers who were studying in a settlement south of Jerusalem. One of the youths managed to call the police before the terrorists snatched away his cell phone. Then, they disappeared.

For almost three weeks, Israel held its breath as the military and police searched for the kidnapped teenagers. Massive prayer services were held for their return and a national emergency hotline was flooded with hundreds of tips about their whereabouts. Eventually, on June 30, their dead bodies were found in farmland outside the city of Hebron. Four days later, a group of Far Right Jewish extremists kidnapped a sixteen-year-old Palestinian boy who was walking down the street in Jerusalem, murdered him, and left his charred body in a wooded area outside the city.

The two horrific acts of terror, each targeting teenagers, launched both sides into a frenzy. Hamas, which had already launched dozens of rockets and mortars toward Israeli communities along the border in June, ramped up its bombardments in the following days. By the second week of July, a full-blown war was underway. Israeli warplanes bombed Gaza, while Hamas fired thousands of rockets and mortars into Israel. Eventually, the Palestinian terrorists who murdered the three Jewish boys and the Jewish terrorists who murdered the Palestinian boy were all caught by Israeli authorities—but by the time that happened, it was too late.

At first, most Israelis, including the residents of Nahal Oz, believed the new war wouldn't be that different from previous rounds of fighting between Israel and Hamas. Rockets would be launched at Israel, and the Iron Dome system would intercept most of them. Israel would bomb targets all across the Gaza Strip; at some point, the civilian death toll would become too much for Israel's Western and Arab allies to stomach, and they would push for a ceasefire.

But the war of 2014 quickly proved to be different. Almost as soon as the war had begun, Hamas started using its new tunnels to carry out attacks against Israeli soldiers on the other side of the border. The organization had used tunnels to attack Israeli military bases inside Gaza before the disengagement, and also for the Shalit kidnapping in 2006, but this was the first time it had successfully utilized this tactic on a massive scale, in order to bring the war into Israeli territory.

There were approximately thirty such cross-border tunnels, most of which were narrow passageways lined with concrete that allowed Hamas gunmen to walk or crawl directly from a point inside Gaza—usually a house or a public building—into fields on the Israeli side of the border. Some of the tunnels were larger and more sophisticated, however—large enough to allow small vehicles to pass through them. Many of them were connected to electricity, their passageways lined with lights, their climate controlled by ventilation systems.

One of Hamas's most successful tunnel attacks took place right outside Nahal Oz: a group of fighters emerged from a tunnel that led into the fields of the kibbutz and attacked a small military post nearby, killing five soldiers. The infiltrators tried to take the soldiers' bodies back into Gaza through the same tunnel—taking an Israeli soldier, dead or alive, would be an opportunity to repeat the Shalit achievement—but they were detected and retreated under fire, leaving behind their ghastly cargo. A similar attempt succeeded in another battle further south: there, a Hamas cell emerged from a tunnel, managed to kill two soldiers, and then spirited away their bodies to an unknown location.

The tunnels created a sense of panic in Israeli communities along the Gaza border. The attacks themselves were horrifying enough, but the fact that some of the tunnels were only discovered after they had been used for a successful cross-border attack also represented a major intelligence failure by the Israeli government—and raised a disturbing question: What if Hamas had other undetected tunnels and ended up using them to attack not just soldiers but also civilians?

The fact that a tunnel had already been used previously for the abduction of Shalit, yet no lessons had been learned, caused people to lose their trust in the authorities. The military promised that by the war's end each and every one of the cross-border tunnels would be found and destroyed—but not everyone in the kibbutz believed that.

———————

During the 2014 war, a few dozen residents chose to remain in Nahal Oz, mostly people whose jobs required their presence on the kibbutz. Families with children, however, were evacuated to other parts of Israel. This was customary: whenever a new round of fighting broke out between Israel and Hamas, one of the first places to be evacuated was Nahal Oz because of its proximity to the border. Usually the evacuation period lasted a week or two at most. But now, as July turned into August and the war continued, the community faced an unprecedented situation in which the majority of the population had been out of their home for over a month.

Inside the kibbutz, the members of the small group that remained tried to keep up each other's spirits. They gathered every evening in a communal shelter at the center of the kibbutz to eat, raise a toast, and break the loneliness. During the first week of the war, they watched the World Cup final together. Senior politicians and military officers stopped by for visits, expressing their admiration at the resilience on display. It was during this period that I first came to the kibbutz myself, to write about the brave residents who had stayed there under fire and continued to work in the fields.

For those who left the community, there was no immediate security threat—no mortars, no rockets, no tunnels—but as the war entered its second month, life away from home was becoming more and more difficult. Most families were either staying in a hotel room or in studio apartments in other kibbutzim. The parents and children all shared the same space—often, the same bed. There was no privacy, no quiet time, and, for most families, no ability to cook their own meals or plan their own schedule. There was no kindergarten or daycare for the children, which meant most parents could not work. "It was becoming a nightmare," recalled Oshrit Sabag, who was away from the kibbutz with her two children, unable to work, while her husband continued to milk the cows back home, under fire.

Inside the Israeli war cabinet, Netanyahu was facing growing pressure from Lieberman and Bennett to finally deliver on the promise he had made five years earlier: to topple Hamas. Lieberman said that without removing Hamas from power, the residents on the Gaza border wouldn't be able to return safely to their homes. Bennett warned that the failure to detect and dismantle the tunnels had made a deeper incursion into Gaza unavoidable: if Israel wanted to put an end to this threat, it would eventually have to treat the root of the problem. While these two politicians challenged Netanyahu from the Right, Lapid and Livni were also pushing for Hamas's removal, outflanking Netanyahu from the Left by calling for the PA's return to Gaza and for the replacement of the extremist Hamas regime with Abbas's more moderate rule.

Netanyahu rejected all of these ideas. He had never believed his own promise to bring down Hamas, but neither could he countenance handing Gaza back to the PA, since that would mean that Israel, for the first time since 2006, would face a unified Palestinian government in control of both the West Bank and the coastal enclave—a scenario that Netanyahu was deeply opposed to, since he feared that it would increase international pressure on Israel to renew the peace process. Ever since Hamas's 2007 takeover of Gaza, Israeli opponents of the two-state solution, like Netanyahu, could easily point to the Islamist regime in the coastal enclave and say: *Are these the people you want us to make peace with?* If the PA were to win back control of Gaza and coordinate with Israel to put an end to Hamas's rocket attacks, it would effectively deny Netanyahu and his ilk of that argument.

On top of that, Netanyahu believed that the split between Hamas and the PA, the former based in Gaza and the latter in the West Bank, also helped ensure that the two-state solution remained practically impossible. In lengthy discussions within the Israeli security cabinet—a small forum that included the most prominent government ministers, military leaders, and intelligence chiefs, who convened regularly to discuss security affairs—he said that whenever the Americans asked him about promoting the two-state solution, he would point at the division between the two Palestinian governments as a major obstacle to reaching a future agreement. As long as the two most prominent Palestinian political entities were locked in their own conflict, Netanyahu thought there would be less pressure on Israel to solve its own conflict with the Palestinians.

In addition to that strategic goal, Netanyahu also feared that intensifying the operation against Hamas and sending forces deep into Gaza would lead to a high number of Israeli casualties. Dozens of soldiers had died in battle during the first forty days of the war; compared to Operation Cast Lead and previous, shorter rounds of fighting against Hamas, this was a relatively large number of fatalities, and it had created a sense of national grief among the Israeli public, reminding people of the dark days of the second Intifada, a decade earlier, during which every morning newscast would start with the announcement of more soldiers who had been killed in battle. Yet the members of the security cabinet were unrelenting, increasing their pressure for a broader operation to topple the Hamas regime.

Then, on August 6, Israel's most widely watched evening news broadcast dropped a bombshell: a source in the government had leaked classified details from a security cabinet discussion about a potential ground invasion of Gaza. The report referred to an internal estimate within the military that "going all the way" against Hamas would cost the lives of not just dozens, but *hundreds* of soldiers. The leak mentioned that there could also be thousands of Palestinian casualties, potentially inviting significant international denunications of Israel.

The leak came in the middle of a security cabinet meeting in Jerusalem. One participant in the meeting recalled that "around seven P.M., after several hours of discussion, Netanyahu said it was time to take a break, and walked across the hallway to his office with a small group of aides. The break lasted for almost an hour, and right before we all had to part with our phones and go back into the larger meeting, everyone began receiving hysterical push notifications from news websites, describing the numbers that had just been presented to us as part of a top-secret briefing."

This leak was well-timed to dismantle Bennett, Lieberman, and Livni's arguments—and it swayed Israeli public opinion against a ground invasion. The war continued, but suddenly Hamas could feel confident that it was going to survive this round of fighting, just like all the ones before it.

———————

As the war entered its sixth week, the evacuated residents of Nahal Oz were beginning to lose patience. "We were exhausted," Oshrit recalled. "People were depressed. We couldn't go on like this for much longer." The kibbutz was still being heavily bombarded but, bit by bit, families began to return. They believed the war would be over any day now: it was clear that Israel wasn't going to initiate a full ground invasion, and Qatar and Egypt were frantically trying to broker a permanent ceasefire.

Oshrit, with her daughter Michal, who was at the time four years old, and her son Noam, then a baby, spent most of that summer in a small kibbutz to the east of Nahal Oz, where there were fewer rockets—in part because the community lay within the reach of the protection of the Iron Dome system. Also staying there were fellow Nahal Oz residents Gila and Doron Tregerman, the parents of three young children: four-year-old Daniel, three-year-old Yuval, and baby Ori. Oshrit and her husband considered the couple their closest friends in the community. "We lived in the same neighborhood, had similar hobbies, and were basically together all the time," Oshrit said. "Our kids were about the same age, so they also became good friends." When Gila called her at the beginning of the war and said they had decided to go elsewhere until things calmed down, Oshrit knew immediately that she was going to join them.

In mid-August, the two families decided to return home. A new temporary cease-fire was announced on August 15, and it lasted for almost four days, during which time many other families also returned to the kibbutz, hoping that life would go back to normal. "We were still afraid of the tunnels, but the military promised us they were taking care of it," Oshrit said. "We felt like it was time to go back."

The ceasefire, however, was not extended and by Friday, August 22, the border region was once more a war zone. Some families that had returned—Oshrit's and the Tregermans among them—found the thought of evacuating again simply unbearable. "I thought to myself: No way I'm packing a suitcase and leaving my house again," Oshrit recounted. "Our mindset was that we just had to get through one or two more days of fighting, and that's it." They decided to stay in Nahal Oz.

That Friday, the chief of staff of the Israeli military, Lieutenant General Benny Gantz, toured the border region. After visiting several other communities, he arrived at Nahal Oz in the early afternoon. Oshrit, who was considered one of the kibbutz's best public speakers, was asked to accompany Gantz as he toured the community. "He was very attuned and kept asking what we needed in order to bring back the entire community," she recalled.

They were walking close to the kibbutz's playground when suddenly a siren went off, indicating an incoming mortar attack. Gantz, his entourage, and the few kibbutz members who had joined the tour all ran to a bomb shelter at the edge of the playground. The chief of staff, who was six foot three, stood directly in front of Oshrit inside the shelter, and she thought to herself that Israel's top general was literally protecting her with his own body. They waited for a few seconds and then heard a large explosion—not very close to their location, but clearly within the community. When they exited the shelter two minutes later, they saw a cloud of black smoke rising from one of the kibbutz's neighborhoods.

The tour of the kibbutz continued as planned, but at the next stop one of Oshrit's neighbors came over and took her aside. "You need to call the Tregermans," the man said. He didn't explain why.

Oshrit felt a chill run down her spine. She took out her phone and called Gila, but her friend didn't answer. She tried Doron, and he picked up after several rings. "What's going on?" she asked.

Doron replied, "You need to come over here."

"Come where?" she asked him.

His answer, and something about the tone of his voice, made her even more scared: "We're at your house. Just get here as fast as you can."

Oshrit left the military delegation and ran home. When she walked in, she immediately understood what had happened. Gila was sitting on a chair, her face and body unharmed but her dress completely soaked in blood. Doron was standing next to her. Their two younger children, three-year-old Yuval and baby Ori, were also in the house, but four-year-old Daniel, their oldest son, wasn't.

There was no need for words. Every parent in Nahal Oz had to work hard, however subconsciously, to always push down one particular nightmare scenario. Now, it had broken loose.

When the siren had sounded, the entire Tregerman family had tried to run into their safe room. But they hadn't made it in time. The mortar had exploded directly outside their house; Daniel had been hit by shrapnel. Gila and Doron, operating on autopilot through their shock, had rushed their two surviving children to their best friends' home, and that's where Oshrit found them minutes later.

Oshrit searched for her husband, Gidi, and learned that he had sprinted to the Tregermans' home immediately after Doron and Gila had arrived at theirs, hoping to use his training as a medic to reverse fate. But soon after Oshrit arrived, her husband returned home, a defeated look on his face. What he had seen at the Tregerman's house left no room for doubt: Daniel had died instantly.

The next hours brought endless agony. Gantz and the officers who had joined him for the visit stopped by the house but could barely find words to respond to the tragedy. Members of the community came over one by one, each asking how they could help. A social worker arrived to speak with the parents, but the living room was too crowded so Oshrit told the three of them to move to another room in the house. It was there that preparations for Daniel's funeral were first discussed.

It was now Friday evening, the starting point of the Jewish Sabbath, which meant that the burial would have to be delayed into the next week. As it grew dark, people began heading back to their homes. "Nobody slept that night," Oshrit said. "Not just in my house, but in the entire kibbutz."

Daniel was a beloved boy, with golden hair and an angelic smile. Nahal Oz had suffered painful events during its history, but never before had a child been killed in such a violent manner. Grief hung over the community for the entire weekend—and all that time, Hamas kept firing rockets and Israel kept bombing Gaza, causing everyone within the community to relive the trauma through the endless explosions.

Gila and Doron decided to bury little Daniel near the home of his grandparents in a community to the south of Nahal Oz, further away from the border. Thousands of people attended the funeral. The family requested that no politicians be present, except for the president of Israel, Reuven Rivlin, whom they had invited to give a short eulogy. After he finished speaking, it was Gila's turn.

"My sweet boy," she began, "I don't even understand what's happening here. I can't believe I'm here at the cemetery to say goodbye to you. We were the happiest family in the world, and I just don't get it. We want to thank you, because you taught us how to love, you taught us how to smile, and you gave us so much happiness. I find comfort in the fact that you were a beloved and happy child until your very last moment."

She continued: "You are the love of my life. A perfect child, the dream of every father and mother. Smart, sensitive, advanced for your age, and beautiful, so beautiful. I'm trying to internalize what happened, and I can't. We were always so proud of you. A minute before the mortar landed, you were helping Dad build a tent in the living room so you could play inside with your sister. The siren didn't save you. It all happened so fast . . . within a second, it was over. We lost you."

Gila concluded by telling Daniel, "We always said you'd be the youngest leader in the world to bring peace. So, if not in your life, maybe in your death."

Two days later, a long-term ceasefire was announced, and the war was over.

CHAPTER 10

"WE'VE ALL HAD A VERY LONG DAY"

OCTOBER 7, 2023

WHEN WE HEARD MY FATHER's voice on the other side of the safe room window, Galia was the first to speak up. "Saba is here," she said simply, using the Hebrew word for grandfather. I could hear the exhaustion in her voice—she had been overwhelmed by the events of the day—but at that moment, she also sounded, for the first time in hours, happy.

My father shouted for us to open the front door. "I'm opening," I yelled back through the metal plate—but it took me a second to actually move. Even after waiting for hours in desperate anticipation of his arrival, I was still surprised to hear him—and I was worried, too. What if a terrorist was still hiding somewhere else in our house, waiting for us to emerge?

The last two hours had been the most difficult of the day. We had been locked into the tightly sealed room together since 6:30 A.M., and the air inside had grown thick, causing Miri and I to worry that we might run out of oxygen. The temperature outside had climbed to around 80 degrees Fahrenheit, and while the thick concrete walls of the safe room kept the interior a bit cooler, by the time we heard my father knocking outside, the heat was starting to get to us. We had agreed to avoid unnecessary speaking, and even tried to slow our breathing. I had been forced to resist a strong, growing urge to crack open the safe room window, just so we could let a little fresh air and light into the room; as the minutes passed, I'd felt that my body was going to betray my mind and that the physical need for light, more than anything else, would cause me to make a terrible mistake. As a precaution, I had decided to sit on the floor on the opposite side of the room from the window. I had still been sitting there when we heard my father's voice.

I took a deep breath and told myself that, if my father was asking us to open the front door, then it must still be locked—meaning it was highly unlikely a terrorist was waiting for us between there and the safe room door. There was no way to be absolutely certain—what if someone had entered through a window?—but at this point, it was a risk worth taking.

I told Miri to put her body in front of the girls, who were both now sitting in the dark on Galia's bed. Then I felt my way through the darkness to the safe room door, and for the first time since we'd closed it almost ten hours earlier, I unlocked it and eased it open.

The burst of light momentarily overwhelmed me, forcing me to cover my eyes. Then I stepped into the corridor that connected the safe room with our living room and crept down the hall.

There were no terrorists hiding in our living room, but I did find a surprise waiting: Pluto, our black Labrador, was standing in front of me, wagging his tail.

Earlier that morning, when my father and I first spoke, he had asked me about the dog, and I said he was probably dead. Pluto hadn't come into the safe room with us and then, as the terrorists had fired into the house, we hadn't heard him bark. This was highly unusual: on most days, Pluto would raise hell anytime someone so much as passed by our house, including neighbors he had known for years. The fact that we hadn't heard him yelping—or heard any other sign of life—even once in the many hours that terrorists and looters had been running around our neighborhood seemed like proof that he was no longer with us. At one point while we were sheltering in the safe room, I had even thought about how we'd explain their beloved dog's death to the girls if we ever managed to get out. But now, here he was, very much alive and looking extremely happy to see me.

Realizing that Pluto had not been outside since the night before, I immediately succumbed to my dog owner's instincts: I ran to the front door, Pluto hot on my heels, and threw it open. The dog raced outside, running past my father and the five Maglan commandos who had accompanied him up onto the front porch of our house. The soldiers didn't try to stop the dog, and neither did my father. He did look shocked to see that

Pluto was still alive, but it was nothing compared to his excitement at seeing me.

My father stepped into the doorway and embraced me. For at least five seconds, we stood there silently, holding each other. Then I pulled back, realizing that he and the soldiers needed to get off our doorstep and into the house.

As I watched my father walk into our living room, it occurred to me that the soldiers alongside him were all in uniform and tactical gear, whereas he was in street clothes, albeit with a helmet on his head and an M16 in hand. I didn't notice at the time that he was wearing a green tzizit, but I did see that there were bloodstains on his jeans. It took me another second to confirm that the blood wasn't his, nor did it appear to belong to any of the five soldiers who had followed him into the house, all of whom seemed to be uninjured.

We hugged again, and now, finally, tears streamed from my eyes. For almost the entire time that we had been locked in the darkness, I had known that he was on his way to us—but it was still unbelievable that he was here, now, standing in front of me. Unbelievable, and a huge relief: After my mother had texted us around noon to say that that he was getting closer, I had been so worried that he'd be hit by an RPG or antitank missile along the way. As the hours passed and we continued waiting in silence, that fear only grew larger in my mind. But now, here he was, alive and seemingly no worse for the wear.

I asked my father where my mother was, and he replied that she was in Ashkelon, and safe—not yet filling me in on the details of their joint operation to rescue the injured soldiers. That could wait; here, now, we had more pressing things to attend to.

While my father and I were talking, the commandos quickly fanned through the rest of our home, searching each room just as they had done in all the homes they had entered beforehand. Finally, after what seemed like an eternity, I heard one of them declare "clean!"

I shouted to Miri, who was still in the safe room with the girls, that we were safe, and thanked the soldiers for coming to save us. Then I looked at my watch, which I hadn't been able to check in the safe room's total darkness, and saw that it was almost 4:00 P.M. I couldn't fathom that it had taken

Bullet holes in the Tibon family's living room window in Nahal Oz. The terrorists had fired into the house from the front porch; some of the bullets exited through a second window in the kitchen.

so many hours for the military to arrive. But at the same time, I felt a huge sense of gratitude to this group of young fighters who were now standing in our living room, studying the damage caused by the terrorists' bullets.

I took a moment to soak in the scene, too, finally able to see visual evidence of the violence that I had heard throughout the day. There were bullet holes everywhere, at least ten that I could count. Broken glass glittered on the floor. Bullets had pierced our chairs, embedded in the walls, and broken two mugs in the kitchen. It was a sad sight, but it didn't matter much to me at that point: the important thing was that we were alive.

My father had gone down the hall to the safe room to see Miri and the girls, and now I headed to the kitchen, careful not to step on all the broken glass, and grabbed two apples and a bag of Bamba—a popular Israeli children's snack made of puffed corn and peanut butter. I took it into the room for Miri to offer the girls, who were now both in the hands of my father, smiling and laughing for the first time that day. A few minutes earlier, I had been the one almost crying while embracing my father; now it was his turn to blink away tears as he hugged his granddaughters. Miri took the opportunity to slip away to the bathroom and fill our water bottles, which despite our careful rationing we had almost emptied after so many hours in lockdown.

Returning to the kitchen, I asked the soldiers if they were hungry. Most of them had left home in the morning without breakfast and hadn't had anything to eat all day. Their commander gave a silent nod, indicating to the men that, yes, they could stop here for a couple of minutes and grab a bite before searching the last few houses in their sector.

Rifling through our kitchen cabinets and refrigerator, I grabbed fruit, cookies, chocolate—anything that could quickly provide the commandos with some energy—and dumped it all in a big pile on our dining table. As the soldiers ate, I also took out glasses and two bottles of water that we had left in the refrigerator overnight. They thanked me, which felt like a ridiculous nicety in light of the risks they'd taken to get here and fight for us.

Inside the safe room, Carmel had heard the commandos' voices, and now she asked Miri who was in the house. Miri took the toddler in her arms and went to the door of the safe room, not yet ready to bring the girls outside. She stood there with Carmel and said, "Look, these are soldiers, they came with Saba to save us."

Carmel pointed at one of the soldiers standing close to the doorway and said, "It's a child."

Miri wanted to correct her: the person our toddler was pointing at was an imposing figure, decked out in battle gear and holding a gun in his hand. But then Miri took another look, saw the soldier making a silly face in an attempt to make our daughter laugh, and realized he was probably nineteen years old, maybe twenty. Legally an adult, but in many ways still a boy—a boy who had come to save our lives.

"Yes," Miri told Carmel, fighting back tears herself, now. "You're right. It's a child."

Galia had finished her green apple and immediately asked for another. I was relieved that all the stress of the day didn't seem to have hurt her appetite. My father was standing next to her, patting her head, but then he stepped out of the room to speak with the Maglan team. They still had a handful of homes to search, but first there was a more urgent problem to deal with.

On our front porch and around the house were five dead bodies, all Hamas terrorists. They had been killed earlier that day by the police team. And one of them, as my father had seen from the street, had died with a rocket-propelled grenade in his hand, aimed at the home of our neighbors, Ilan and Sharon.

Israeli warplanes were flying overhead now, on their way to bomb targets in Gaza, and from time to time mortars were still being launched at the kibbutz. The soldiers worried that the blasts caused by the Israeli bombs falling on Gaza or by Hamas's mortars landing inside the community could shift the dead terrorist's body and release the RPG still in his hand, potentially destroying Ilan and Sharon's house and hurting anyone still inside.

My father and the Maglan commander agreed that the best idea was to bring the family from next door into our home. Trying to move the RPG or disable it was deemed too risky and slow at a moment when safety and speed were of the essence. Wasting no time, the soldiers immediately went to Ilan and Sharon's house, leaving my father with us.

As we waited for the troops to return, my father told me to "take a peek" outside. I stepped out the door and couldn't believe my eyes. There were dead bodies everywhere, scattered around the neighborhood where they had fallen. There was blood on the sidewalks and broken glass on the road. No car on our street had been left undamaged and every home, including our own, was pocked by the impact of dozens of bullets. It looked like a scene out of a Clint Eastwood western, but it wasn't a movie—this was real life, right here in front of me.

As I stepped outside, I realized that I was still wearing only underwear— the unavoidable result of dashing straight from bed to our safe room at 6:30 that morning. I ducked back inside, got dressed, and also brought some clothes for Miri from our bedroom so that she could finally get out of her pajamas. We also put new clothes on Galia and Carmel, and brought them some toys and puzzles. My father sat for a minute on a chair in the living room, with his pistol on his lap and the dog, who had come back from outside, resting next to him. I took Miri's phone and snapped a picture—and then tried, unsuccessfully, to send it to my mother in an

Noam Tibon resting in Amir and Miri's home in Nahal Oz, ten hours after he left his house in Tel Aviv and raced toward the Gaza border area. Bloodstains are visible on his jeans, and a bullet hole can be seen in the window at top left.

attempt to let her know we were all alive. There was still no cell phone reception in our neighborhood.

At last, the soldiers returned. With them were five people—but not exactly the five we were expecting.

When the soldiers had told my father that they were going to bring the neighbors, I thought they'd come back with Ilan, Sharon, and their three daughters, two of whom went to preschool with Galia. But instead, the soldiers were now ushering in Sharon, the girls, and a twelve-year-old boy named Ariel, whose family lived on the other side of the kibbutz. Sharon had a worried look on her face. When she recognized my father, the first thing she asked him was, "Have you seen my husband?"

Approximately 1,600 feet to the north, on the other edge of the kibbutz, the second Maglan team was also about to finish searching its assigned zone. Within the space of two hours, they'd saved an entire family from slaughter and had killed three mehablim at close range; they had also made the chilling discovery that they were too late to save another family from being kidnapped. But the most horrific experience of the day was still ahead of them. It waited in the last house they needed to search, right next to the front gate of Nahal Oz.

This corner home, on a knoll in the kibbutz that overlooked Gaza City, belonged to the Zohar family: father Yaniv, a news photographer who had worked for the Associated Press for many years, documenting Israel's wars with Gaza from his home on the border; mother Yasmin, born and raised in Nahal Oz, who was about to obtain her PhD in education; their two daughters, Keshet, twenty, and Tchelet, eighteen; and their youngest son, Ariel, the twelve-year-old who had found shelter in my neighbors' home.

The commandos had no idea what to expect as they entered the home, but they didn't have much reason for optimism: the door was broken and the windows smashed. It was clear that someone had been there before them.

Finding the living room empty, the soldiers moved deeper into the house, weapons in hand. They crept down a dark hallway that led to several bedrooms. The first room was empty, as was the one next to it. The main bedroom, used by the parents, was the same. But the troops still hadn't checked the safe room, which was completely dark and silent—the door closed but unlocked.

When the Maglan commandos opened the safe room, they saw blood on the floor, dozens of bullet holes all over the walls, and four bodies, almost huddled together: Yaniv, Yasmin, and their two daughters. They were all dead, killed by close-range gunfire. Helpless to do anything more, the men covered their bodies with blankets.

Elsewhere in the house, the commandos had seen family pictures with five people in them, but inside the safe room, there was no sign of one of those family members: the young boy. The soldiers feared that he, too, had been kidnapped.

Shaken by what they had just seen, the young men wanted to leave this house and never come back—but instead, they had to stay there: the house offered them a direct line of sight to the community's front gate, which they now had to protect in case more mehablim from Gaza tried to enter Nahal Oz. So the commandos stayed on the front porch for the next two hours, with the bodies of the family mere steps away from them.

———————

Back at our house, twelve-year-old Ariel Zohar walked through the door and, just like Sharon Fiorentino, began asking us questions. He wondered if we had heard anything about his family—if anyone in the kibbutz had been able to contact them. As gently as we could, we told Ariel that we had just gotten out of our own safe room and hadn't had any cell phone service or battery power for many hours. We had no more idea than he did about what was happening elsewhere in the community.

In a quiet voice, Ariel explained how he had ended up spending the day with Sharon, our neighbor. Early in the morning, just before the mortars started landing on the kibbutz, he had gone out for a jog. As the explosions had begun, his mother had called Ilan, the security chief living next door to us, and asked for his help in finding her son. Ilan found Ariel on the internal ring road surrounding the kibbutz and brought him to his own home, telling Sharon to take care of him in the safe room together with their daughters. For the long, intervening hours, while the sound of gunfire echoed across our neighborhood, Sharon sat in the darkness of the safe room, hugging her daughters with one arm and holding Ariel's hand with her free hand.

That morning, Ariel had been able to update his parents via his phone that he was relatively safe and had heard that they were also hiding in their safe room with his two sisters, alive. But once noon passed, he heard nothing more from them—and he was growing increasingly concerned.

Sharon was equally worried for Ilan, who had left their home with his M16 shortly after bringing in Ariel and had not returned since. His phone kept ringing and ringing whenever she tried to call, but he did not pick up or respond to any messages. With tears in her eyes, she told us—in English, so the girls wouldn't understand—that he must be dead.

No one could say for sure what was happening, I reminded Sharon; we had to hold out hope. She nodded in agreement, but I could see she didn't truly believe it. Sadly, after what I had seen outside our front door, I shared her skepticism.

The Maglan team had left our home by now in order to search the last row of houses in our neighborhood. Before they'd departed, my father had handed the commandos Hen Bukhris's rifle and helmet; he was staying with us now and no longer needed them. But he held on to his pistol, just in case they had somehow missed a terrorist in their search of the neighborhood.

After the Maglan troops left, my father also instructed everyone who remained in the house to stay as still as possible. He was afraid that if the commandos outside, who were still on high alert, detected any quick, unexpected movements from the windows, they could accidentally shoot in our direction. His fear was justified: although my father had no way of knowing it at the time, in another part of the kibbutz, at around the same time that Sharon and the kids were brought over to our house, a tragedy occurred when a group of soldiers from the Givati Brigade accidentally shot to death a member of our community.

Forty-eight-year-old Ran Poslushni was a father of four whose oldest son was a soldier and had a gun at home but wasn't with the family that morning. Ran took his son's gun, sent the rest of the family to the safe room, and stayed near the door of the house. Several times that day he fired at terrorists who got close to his home, driving them off. But in the afternoon, as the IDF was securing the kibbutz, the Givati soldiers saw a suspicious figure running near the Poslushni family home. They began shouting that they had spotted a mehabel—a terrorist.

Ran was still inside—but with his son's gun in hand, he dashed to his second-floor balcony, wanting to assist the soldiers. One of them, however, thought that Ran was the terrorist they were chasing. In the heat of the moment, the soldier shot Ran, killing him. He was the only person from the kibbutz to die after the arrival of the military—an accidental tragedy that compounded all the others the community endured that day.

And the tally was steadily mounting. When a group of soldiers from the Givati Brigade arrived at the Idan family home, in the southwestern part of the kibbutz, not far from the pool, they were shocked by the sight awaiting them. Huddled on the floor of the house, alive but visibly traumatized, were two women and four children: a baby, a toddler, a nine-year-old boy, and a teenage girl. There were no men with them. The floor was covered with broken glass and smeared with blood.

Expressions of fear and desperation were fixed on the faces of the adults in the home: Gali, forty-nine, and Lishay, thirty-eight. One of the soldiers found the courage to ask what had happened. The women could barely find the words to recount their story.

They were both mothers, from different families in different households. Earlier that day, they and their families had each been pulled from their safe rooms—but not before the terrorists had murdered Ma'ayan, Gali's eighteen-year-old daughter. They had then opened a Facebook Live broadcast to show the world that Hamas now held the family hostage. Another team of terrorists had brought over the Miran family: father Omri, mother Lishay, and their two daughters Roni and Alma. That same team had also taken Judith Ra'anan, fifty-nine, an American citizen from Illinois who had come to Nahal Oz to visit her mother, and Natalie Ra'anan, her teenage daughter, to the same house.

The entire group was held at gunpoint for more than an hour. Then, as the Hamasniks became aware that the military was approaching the kibbutz, they decided to take whichever hostages they could and leave. Tzachi and Omri were handcuffed and separated from their families; Judith and Natalie, who spoke with the terrorists in English and had mentioned several times that they were US citizens, were ordered to get on their feet, too.

Shortly after 1:30 P.M., the mehablim marched the four out of the kibbutz. Omri's two-year-old daughter, Roni, tried to run after her father; Lishay stopped and hugged her as the girl desperately cried, "Daddy, Daddy! Don't take him!"

Laser-focused on the most important priority—staying alive—Lishay yelled one last sentence to her husband: "Don't be a hero. We're waiting for you." He walked to the car with his back straight and his head held high.

Roni continued to cry for several more minutes but then calmed down and started entertaining her baby sister Alma. It was as if the toddler understood that after what had just happened, her mother and sibling needed help just as much as she did.

———————

The Maglan soldiers completed their search of our neighborhood at approximately 6:30 P.M. By then, we finally had cell phone coverage again, and I had succeeded in getting through to my mother. We both had so much to tell one another—but my phone barely had any battery, as we still had no electricity and I could only charge it by connecting a USB cable to my laptop, which still had some juice. I told her that we were alive and my father had reached us. She asked me how the girls were doing, and I said they looked OK, considering everything they'd been through. We now had soldiers in our neighborhood, I told her, but Miri was still with Galia and Carmel in the safe room.

I could hear through the phone how excited and relieved my mom was to hear my voice and to learn that her daughter-in-law and two granddaughters were alive. "I was so worried," she said. "I couldn't imagine my life without the four of you." She asked if we knew anything about the fate of our friends, and I replied that she was the first person I had called and that I still had no access to data roaming on my phone, so we were in the dark about the broader situation in the community.

My mother asked me to tell my father that all the wounded soldiers were alive—a reference I didn't yet understand but promised to pass along—and that, after dropping them off at the hospital, she had returned to Sderot and brought water bottles to people who were stranded in the bomb shelters along Route 232. I moved the phone from my ear and went over to the safe room, to relay the information to my father. He asked me to tell her to go back to Tel Aviv—there was no chance of her getting to Nahal Oz with their Jeep at that point, and it would be much safer for her to head back home than to wait for us in the border region. He estimated it would be many hours before we could get out of the kibbutz.

I also noticed that he seemed surprised—happily so—to hear my mother's report about the wounded soldiers. Only after the call did he relate to me, briefly, the story of how he had ended up evacuating three fighters from the battlefield on the road leading to Nahal Oz. One of

199

them, he said, had already been on the verge of death when they had put him in my father's car.

Next, I called Miri's mother, Irena, and told her that all of us were alive. She had been in touch with my parents in the morning and knew about the journey they had made to the border area and some of the horrors they had seen along the way. I could hear her struggling mightily to keep her composure as I explained, in a few sentences, what had happened in our neighborhood.

Right before the phone shut down completely, I made two other phone calls. The first was to my sister-in-law, Jessica, a resident of Tel Aviv. I assumed that Uri, my younger brother, wouldn't answer—as a combat doctor in the Israeli military, he had rushed to join his unit that morning and I knew he would be busy at work. She told me that he was okay, that she was in contact with him, and that she'd pass along the message that my father had made it to Nahal Oz and rescued us.

Next, I called my friend and colleague Amos Harel, *Haaretz*'s military analyst, with whom I had spoken first thing that morning as the gunfire began in our neighborhood. Amos was relieved to hear my voice and asked if the kibbutz had been secured; I told him that we were safe and that my father had arrived but that I still could hear gunfire nearby, meaning that the battle for Nahal Oz wasn't over yet.

With the sun setting, the soldiers began assembling more and more neighbors in our house. They told my father that in every area of the kibbutz, they were trying to place as many people as they could under one roof to decrease the likelihood of a roving Hamasnik entering a home they had already declared clear and surprising a helpless family inside.

After Sharon and the children, the next person the soldiers brought in was Yonchi, the elderly man living two houses behind us. I saw the bloody wound on his hand, realized that his wife Shoshi wasn't with him, and understood immediately what this meant.

Shoshi had arrived at Nahal Oz in the early 1980s, after falling in love with Yonchi, who was already living in the kibbutz when the couple first met. They got married and raised four children, who in turn, made her a proud grandmother of eight. She worked as a teacher, and later became the secretary of a large factory in the border region. By the time we had become her neighbors in Nahal Oz, she had retired but continued to volunteer constantly within the community. I used to meet her almost every morning around 7:15 A.M., when I walked with Galia and Carmel to their daycare and passed by her house. She always smiled at the girls, asked them questions, and patiently waited for them to reply. Now, I realized, we would never see her again on our morning route—and my heart felt heavy as I tried to digest the horrible news.

Accompanying Yonchi were Ruti and Yossi, a couple in their seventies who lived across the street and had a view of our front door from their kitchen. The soldiers had reached their home before ours, and Ruti, it turned out, had seen me through her window when I glanced outside our door to see the mayhem in front of our house. Now, she looked at me with a smile and said, "Why did you go out in your underwear earlier? Don't you have any manners?" As sad as I was at that moment, her joke managed to briefly raise my spirits—exactly as Ruti, a social worker, had intended.

Around 7:30 P.M., Beri Meirovitch—the member of the security team who had been out fighting all day alongside Nissan Dekalo and the police troopers—stopped by our house to speak with my father and the soldiers. They all agreed that it was time to start planning the evacuation of the kibbutz's residents. The Maglan and Givati forces had killed almost thirty terrorists in different parts of the community and were close to declaring it safe, but it was clear to everyone that all the residents had to leave as soon as possible: the entire border area had become a war zone and the military didn't want any civilians—especially not children or elderly people—to be stuck in their homes as tanks rolled into the region and Hamas intensified its mortar attacks.

But how to evacuate everyone? There were roughly 450 full-time residents of our kibbutz, most of whom, miraculously, still seemed to be alive. Getting a bus into Nahal Oz to start taking people away would be a complicated task: the roads leading to the kibbutz were still not fully under Israeli control, and it would be difficult to find drivers who would agree to make the trip.

When Sharon spotted Beri, she approached him and asked if he knew anything about Ilan's situation—she still couldn't reach him on the phone. Beri told her he hadn't seen or heard from him since the early morning but that he had no evidence that he was dead. It was the best and most honest answer he could offer.

By 8:00 P.M., we had more than forty people in our house, including about ten young children. The safe room was too small to fit everyone inside, so we decided that only the children would stay in there—with an adult or two watching over them at all times—while everyone else spread out in our living room. Now and then gunfire could still be heard outside, and every thirty minutes or so we heard a mortar explode nearby, but most of us didn't bother to run into the safe room anymore. After everything we had been through, the explosions barely registered.

As darkness descended over the kibbutz, the electricity had finally returned, and we could turn on the lights and charge our phones fully for the first time that day. Soldiers came in and out of the house, still unable to predict when exactly we would be evacuated. Inside our safe room, one of Ilan and Sharon's daughters had found a book that belonged to Galia, *With My Daddy* by James Brown and Cally Johnson-Isaacs—a story focusing on the loving relationship between a child and a father. Sharon couldn't bring herself to read this book out aloud to her daughter while she was still worried about Ilan; I volunteered to do it instead, barely suppressing the tears that were about to run down my face as I scanned through the pages.

The restoration of power meant the return of other amenities, as well. Ruti, with a dead-serious look on her face, approached Miri in the living room. In front of everyone, she asked where she could find a pot for cooking pasta. Miri seemed confused. "Pasta? What are you talking about?" she asked. But Ruti insisted. "I know we've all had a very long day," she said, "but there are ten children sitting in that little room, and they need to have dinner."

Miri accompanied Ruti to the kitchen and the two of them, along with Shimrit, another neighbor and a mother of four, prepared dinner for everyone in the house: children, adults, and soldiers. There was pasta with tomato sauce, meatballs that we had cooked the day before with the intention of eating them for lunch that Saturday, and some freshly cut vegetables. As I watched people eating—the children sitting on the floor of the safe room, their parents in the living room, and the soldiers out on the porch, visible only through the cracks that the terrorists' bullets had left in our windows—I realized that Ruti had just done us all a huge favor. She had told us, in very few words, that since we were alive, we were going to have to live.

As more people filtered into our home, we began to hear rumors of the atrocity that had unfolded on the other side of the kibbutz, in the Idan family's house, and the unthinkable result: Ma'ayan was dead, and several of our friends and neighbors had been taken into Gaza. We hoped it was a mistake—that maybe the military was waiting at the border fence, ready to stop the terrorists and free Omri and Tzahi. But there was little reason for hope. My father kept silent as we began sharing the disturbing information with him. Nothing he had seen that day indicated that anything good was in store for the hostages.

There was still no information about the whereabouts of many other people in our community. No one had heard from Shlomo Ron, an elderly member of the community, who lived in a house not far from the communal dining hall. Later that evening, we learned that he was murdered by Hamasniks in his living room, while his wife and two daughters—who had arrived that weekend to visit their parents—were hiding in the safe room. The terrorists entered the home, saw an old man sitting alone on his sofa, shot him to death, and kept moving into the next house, bypassing the rest of the family. By choosing to stay seated in front of the door, Shlomo had saved the lives of his loved ones.

We also had no information about Ilan, and no one knew anything about the fate of Dikla Arava, her boyfriend Noam Elyakim, and his two daughters Dafna and Ela. As we were trying to collect bits and pieces of information, I turned on my phone, finally fully charged, and saw more than two thousand unread messages and emails—most of them containing different variations of the same question: *Are you OK?* I didn't have the time or energy to answer everyone, so I only wrote back to a handful of friends and relatives, and then put the phone down, planning to post a message on social media later in an attempt to answer everyone at once.

At approximately 8:30 P.M., the soldiers told us they believed we'd be evacuated soon—but another hour passed and nothing happened. I glanced at the top headlines of Israel's different news websites on my phone and realized that even then, after an entire day of fighting, the situation was still not under control everywhere along the border. There was still active fighting in Be'eri, Kfar Azza, and other communities around us. One headline indicated that the military was preparing for the fighting inside Israel to last for at least forty-eight hours. There were already public estimates that more than 250 people had been killed or murdered in the Hamas attack; my father told me that he thought the real number was significantly higher, judging by the number of bodies he had seen on his way to Nahal Oz.

Then, at around 10:00 P.M., after hours of waiting, things began to happen—fast. Three roofless military Humvees pulled up in front of our house, and one by one, the families we had hosted that evening were all ferried to a large building near the main gate of the kibbutz that for years had been used as tractor depot and was large enough for everyone to wait in together until the evacuation bus arrived.

Miri, my father, and I decided that we would wait behind with Galia and Carmel and leave last—making sure that everyone else in the house was safe. Sharon and her daughters came with us in the final convoy. Until the very last second, she still hoped that Ilan would show up and join them.

As we were preparing to leave the house, we ran into a moral and practical dilemma. It was clear that Pluto, weighing close to ninety pounds, wouldn't be able to come with us on the bus that, later that night, was supposed to lead us from the tractor parking area to safety. He was too large and too energetic, and taking him on the bus would mean forcing a human being, a neighbor, to wait for the next bus—which might not arrive for hours. We realized our dog would have to stay in the house and that we'd need to return for him the next day, assuming we could make it back at all. But how could we leave him behind after everything he had gone through that day, knowing that mortars were still falling on the community?

I decided to talk with the Maglan commandos, who, I understood, were planning to stay at the kibbutz for the next few days. I approached a soldier named Idan and told him we had to leave the dog behind for a day, perhaps two, until it would be possible for one of us to return to the kibbutz with a car and take him out. We knew this was a risky bet and that Pluto could end up alone in the house for much longer, but we had no better option.

Idan told me he'd be more than happy to take Pluto out for a walk once a day and give him food. I filled our bathtub all the way to the top so that Pluto would have enough water to drink, gave him a hug, and promised him we'd be back to collect him—hopefully tomorrow and, if not, then certainly the day after. Idan told me not to worry and reiterated that they'd take care of him. Then we hastily grabbed the girls' favorite blankets and the dolls they slept with and walked with my father to one of the Humvees.

The open-air drive lasted for two minutes, but it felt like a lifetime. We were on high alert: everything around us was dark, and we could still hear the sounds of battle, now mostly coming from the direction of Gaza. Despite the fact that our home's electricity had been restored, the streetlights in our neighborhood weren't working, something I assumed was deliberate—an effort by the soldiers to better protect the convoys that were shuttling people to safety. My father gripped his pistol while Miri and I did our best to shield the girls with our bodies.

When finally we arrived at the tractor depot, we jumped out of the Humvee and found more than seventy of our friends and neighbors already there, waiting for the evacuation bus. It was probably both the happiest and saddest moment of the entire day. We were overjoyed to see so many friends we had been worried sick about, but we also knew by then that many other members of our community had died or were missing. Every hug and handshake was an emotional rollercoaster.

The Maglan commandos were sent out into the fields of the kibbutz to search the surrounding area and get into firing positions so they could protect the bus that was about to arrive and take us to safety. The Givati soldiers remained with us at the tractor site, but at one point their commander called them together for a briefing and the door to the depot was left unguarded. My father, with his pistol, stood there for several minutes until the soldiers returned. One of them, who hadn't recognized my father, asked if he was a member of the local security team, to which he replied, "Yes, sort of."

The bus arrived shortly after 10:30 P.M. We were the second group to leave the kibbutz—the same bus had previously left full of residents shortly after 9:00 P.M. and had dropped them at a military base forty minutes to the east, near the city of Be'er Sheva. Now we all climbed in—at least those of us who were lucky enough to have made it to the tractor depot. More than two hundred people were still left behind: some in their homes, some in the houses of neighbors, all waiting for their turn to be evacuated. The soldiers hurried us into the bus so they could begin the process of bringing over the next group of evacuees. Their goal was to get everyone out of the kibbutz by 2:00 A.M.

Inside the bus, our family squeezed into three seats within the same row. I sat with Carmel on my lap, while Miri held Galia and my father sat by the window.

As the bus started moving, we took one last look at Nahal Oz. In the distance, near the area of the kibbutz's cowshed, a huge fire was raging, lighting up the night sky and casting our surroundings in a surreal sheen of golds, oranges, and yellows. Our community was burning, and we were literally leaving it behind in flames.

———————

The bus ride was tense. Most of us had heard by now of the horrors that took place along the region's main roads that day. The girls fell asleep, as did most of the other children. The adults were all silent. Nobody seemed to be able to let their guard down enough to sleep, but neither did we know what to say; it was as if words had simply lost their meaning.

I was still getting messages from concerned friends in Israel and abroad, and as the bus arrived at the same military base where our neighbors had already been dropped off earlier that evening, I felt it was time to finally answer everyone at once. I opened my X account and posted a brief message in Hebrew: "We're alive. Our daughters are heroes. They waited silently in our safe room for 10 hours with no food or electricity. The soldiers who arrived are heroes. And the biggest hero is my father, who came from Tel Aviv, led the soldiers to us and helped kill the bad guys. We'll tell more later. We are praying for our injured and missing neighbors."

The post went viral within seconds, eventually reaching almost three million views. In retrospect, I regret not waiting until the next morning before publishing it. When I clicked "post," I had not yet heard the full story of my parents' journey and wasn't aware of everything that had happened that day in the kibbutz: the heroic battle that Nissan, Beri, and the police team had fought for hours, alone, against more than a hundred heavily armed terrorists; the careful, methodical search that Eshel had led through the kibbutz in the afternoon hours; and the full, horrid details of the tragedy that had occurred at the home of the Idan family.

But at that point, I felt I had to tell the people in my network, in general terms and under the 280-character limitations of the X platform, what had happened and that we were now safe. I already knew that I would eventually have to write a longer, fuller description of what we had all been through on that day. This, perhaps, was a start.

Two minutes later, my father's phone rang. On the other end was a producer for Channel 12, the leading TV news channel in Israel, asking to interview him by phone. My dad said yes and was immediately transferred to the studio.

The call had caught him while we were walking from the bus to a large hangar, where dozens of mattresses were spread on the floor and long tables full of snacks and sweets had been organized for us. Now, sitting on a mattress on the floor next to Galia as she ate chocolate pudding with a plastic spoon, my father recounted in brief the dramatic events he had just experienced. Hundreds of thousands of people in Israel were watching the broadcast, and the journalists in the studio expressed amazement at the details he was now sharing: the rescue of the couple from the Nova party; the battle along the road to the kibbutz; the evacuation of the wounded soldiers; and finally, the scores of dead terrorists in our neighborhood, some of them almost literally on our doorstep.

The second my father hung up, my phone lit up with dozens of calls and messages. Every news producer in the country, it seemed, was either calling or texting me to ask for an interview. Other people were simply reacting to the story as my father told it on television, writing to me about his heroism and determination.

I didn't answer any of these calls or messages. I had no intention, at that point, of doing any interviews. Instead, for the first time since the whistle of a mortar had woken us up that morning, I closed my eyes, laid my head on the mattress, and slept.

CHAPTER 11

PARTNERS

2015–2023

IN THE DAYS AFTER DANIEL Tregerman's funeral, calm returned to the Gaza border thanks to the ceasefire that ended the 2014 war. Netanyahu declared a new, postwar policy toward Gaza, summarized in a simple catchphrase: "Quiet will be met with quiet." He had long since abandoned his promise to topple Hamas in favor of a deal that its leadership, for the time being, was willing to accept: the organization would halt its rocket attacks on Israel, and Israel would avoid any military action against Hamas. The unspoken part of this arrangement was that both sides would continue preparing for the next round of war, which everyone assumed would eventually arrive—a question of when, not if.

And so, while the region at large remained quiet, a storm was raging inside Nahal Oz: the community was on the verge of collapse. In early September, just days after the ceasefire began, more than fifteen families announced they were leaving the kibbutz and moving somewhere else—somewhere safer. Most of them were parents of young children, who simply couldn't explain to their kids why their friend Daniel won't be showing up for the first day of preschool that year.

Almost overnight, a quarter of the population had left. Ever since the community's first babies were born, in the mid-1950s, the sound of children—crying, laughing, singing, and playing—had always been heard at Nahal Oz. Now, however, there was doubt if there would be enough kids in the kibbutz to reopen the education system.

The families that left were impacted not just by the trauma of little Daniel's death but also by the hopeless result of the war. For two full months, Israel and Hamas had fought each other in a bloody contest that eclipsed all the previous rounds of violence between the two sides: more than two thousand people had died in Gaza, approximately half of them civilians; thousands of homes had been destroyed; Nahal Oz had been bombarded incessantly for more than sixty days. Yet when it all ended, Hamas remained in power in Gaza; Netanyahu remained the prime minister of Israel; and the next war was already being discussed as an unavoidable certainty.

For Oshrit Sabag, this crisis was especially personal—and not just because Doron and Gila, Daniel's parents, were her best friends in the community and were among the families who left Nahal Oz after the tragedy. Two years earlier, Oshrit had been appointed to lead the kibbutz's "demographic growth team"—a small crew responsible for attracting new families to join the community. Her job, for which she received a salary from the kibbutz, was to help expand Nahal Oz by convincing people from other parts of Israel to move there, despite the security risks.

When she first got the job in 2013, many in the community had raised an eyebrow. Who would choose to move to one of the only Israeli communities not protected by the Iron Dome? But Oshrit believed that just as she had fallen in love with the place a decade earlier, so would other Israelis, too, once they actually saw it with their own eyes. She also knew that Israel's real estate prices had been surging since 2005, as had the costs of daycare as well as preschool and afternoon activities for children. Oshrit was convinced that Nahal Oz, where homes were cheaper compared to most of the country and where the excellent early education system—the daycare, preschool, kindergarten, and afternoon educational activities for school-aged children—was subsidized by the kibbutz, still had much to offer young families.

In 2013 and 2014, before the latest war had erupted, the kibbutz indeed accepted a handful of new families, and a few weeks before the conflict broke out, Oshrit had updated the kibbutz management that twelve other families had expressed interest in joining. But the war had put an end to all that. One by one, the new families she'd been expecting called to tell her that they'd changed their minds.

It was a dark period for Oshrit, by then a mother of two. But out of the grief—over the death of Daniel, the departure of Gila and Doron, and the larger social crisis in the kibbutz—she reached two important decisions. The first was to stay in Nahal Oz. Her mother had arrived in Israel decades earlier as a refugee from Libya, after that country had expelled all of its Jewish population; leaving her home due to Hamas's violence seemed to Oshrit like a betrayal of her family's legacy.

The second decision was to return to her job and lead the demographic growth team. "People told me it was a suicide mission," she recalled, wryly. But she thought otherwise.

She wrote down a detailed plan on how to attract new families to the kibbutz—with an ambitious goal: to overcome the entire population loss within two years. In a series of talking points for prospective families, she sought to turn the community's crisis into an opportunity:

Many families with children left the education system? Yes, and now every new child that arrives will get much more attention from the educational staff.

Homes all over the kibbutz had been abandoned, still damaged by the fighting in the summer? True—and with a small repair, they could become your dream home in a beautiful kibbutz just an hour's drive from Tel Aviv.

On top of the practical arguments, she decided to also make an ideological appeal to people interested in strengthening the border region, highlighting in media appearances that rebuilding Nahal Oz was a national mission in the aftermath of the war.

Every new family she'd be able to bring to the community, she told herself, would be one small act of payback against Hamas—a proof of Israeli resilience and determination. "I wanted Hamas to see that we were bringing new people here," she explained. "This became my life's mission."

Miri and I were one of the first couples to move to Nahal Oz in the fall of 2014, mere weeks after Daniel Tregerman's funeral. For several months before the war, we had been discussing the idea of leaving Tel Aviv for a smaller, quieter place, but originally, we didn't think of the Gaza border area as an option. Only after my visits there during the war did we decide to give it a try.

Oshrit was the first person we met in the community. She took us on a tour of the available homes, while telling us about the local education system and different aspects of the communal life in the kibbutz. We had no idea at the time what a trauma she had just endured—how close she was with the Tregerman family and how the aftermath of that day's tragedy had unfolded inside her very own home.

In early November, in the weekly update sent to Nahal Oz residents by the community manager, there was a black-and-white photo of Miri and me and, next to it, a short paragraph announcing that we had moved to the kibbutz. Our friends in Tel Aviv thought we were crazy—but we weren't the only ones.

Over the coming months, more and more young couples and families arrived at Nahal Oz, many for reasons similar to ours: patriotism and defiance of Hamas, for one thing, but also a desire for community, for a slower lifestyle, and for proximity to nature. By the summer of 2015, the community was close to regaining the number of people it had lost only a year earlier—an incredible achievement that we felt proud to be a small part of.

Throughout 2015, several rockets and mortars were launched at the kibbutz, but these were isolated incidents that didn't have much of an impact on our lives. The "quiet for quiet" formula was being honored, for the most part, by both Israel and Hamas—allowing the kibbutz to continue rebuilding after the exodus of the year before.

Meanwhile, inside Gaza, a reconstruction process was also underway—and once again, Qatar had emerged as a dominant force behind it. During the war, Israeli officials, including Netanyahu, had criticized the country for its support of Hamas, but just months into the precarious ceasefire that criticism was forgotten as Qatar once again flooded Gaza with money, with the tacit support of Netanyahu's government.

Netanyahu claimed credit for the enduring calm along the border, but when a new Israeli election appeared on the horizon in 2015, the inconclusive results of the war came back to haunt him. Naftali Bennett and

Avigdor Lieberman, the two right-wing ministers who had failed to convince him to topple Hamas, now blamed him for failing to "finish the job" in Gaza. In the final weeks of the campaign, Netanyahu was losing support in the polls, mostly to his rivals on the Right. Pundits expected that if this trend continued, the left-leaning Labor Party—which overall was poised to win more seats than Likud—would get to form the next government.

On the verge of losing power, Netanyahu did something unprecedented. Two weeks before Election Day, at the invitation of Republican lawmakers in Washington, DC, he appeared in the US Congress and delivered a combative speech against the policies of President Obama, assailing his broader Middle East agenda and his negotiations with Iran over a nuclear deal, in a desperate bid to rally nationalists back home. It was the first time ever that an Israeli prime minister had publicly attacked the leader of Israel's closest ally in his own capital, in front of hundreds of American lawmakers.

The move worked: Likud regained popular support at the expense of the other right-wing parties, and on election night, it was once again Israel's largest party, dashing the Labor Party's hopes of returning to power. As right-wing voters drifted back to Netanyahu, his rivals Bennett and Lieberman ended up losing seats, a humiliating result for them and their parties.

Miri watched the election results come in amid throngs of our neighbors in the kibbutz's pub while I was still at work. Around 11:00 P.M., she called me in tears and said that the festive atmosphere at the watch party had turned to despair. Close to 90 percent of the local votes had gone to parties opposing Netanyahu, and even the few right-wingers within the community mostly had given their votes to Bennett and Lieberman. "How could people in this country vote for him again, after everything that just happened?" she asked. I had no good answer.

Depressed by the general direction of the country, we found comfort among our growing group of friends and neighbors inside Nahal Oz, most of whom shared our dismal view of the situation.

Every weekend, we took long hikes in the fields and woods around us, feeling like tourists in our own country as we discovered hidden spots of beauty in the region. Outside Kibbutz Nirim, twenty-five minutes to the south of us, was a well-preserved mosaic floor from the Byzantine era, with incredible depictions of wild animals; in the fields of kibbutz Nir Yitzhak, farther south, thousands of buttercups blossomed in late April, stretching into the horizon in bright shades of red, pink, and orange. Friends from Tel Aviv who'd come to visit us were amazed to see these magical places. More and more, we began hearing different variations of the same sentiment: *We get it—we understand why you moved here.*

In October 2015, exactly a year after we moved to Nahal Oz, I got a phone call from Oshrit. "There's a new couple coming to the kibbutz," she said. "They're incredible people. Can I ask you guys to host them for Friday night dinner?"

She told me briefly about these latest transplants: Avishay Edri, thirty, was studying for a PhD in biology, focusing his research on ways to fight the spread of the Ebola virus. His wife Brit, thirty-one, was a psychologist working for the Israeli police. I said we'd be happy to meet them.

From the moment they sat at our table, I knew we'd be friends. Avishay had grown up in Kiryat Shmona, a border town in northern Israel, less than two miles from Lebanon. Like most of the town's residents, his parents hailed from families that had immigrated to Israel from the Middle East—in his case, Iran and Morocco.

I grew up not far from Avishay's hometown: my father was stationed for most of my childhood along the Lebanese border, and so our family lived in the north. Both Avishay and I, as children, had experienced rocket attacks on our communities. Until I sat next to him that evening, however, it had never occurred to me that perhaps that period of my childhood had shaped my relatively calm approach to the threats associated with life at Nahal Oz.

Brit was very interested in our decision to move from Tel Aviv to the kibbutz; she seemed to share our view of life on the border as a sort of a mission—especially after what had happened in Nahal Oz a year earlier. She and Avisahy, however, weren't nationalists or religious extremists—the opposite was true. Like us, they believed it was important to protect Israel's borders—and just as important to reach peace with our neighbors and end our decades-long conflict with them.

Toward the end of the night, we told them about the group of young families that had already moved into the community, and how easily they'd fit in. Soon, they moved into a house right across from ours, and half a year later Brit gave birth to their first daughter, whom they named Negev, after the Israeli desert region that began just to the east of the Gaza border area. At the time, we had not had Galia or Carmel yet, and most of our friends on the kibbutz were still childless, too. So we watched and learned from our new neighbors as they set about raising Negev—and facing the unique challenges that we quickly realized came along with the joys of parenthood in Nahal Oz.

Things began to heat up again toward the end of 2017. In December of that year, the new US president, Donald Trump, announced his intention to change a decades-old American policy and recognize Jerusalem as the capital of Israel. Ever since Israel's creation in 1948, the US, and with it most Western countries, had rejected Israel's designation of Jerusalem as its capital city, choosing instead to place their embassies in Tel Aviv. Their decisions were born of a concern about the religious sensitivity around Jerusalem and fear of igniting unnecessary tensions with the Islamic world.

The US Congress had passed a law recognizing Jerusalem as Israel's capital in 1995, but the three American presidents who held office after its passage—Bill Clinton, George W. Bush, and Barack Obama—all delayed its implementation, citing national security concerns. Trump promised to end that policy, and on December 6, 2017, he announced that the US would soon move its embassy in Israel to Jerusalem. The decision was celebrated widely in Israel, but along the Gaza border, it led to an immediate surge of violence, as Hamas launched more than thirty rockets and mortars at Nahal Oz and other communities—more than the organization had launched in the entire year prior to Trump's declaration.

The situation escalated further in 2018. In late March of that year, a massive demonstration was organized on the Gazan side of the border fence. The date chosen for the event, March 30, a Friday afternoon, was known to Israel in advance, and so was the plan: tens of thousands of Palestinians—mostly citizens, and among them many children—would march from Gaza City toward the fence and try to get as close to it as they could. What would happen once they got there was anyone's guess, but the military feared they'd try to take down the fence and enter Israel. The demonstration was at first organized by local activists who had no direct connection to Hamas, but by the time it was about to get underway, the organization controlling Gaza had forced the organizers to accept its involvement.

Three years earlier, shortly after Miri and I had moved to Nahal Oz, a senior military commander in the border region had knocked on our door one Saturday morning, surprising us in our pajamas. He was touring the area near Nahal Oz and wanted to see with his own eyes the journalist who had moved to the kibbutz from Tel Aviv. I invited the officer in, and we sat for coffee in our small living room. At one point in the conversation, I asked him what was keeping him up at night. I expected him to say something about the tunnels that Hamas was once again digging under the border or perhaps the development of new rockets that could outsmart the Iron Dome. His answer surprised me: "I'm afraid things will get so bad over there, that at some point, hundreds of thousands of people will just start marching to the fence. What will we do then?" Now, this commander's nightmare was about to come true.

The organizers of the march described it as a desperate cry for help. Almost four years after the 2014 war, Gaza remained impoverished, the war's destruction was still visible in many parts of the Strip, and the unemployment rate was over 50 percent. The Qatari money helped Hamas hold on to power, but it didn't do much to help the ordinary Gazan citizens suffering from the joint Israeli-Egyptian blockade.

For the Israeli commanders on the ground, however, the march presented a terrible dilemma. The military was deploying hundreds of soldiers on the Israeli side of the border in an attempt to deter the crowd from reaching the fence. But what were those soldiers supposed to do if the masses continued marching forward?

One option, of course, was to simply let the demonstrators get to the fence—and risk the crowd trying to break through it and run toward Nahal Oz. Israeli intelligence had secretly warned the government that among the unarmed protesters would be hundreds of armed men from Hamas; their mission, if the crowd managed to break through the fence, would be to take advantage of the chaos by slipping across the border, entering the kibbutz, and killing or kidnapping Israeli citizens.

The commanders' other option was to try to hold the crowd away from the fence with tear gas and rubber bullets—and if they kept moving, to resort to gunfire. This was a gruesome choice that would almost certainly lead to the death of unarmed civilians.

There were only bad choices, in short—and there was a high risk that no matter what happened, a new round of fighting would break out in the aftermath of the protest.

That Friday afternoon, as the demonstration got underway, the entire world was watching—literally, thanks to television cameras documenting the event from both sides of the border. Near the fence, the demonstrators erected six large tents, where activities for families and children began taking place; kites were flying in the sky and music was playing from loudspeakers. But then, just hundreds of feet away from this peaceful scene, men began throwing stones and Molotov cocktails toward the Israeli soldiers on the other side of the fence. Some of these Palestinians tried to reach the fence itself and cut parts of it.

The Israeli soldiers guarding the border received an order to open fire at anyone they felt was posing a threat to them—which, in this scenario, would include breaching the fence separating Israel from Gaza, to say nothing of hurling rudimentary bombs or carrying weapons. It didn't take them long to open fire.

By the late afternoon, the scale of the disaster was becoming clear: the border fence was still intact, but sixteen Palestinians had died from the military's bullets. Israel claimed that almost all of them were armed Hamas militants; Hamas denied this and accused Israel of massacring peaceful protesters. That evening, the organization launched a new barrage of rockets at Israeli border communities. Netanyahu's "quiet for quiet" policy had just gone down in flames.

———

The months that followed were difficult for those living along the border—on both sides. Almost every week, a rocket was launched at one or more of the communities on the Israeli side of the fence, and Israel struck back at Gaza with war planes and attack helicopters. It wasn't a full-blown war yet, but it felt like the region was on the verge of one.

But the day things truly seemed to spiral out of control was November 12, 2018. The night before, an Israeli secret operation inside the Gaza Strip, carried out by a special intelligence unit, had been detected and thwarted by Hamas. The Israeli soldiers had been trying to install listening devices and gain access to Hamas's internal communications network; their discovery touched off a pitched battle in which seven Hamas fighters and one senior Israeli officer were killed.

Residents along the Israeli side of the border heard the battle raging inside the Strip, with long bursts of gunfire followed by unusually heavy aerial traffic as Israeli warplanes and rescue helicopters arrived at the scene. By early morning, the battle was over—but Hamas would have the last word. Within a few hours, more than fifteen rockets were launched into southern Israel, including several aimed at Nahal Oz.

Soon, our regional council, containing eleven communities located close to the border, sent a text message to all its residents announcing that there would be no school, kindergarten, or daycare services that day and that families should stay home and remain close to their safe rooms.

At this point, our friends Avishay and Brit Edri had settled into life in the kibbutz, and their family had grown since our introductory dinner: little Negev was now two and a half and had a new baby sister, Teva (Hebrew for "nature"). After getting the alert from the Nahal Oz security team, Avishay called his boss and explained that he had to stay at home with his kids, since all their classes and activities had been canceled; he and Brit would spend the coming hours with the two girls inside the safe room, struggling to entertain them.

This was getting to be a familiar routine: there had been a handful of frightening incidents soon after Negev's birth during which Avishay and Brit had to run to their safe room with the baby in their arms, but as the tensions along the border had increased and these experiences became more common, they also became more familiar. As Avishay and Brit would soon discover, this could prove dangerous.

On that morning, everybody had expected the mortar fire to last all day—but after the early barrage, Hamas stopped firing. There were no more sirens, and the only noise Avishay could hear from the safe room was the humming of Israeli drones in the sky. *This is strange*, he thought to himself. *What's the catch?* But hours passed, and the rockets still hadn't started up again.

At 4:00 P.M., Avishay finally decided that it was safe to get out. Perhaps, he thought to himself, Hamas was satisfied with foiling Israel's operation the night before and then firing some rockets at sunrise? Could this round of escalation now be over?

Negev was hungry, so Avishay and Brit decided to drive the family to Sderot and get pizza for dinner. After a long day in the safe room, they needed some fresh air. They were putting the girls in their car seats when Avishay received a disturbing push notification from an Israeli news site: Hamas had fired an antitank missile at a bus along Route 232, close to kibbutz Mefalsim.

"We can't go," Avishay told Brit. No sooner had the words left his mouth than the sirens began wailing.

The barrage that fell on Nahal Oz moments later caught Avishay, Brit, and their children too far from their home, unable to reach their safe room. Instead, they grabbed the girls and ran to a small bomb shelter at the edge of the parking lot—a fifty-square-foot rectangular structure built of thick concrete. Inside it they found another neighbor already hiding with her daughter, a friend of Negev's from kindergarten. The girls cried as a powerful rocket exploded right outside the shelter.

The six of them stayed inside for more than an hour. Darkness began to descend over the kibbutz, but the bombardment continued. Avishay read on his phone that the entire border region was under attack, with hundreds of rockets and mortars launched at different communities.

When things finally got quiet, Brit and Avishay ran home with Negev and Teva, as did the other mom and her daughter. They made it back without a scratch, but Avishay and Brit spent the rest of the night in their safe room with the girls, having learned a painful lesson: when security tensions began to rise along the border, complacency—or even a simple desire for normalcy—could kill.

While the border was under attack, the Israeli security cabinet convened for an urgent meeting in Jerusalem. Avigdor Lieberman, who had been appointed defense minister two years earlier, pushed once again for a large military operation against Hamas, with the aim of toppling the regime in Gaza once and for all. He also reminded Netanyahu of a document he had personally handed to him in late 2016, warning of a catastrophic danger to Israel: a secret plan by Hamas to cross the border fence at several points simultaneously, attack a long list of Israeli communities near Gaza, murder hundreds of citizens, and take dozens of hostages into Gaza.

The architect of this horrifying plan was Yihyia Sinwar, one of the most prominent terrorists whom Israel had agreed to release from prison as part of the 2011 Gilad Shalit deal. Upon his return to Gaza, Sinwar had promised that he wouldn't "abandon his brothers"—the thousands of Palestinian prisoners still left in Israel's jails. He immediately began working on a plan that would, he believed, eventually force Israel to release each and every one of them.

Lieberman's document explained in great detail what Sinwar was plotting—from the opening act of breaching the border fence, to the final step of bringing Israeli hostages into Gaza and placing them in tunnels underneath Gaza City. Unless Israel took down Hamas, Lieberman warned, the organization would continue preparing for this attack.

Netanyahu heard the arguments but once again ruled out the kind of operation that Lieberman was demanding—and just like in 2014, the senior ranks of the military were on Netanyahu's side, explaining that Israel had more urgent defense priorities, such as stopping Iran's massive shipments of weapons to Hezbollah in Lebanon. The discussion ended with a decision to deescalate the situation in Gaza, preferably by requesting that Qatar bring more money into the Strip in an attempt to pacify Hamas.

Qatar's support for Hamas had gone through several evolutions since Netanyahu had reclaimed the role of prime minister in 2009. Early on, the rich oil kingdom pledged to deliver as much as $400 million to the Gaza Strip and to invest the funds in the construction of specific public-works projects—schools, hospitals, and the like. Israel closely monitored the money that entered Gaza's banks, however, and there were indications that some of it, despite Qatar's promises, was eventually making its way into the hands of Hamas's military wing. The same was true of construction materials, often bought with the Qatari funds that were supposed to go directly to specific projects—but ended up being used for the construction of tunnels and rockets instead. Yet Netanyahu didn't take any concrete action to stop the Qatari cash flow.

After the 2014 war, Israel tried to exert more control over new construction projects in Gaza. Qatar once again emerged as the chief financier of the postwar reconstruction, but this time Netanyahu and other senior Israeli officials promised that Israel would ensure that construction materials funded by Qatar and delivered into Gaza—via either the Israeli border crossings at Erez and Kerem Shalom or the Rafah crossing between Gaza and Egypt on the southern edge of the Strip—did not end up being used by Hamas for military purposes.

Now, four years later, the government was considering a new kind of arrangement: one that would do the opposite. They would loosen Israeli controls and allow Qatar to simply bring cash into Gaza. This, of course, would be much preferable for Hamas, and Netanyahu's government knew it. Indeed, they had worked it out with Hamas indirectly: the idea had been discussed between the Israeli and Qatari governments and also presented to the leadership of Hamas, with Netanyahu's approval. Netanyahu and his closest aides thought this gambit could bring back quiet along the border. But Lieberman said it was a disgrace.

The day after the security cabinet meeting, Lieberman organized a press conference and declared his resignation. "It's time for new elections," he declared. "What we are doing right now is buying short-term quiet at the price of our long-term national security." Without the outgoing defense minister's party, Netanyahu's governing coalition was left with a bare-bones, single-vote majority in the Israeli Knesset. Netanyahu feared that in such a scenario, any single member of the governing coalition could bring it down at their own initiative and decided it was better for him to set the national agenda and put an end to this unstable government. Israel was headed to new elections, in which Gaza would once again play an important role.

Three weeks after the dramatic sequence of events that led to the fall of Netanyahu's government, a small convoy of black vehicles arrived at the Erez Crossing at the northern border of the Strip. In one of the vehicles sat Mohammed al-Emadi, a special envoy of the Qatari government. Sporting a short mustache and wearing a traditional keffiyeh, al-Emadi was there on an important mission: he was about to bring into Gaza dozens of suitcases containing a staggering amount of cash—$15 million in total, all a gift from the government of Qatar to the government of Gaza.

Emadi's official title was "head of the Qatari Committee for the Reconstruction of Gaza," and his job was to transfer money from the rich Gulf country into the impoverished Gaza Strip, with the full authorization and support of the Israeli government. His arrival was part of a three-way deal involving Israel, Qatar, and Hamas, in an attempt to end the months-long period of fighting that began with the "march of return," which reached its peak in November 2018 with the same spate of missile attacks that almost killed our friends, the Edri family. This deal was the one Lieberman had railed against weeks earlier at the security cabinet, to no avail.

Israel, as part of this deal, was allowing Qatar to bring millions of dollars in cash into Gaza on an almost monthly basis. This was an unprecedented development: beforehand, Qatar had sent money into Gaza via banking transactions, which were relatively easy for Israeli intelligence to trace. Hamas still found ways to maneuver the money toward its military needs, but Israel had its ways of monitoring the situation and acting when terror funding was suspected. Now, however, the Qatari envoy was about to deliver a literal mountain of money into Gaza, effectively with almost no strings attached.

Officially, this cash transfusion was meant to cover the salaries of thousands of government workers in the Gaza Strip, who until recently had been paid by the Palestinian Authority despite the fact that Gaza had been under the control of Hamas since 2007; that arrangement worked well for over a decade, allowing PA leader Mahmoud Abbas to claim he still had influence over some aspects of life in Gaza despite Hamas's control of the Strip. But by mid-2018, this pretense—and the payments that had sustained it—had come to an end. Abbas had changed his mind and decided he needed to place economic pressure on Hamas, hoping he could force the Islamists to accept his rule and give up power. His gamble failed, however: Netanyahu's deal with Qatar released a good amount of that pressure by allowing more money to flow into the Strip than ever before.

Once inside Gaza, the money was indeed delivered to the thousands of government employees there, exactly as Israel, Qatar, and Hamas had agreed. But Israeli intelligence had warned from the earliest days of the controversial arrangement that some of the money would eventually reach Hamas's military wing, just as had happened when Qatar had sent money through other channels in the past. In addition, there were disturbing indications that caused Israeli officials to suspect that alongside the official money route handled by the Qatari diplomat, there could have been a parallel track through which money from Qatar went directly to Hamas, without any safeguards.

In return for the Qatari cash, Hamas agreed to give Netanyahu what he most urgently needed ahead of the upcoming Israeli election: quiet, bought and paid for with the help of Qatar. When Lieberman blasted Netanyahu for "buying short-term quiet," this was exactly what he was alluding to. But he was one of the only voices in Israel's senior ranks who objected to this arrangement.

For Netanyahu, short-term quiet was one good reason to proceed with this deal; another was his wish to weaken the Palestinian Authority as a way of ensuring that the dream of a two-state solution remained just that. In March 2019, at a meeting of Likud lawmakers in the Knesset, Netanyahu laid out his view. "Whoever is against a Palestinian state," he said, "should be for [the Qatari money]."

Netanyahu explained that the Qatari handouts helped Hamas remain in control of Gaza—and that keeping the organization in power was essential in order to avoid renewed pressure on Israel to seek a two-state solution. The Palestinian split between the PA-controlled parts of the West Bank and the Hamas-controlled Gaza Strip, he said, was good for Israel at that point—and had to be maintained.

But still, giving cash to Hamas was a highly unpopular move. It was blasted not just by Lieberman and other right-wing leaders, like Naftali

Bennett, but also by Netanyahu's main challenger in the new election, set for April 2019: Benny Gantz, the former military chief of staff who had been visiting Nahal Oz the day of Daniel Tregerman's death, and who was now heading up a new centrist party. Gantz accused Netanyahu of emboldening the enemy and promised to promote new ways of bringing humanitarian aid to the civilian population of Gaza if he were to be elected—without funneling money to Hamas.

As Netanyahu faced growing criticism over the Qatari payments, his mouthpieces in the Israeli media—pundits who had been loyal supporters of his for years, some of whom were later appointed to different positions in his government—used his argument about the internal Palestinian split to defend his unpopular policy. "Mark my words: Netanyahu is keeping Hamas on its feet so that our entire country doesn't become like the Gaza border communities," one of them wrote in late 2018. "If Hamas falls, Abbas will take over Gaza, and then people on the left will push for negotiations and the creation of a Palestinian state. This is why Netanyahu isn't eliminating Hamas."

Just as the prime minister's support from his own countrymen was slipping, however, he found an unlikely partner on the other side of the border.

———

In late 2018, Yihyia Sinwar, who by then had established himself the undisputed leader of Hamas in Gaza, began sending messages to Netanyahu. Communicating through both Qatari and Egyptian interlocutors, Sinwar said that he was willing to discuss an even larger deal, going beyond the suitcases: a longer ceasefire in return for the removal of the Israeli blockade over Gaza.

This wasn't an offer for a peace process, and if Netanyahu were to accept it, there would be no Oslo-like signing ceremony at the White House. But Sinwar was offering Netanyahu stability and quiet, in return for which Netanyahu wouldn't have to redraw any borders or remove any Israeli settlements from the West Bank. The prime minister instructed his national security adviser, Meir Ben-Shabbat, a loyal confidant, to pursue the secret channel with the Hamas leader.

Once he realized that his messages had indeed reached Netanyahu, Sinwar gave a senior Egyptian official a handwritten note to pass to Ben-Shabbat. On it, inscribed in perfect Hebrew, was one sentence: "Take a calculated risk." The note soon made its way to Netanyahu's desk.

Sinwar was no moderate: In the late 1980s, he had received five life sentences from the Israeli judiciary for murdering Palestinians suspected of collaboration with Israel. The indictment included shocking details of the violence he had used to punish his victims, such as choking people to death with his bare hands. Once in prison, he assumed a leadership role among the thousands of Palestinians jailed by Israel. By the time of his release in 2011 as part of the Shalit deal, he had taught himself fluent Hebrew and even translated several books from that language into Arabic—mostly autobiographies written by famous Israeli generals and intelligence chiefs. He considered himself a student of Israeli society, determined to better understand the enemy in order to identify its weak spots.

But although he was an implacable foe of Israel, Sinwar was also a patient man. His main objective was to build up Hamas's military capabilities without losing its greatest achievement since it had been founded: governmental control of the Gaza Strip. The Qatari arrangement, even if it forced him to temporarily avoid attacking Israel, was allowing Sinwar to achieve both goals. But if Netanyahu took the bait that Sinwar was now dangling before him, the gains for Hamas would be even greater.

Thus, as the Qatari envoy had continued to ferry suitcases of cash over the Israel-Gaza border in late 2018 and early 2019, Sinwar saw an opportunity to extend what had proven to be a mutually beneficial relationship: Netanyahu needed quiet, and Hamas needed money. That had been the basis for the "smaller" Qatari deal—and it now formed the basis for the larger agreement that Sinwar was proposing.

Netanyahu was willing to consider Sinwar's proposition, and even made some policy changes in order to show he was serious about it. In 2019, his government allowed approximately five thousand Gazans to receive special permits and enter Israel on a daily basis in order to work in agriculture and construction. This was a small step, which made very little difference for the millions still living under Israel's ongoing blockade in Gaza, but it helped convince Hamas's leader that Netanyahu was willing to do business with him.

But before making any more gestures, Netanyahu first of all had to win the upcoming election. That task became much more complicated, however, when Israel's attorney general announced his intention to indict the prime minister for bribery, fraud, and breach of trust in three different court cases involving his allegedly corrupt ties with powerful business tycoons, two of whom also owned influential media outlets. Unlike Olmert, who had resigned under similar circumstances a decade earlier, Netanyahu decided to stay in power, and battle the indictment in court while continuing to serve as prime minister.

On election night, the exit polls showed Netanyahu securing another term in office. But the celebration at the Likud headquarters turned out to be premature: Lieberman, who had won only five seats (out of 120 in the entire Knesset), emerged as the kingmaker. Without his small party, Netanyahu was short of the needed majority to form a government. The former defense minister had finally gotten his revenge—but while he'd refused to join another Netanyahu-led government, he also refused to join Gantz, saying that the ideological gaps between their parties were too large. As a result, no one managed to form a government, and for the first time in Israeli history, the country was forced to hold a second election within one year.

The follow-up election, held in September, brought another deadlock. Netanyahu remained short of a governing majority without Lieberman, but his opponents had also failed to form one of their own. A third election in March 2020 also ended with an inconclusive result; but this time, because of the rapidly escalating COVID crisis, Gantz agreed to join Netanyahu in a short-lived emergency government, which eventually fell apart after less than a year. Another election, the fourth in less than two years, was set for early 2021.

During this period of internal instability in Israel, one thing remained steady: the Qatari payments to Gaza. Before the third election round, in early 2020, there was a brief escalation between Israel and Gaza, but Netanyahu sent the chief of Mossad to Qatar with an urgent request to increase the monthly payments to Hamas in order to maintain calm on the border. Qatar announced that it was planning to send $360 million to Gaza in the coming years.

The March 2021 election delivered, at long last, a verdict. Netanyahu had once again failed to reach a majority, and his opponents—Right, Left, and Center—decided to form a government without him, even at the cost of once unthinkable political collaborations. Bennett emerged as the top candidate to lead that government, the result of a deal with the centrist leader Yair Lapid, re-creating an alliance they had first formed a decade earlier. Their prospective coalition also included Gantz, Lieberman, the Labor Party, and the liberal leftist Meretz Party. On top of all that, a small party representing the Arab citizens of Israel was slated to join them.

The talks about the formation of this diverse coalition had been going on for weeks and significant progress had been made, to the point that political pundits began writing columns about the end of the twelve-year-long Netanyahu era. But just when it seemed like he was finally going down, Netanyahu received an unexpected assist—from Gaza.

It was Monday, May 10, and the Edri family was on the move. For several days now, there had been violent confrontations between the Israeli police and Palestinian residents of Jerusalem, as tensions in the holy city reached a boiling point. Usually, whenever violence broke out in Jerusalem, it meant that an escalation in Gaza was likely coming next. This time, however, there was no need to guess what Hamas might do; the organization had given Israel a public ultimatum, saying that it would launch a barrage of rockets at 6 P.M. if the police in Jerusalem didn't stop what Hamas had described as the harassment of the city's Muslim population.

Miri and I had already left Nahal Oz earlier that morning, sensing that the situation in Jerusalem was soon going to spill over to our region. We were now parents ourselves—Galia had been born a year earlier—and we had no desire to spend several days under fire, stuck in our safe room with a crying baby. I texted Avishay that we were going to Tel Aviv for a few days, and recommended that they do the same. But I needn't have bothered: by the time my message came through, he and Brit were already packing.

The tensions had started with an Israeli court order to evict several Palestinian families from their homes in the Sheikh Jarrah neighborhood in East Jerusalem. These homes had mostly been built on lands that belonged to Jewish families before the foundation of the State of Israel; they were handed over to Palestinian families after the 1948 war, as the neighborhood came under Jordanian control; and they were then handed to descendants of the land's Jewish owners after Israel conquered East Jerusalem in 1967. The Palestinian families remained in the homes, many as renters, for decades, but in the 1990s the properties were sold to a Far Right Jewish group working to "Judaize" Palestinian parts of Jerusalem by purchasing houses there, evicting the Palestinians living in them, and bringing in Jewish families instead.

The Palestinian families battled the eviction order, taking their case all the way to the Israeli Supreme Court. Their fight became the center of national and international attention—a symbol of the larger struggle over the fate of Jerusalem and of the region.

Adding fuel to the fire was Itamar Ben-Gvir, a Far Right Jewish politician who had become a close ally of Netanyahu's. Ben-Gvir had first made a name for himself during the wild demonstrations against Rabin in the 1990s. Later in his life, he was filmed harassing Palestinian civilians in the streets of Hebron, organized anti-LGBT demonstrations in which the participants of the Jerusalem pride parade were compared to beasts, and hung an image of Baruch Goldstein, the perpetrator of the 1994 Hebron massacre, in his living room. Israeli courts had found him guilty of supporting terrorism, due to his ties to Kach, a Far Right group labeled as a terror organization by the Israeli government. For years, the entire Israeli political system had boycotted Ben-Gvir, and he had tried and failed multiple times to enter the Knesset. But ahead of the 2021 election, Netanyahu pressured another Far Right leader, a close ally of his, to accept Ben-Gvir into his party, thus paving the way for the violent provocateur to become a lawmaker.

In the wake of the March 2021 election, while Netanyahu's political rivals were busy negotiating the outlines of their diverse new coalition government, Ben-Gvir repaid Netanyahu handsomely for his support. He arrived one morning in Sheikh Jarrah, set up a tent in the middle of the neighborhood, and announced that this was going to be his new office—from which he would oversee the eviction of the local Palestinian families. The Israeli police warned that his incendiary behavior threatened to ignite the city, and with it the entire country; for Ben-Gvir, this was all the more reason to stay put.

In the following days, these warnings came true. Riots quickly spread from Jerusalem to the West Bank and, most dangerously, to Arab cities and neighborhoods inside Israel. With every passing day, the violence escalated, yet the Gaza border remained quiet—until the publication of Hamas's ultimatum.

By the time Avishay and Brit were driving out of the kibbutz, in the early afternoon hours, the roads in the border region were jammed in both directions: civilian cars were heading out of the area, trying to leave before the rockets began falling, while military vehicles were heading the other way, preparing for battle.

When 6:00 P.M. arrived, nothing happened. A minute passed and, still, no rockets. Then, two minutes past the deadline, Hamas delivered on its promise, firing hundreds of rockets simultaneously toward different parts of Israel, including Jerusalem. Forced to choose between the pragmatic arrangement he had reached with Netanyahu and an opportunity to present himself to the Palestinian people and the wider Arab-Muslim world as a "defender of Jerusalem," Sinwar had chosen the latter. Israel and Hamas were now at war once again—and before a single bullet had been fired, one man had won: Netanyahu.

The massive Hamas attack caused Bennett to immediately suspend the coalition talks, and announce that, with a war now raging, this was not the time to bring in a new government. The vast ideological differences between the right-wing flank of the coalition-in-the-making (Lieberman and Bennett) and its left-wing elements (the Labor Party and Meretz) had already proven difficult to overcome. Now, with rockets landing all over the country and riots erupting in Arab cities from north to south, bridging these divides seemed impossible. Netanyahu had lost the election—yet somehow was on the verge of staying in power, thanks to Sinwar and Ben-Gvir.

The war lasted almost two weeks but seemed poised to last longer and to spread wider than previous rounds of fighting between Israel and

Hamas. In the last days of the conflict, as rockets were being launched into Israel from Lebanon and the region seemed on the verge of an all-out war, the new US administration, led by President Joe Biden, intervened and orchestrated a ceasefire.

Miri and I returned to Nahal Oz with Galia, and so did Brit and Avishay with Negev, Teva, and their third daughter Hesed. On our first evening back home, after the kids all fell asleep, we sat on our porch, sipping herbal tea and eating ice cream. "I've never been more pessimistic about the country," Miri said. Avishay seemed to agree. We all couldn't fathom the sudden collapse of the talks to create a better government.

But then, just as we were running out of hope, things suddenly shifted in the opposite direction. A few days after the end of the war, Bennett announced he was renewing the coalition talks. By mid-June, the thing that many Israelis had considered impossible finally happened: for the first time in a dozen years, Netanyahu was no longer Israel's prime minister.

Bennett had taken over, leading the most diverse governing coalition in Israeli history: Jews and Arabs, religious and secular, left-wing and right-wing, all united by one goal—replacing Netanyahu and his Far Right, ultrareligous allies so as to bring stability to Israel after two years of chaos. The idea that Israel would be forced to go into another election, the fifth in two and a half years, after just emerging out of a pandemic and then a war, pushed the politicians who had formed this coalition to put aside their ideological differences and focus on literally saving the country. We were only sorry that they hadn't done it two election rounds earlier.

Avishay felt a huge relief once the new government took over. He had grown up in a Likud-supporting family, and his parents had continued to vote for Netanyahu throughout the four election rounds. But Avishay himself had grown disillusioned with the man over the years, coming to see him as motivated by nothing but power, which Netanyahu seemed determined to hold on to at all costs. That desire had led Netanyahu to allow the Qatari cash payments to Hamas on the one hand and to legitimize the racist, violent Ben-Gvir on the other. The new government included some parties that Avishay disagreed with on policy issues, but it was led by "competent people," he said, which was what mattered most to him at that point. The majority of Israelis seemed to agree: public opinion polls showed the new coalition entering office with the strong backing of most of the country.

After the US-brokered ceasefire and the rise of the Bennett coalition government, the border region became quiet again, and life in Nahal Oz began to go back to normal. This time, unlike what the community had experienced in 2014, no families had left at the end of the fighting. Instead, as summer arrived, we were all swept up by a sense of great excitement, preparing for a groundbreaking event: the kibbutz's first-ever LGBT wedding.

In the years after the 2014 war, as part of Oshrit's efforts to bring in new families, Nahal Oz had become home to several LGBT couples—but hosting a same-sex wedding on the grounds of the kibbutz was something different. It was not just an act of acceptance but a statement by the kibbutz that all couples getting married within our community were equal, something that sadly was still not a consensus in Israel, where same-sex marriage is not legally recognized by the state, due to a veto by several religious parties. When Carine Rachamim, who had grown up in the community, announced her plans to marry her girlfriend Na'ama that summer, everyone realized that it was going to be a watershed moment.

Hundreds of guests arrived at the event, which took place on a Thursday evening on the big lawn next to the communal swimming pool. Even national media expressed interest in the event: Carine and Na'ama gave an interview to one of Israel's top-rated television channels, during which the host mentioned Carine's distinguished career in soccer; by that point, she had won several championships with her team and had played on the Israeli national women's team.

The party began at sunset and lasted long past midnight. Dani, Carine's father, was positively glowing as he walked around the compound with a proud smile on his face. More than a dozen years had passed since he first learned of his daughter's attraction to women; at first he had been worried about how people in the kibbutz would react, but now, seeing her surrounded by loving friends and neighbors, those fears seemed like a distant, irrelevant memory.

Another person who felt immensely proud to see Carine in her white dress was Dikla Arava, her former teacher and the first adult with whom

Dikla Arava (left) and her former student Carine Rachamim at the June 2021
wedding of Carine and Na'ama in kibbutz Nahal Oz.

Carine had felt comfortable enough to share her sexual identity. Now,
they were hugging and laughing on the dance floor, recalling how, when
Carine and Na'ama had only started dating, she told Dikla of the new girl
she was seeing, and added, "It's early, but I think she's the one."

The wedding photographer snapped a picture of their conversation—
Carine full of joy, and Dikla with a huge smile on her face, wrapping her
hands around her beloved former student.

———

Roughly a year later, Avishay was sitting in his car on the Israeli side of the
Erez crossing. This was the same spot where the Qatari envoy had once
carried cash into Gaza, and it was only about a twenty-minute drive from
Nahal Oz. Avishay wasn't planning to enter the Strip—that was forbidden
for all Israeli civilians—but he *was* waiting for someone to emerge from
it. Two people, actually: a woman and a child.

It was June 2022, a year since the rise of the Bennett government, and
except for one incident in August the previous year in which an armed
Palestinian had shot to death an Israeli soldier, the border had mostly

remained quiet. Still, Avishay was somewhat tense as he waited in the border crossing's parking lot.

Eventually, the woman—a grandmother in her late sixties—and the child, a young boy, showed up, and Avishay invited them into his car. They had arrived at the Palestinian side of the border crossing with a relative, crossed into Israel by foot after a lengthy examination by Israeli soldiers, and were now relying on Avishay for the next leg of their trip. He was there to drive them to Jerusalem, where the child, who suffered from kidney failure, was scheduled to receive dialysis treatment.

The woman and the child didn't speak any Hebrew, but with a few words in English and Arabic, Avishay was able to explain to them that he was going to take them to the hospital. Ahead of their arrival, he had cleaned the car and removed one of the baby seats in the back, to make more room. He wanted them to feel comfortable; as a father with young children of his own, he could only imagine how frightened and anguished they both must be.

This was the first time that Avishay had embarked on such a mission, which was organized by an Israeli organization called Road to Recovery. Founded thirty years earlier by an Israeli peace activist whose brother had been murdered by Hamas, the organization recruited Israelis who wanted to help sick Palestinians receive treatment in Israeli hospitals, which were better equipped and had more experts on hand than those in Gaza. The organization had dozens of volunteers in communities along the Gaza border; Avishay had first heard about it a few months earlier, and after signing up to join, he was given his first assignment: driving the boy and his grandmother to Jerusalem.

Most of the hour-plus trip passed in silence. There was so much that Avishay wanted to ask his passengers about life in Gaza and so much he wanted to share about Nahal Oz, but the language barrier made any meaningful conversation impossible. After dropping the woman and child off at the hospital, he drove to his workplace—also located in the Israeli capital—and then returned to pick them up at the end of the day, driving them back to the border crossing before returning to the kibbutz.

In the coming weeks, the Road to Recovery organizers asked Avishay again and again to drive more people to Jerusalem. He did not expect any gestures of gratitude from the Palestinians he took in his car, and for the most part, he received none. "I realized that from their point of view, I was part of the country that had placed them under this blockade to begin with," he explained. "I didn't think that because I gave them a ride to the hospital, they were suddenly going to become Zionists." But helping these people, especially children in need of expensive medical care that was unavailable in Gaza, wasn't about politics; it simply seemed to him like the right thing to do.

At least ten times in 2022 and early 2023, Avishay made the same trip, taking patients from the Erez Crossing to Jerusalem and then bringing them back to the border. One time, he drove a father from Gaza with a young boy who had been diagnosed with cancer. The father had worked in Israel in the past and spoke some Hebrew. He told Avishay how much he hated Hamas for "stealing all the money that came into Gaza" and using it for their military instead of helping the civilian population. Avishay nodded in agreement, but he couldn't be sure if the man was sharing his real views or if he was just trying to say what he thought the Israeli now driving him wanted to hear.

Politically, Avishay's views had always tended toward the center-right. His disappointment with Netanyahu and Likud did not mean he had turned into a pacifist; on the contrary, he wanted Israel to topple the Hamas regime and was angry at Netanyahu for spending twelve years in power and failing to do so. He hoped that Bennett's government would complete that task and help a more moderate Palestinian entity, perhaps the PA, to take over in Gaza.

But that hope was dashed in the summer of 2022, when the Bennett government disintegrated. The contradictions between its diverse ideological elements, on issues ranging from the relationship between religion and the state to the construction of West Bank settlements, had been surmountable when the coalition partners had been united by a desire to bring down Netanyahu. But once they were in power, their internal policy disagreements eventually brought about their own downfall.

For residents of the Gaza border area, the collapse of the governing coalition was bad news: its year in power had been incredibly quiet along the border. The Bennett government had raised the number of

Palestinians who received permits to come and work inside Israel but, at the same time, responded forcefully from the air whenever Hamas or another Palestinian faction had fired even a single rocket toward Israel. "They created some hope for ordinary people in Gaza with the work permits, and were tough on Hamas militarily," Avishay later explained. "I thought it was better than Netanyahu's approach."

But in November of that year, Israel held another election, and the parties that had ruled the country under the outgoing government lost five seats; Netanyahu and his Far Right, ultrareligious partners returned to power with a stable majority. For the first time since his criminal trial began three years earlier, he had decisively won an election.

On election night, Netanyahu announced that he intended to lead a "fully right-wing coalition," consisting of Likud, two ultrareligious parties, and a new party led by Ben-Gvir, which had won fourteen seats—an all-time high for the Israeli Far Right. This unprecedented result was an even greater shock than Netanyahu's return to power.

The next morning, for the first time since we'd moved to Nahal Oz, Miri and I spoke about the possibility of leaving—the kibbutz, and perhaps even the country—for good. We were scared of what this new, extremist government would bring and of the kind of future that our daughters would have in a country where a man like Ben-Gvir could hold power.

Across the border, from a small office in the center of Gaza City, Yihiya Sinwar was closely following the political turmoil in Israel—and patiently planning his next move. Netanyahu, he told his people, was returning to power a weaker man than he had been before, totally reliant on his Far Right coalition partners. The person who would truly set the tone in the new government, Sinwar estimated, would be Itamar Ben-Gvir. For Hamas, that wasn't necessarily a bad development.

In mid-December, a month after the Israeli election, a massive rally took place in Gaza, marking thirty-five years since the creation of Hamas. Tens of thousands of the organization's supporters attended. There were speeches by Hamas's political leaders, and a military parade showcasing the organization's fighting forces, but the man the crowd was truly waiting for—Sinwar—took the stage only an hour and a half into the event, to deafening cheers from the audience, which was waving Hamas's green-and-white flags.

Wearing a jacket and a buttoned shirt with no tie and reading from printed papers that he had brought with him to the stage, Sinwar delivered a rumbling speech in which he highlighted again his commitment to securing the release of all Palestinians held in Israeli prisons. He also said that the rise of the new Far Right government in Israel would lead to an "open confrontation" in 2023 and that Hamas was planning to "ignite" the West Bank.

But the most important part of the speech, which came midway through, was devoted to what Sinwar described as "the flood"—a massive attack against Israel, which he warned would come from inside Gaza itself. "We will come to you, God willing, in a roaring flood," he said, addressing the Israeli government. "We will come to you with endless rockets, we will come to you in a limitless flood of soldiers, we will come to you with millions of our people, like the returning tide."

Four years earlier, Sinwar had urged Netanyahu to "take a calculated risk" by ending the Israeli blockade on Gaza; Netanyahu had been willing to engage with him but soon lost his governing majority and hadn't recovered politically until 2023. Now, Sinwar no longer seemed interested in the formula that he and Netanyahu had once discussed through foreign interlocutors. His speech couldn't have been clearer: he was preparing for war.

Yet Netanyahu and the top echelons of the Israeli military, it seemed, simply weren't listening. Sinwar's explicit threats were ignored, or worse, treated as empty bravado. "Hamas is deterred and afraid of us," Netanyahu explained in a briefing to Likud members of the Israeli Knesset. "They have stopped firing rockets into our territory." He repeatedly claimed that since the end of the 2021 war, Hamas had not launched a single rocket toward Israel, "because they're scared." He repeated that message throughout 2023, saying mere weeks before the October 7 attack that his government had "turned the clock back ten years on Hamas."

To make things worse, Netanyahu's new coalition ally, Ben-Gvir, whom the Israeli police had accused two years prior of igniting religious tensions in Jerusalem ahead of the 2021 war, was now appointed by

Netanyahu to be the minister in charge of the police—and on his first week on the job, he visited the Temple Mount compound, known to Muslims around the world as Haram al-Sharif. This was the same holy site that, in the fall of 2000, Ariel Sharon had also visited, triggering the second intifada—an outpouring of violence that still loomed large in Israeli and Palestinian imaginations some two decades later.

For years, Ben-Gvir had called for a change to the delicate status quo that had long been maintained at the sensitive compound. Specifically, he wanted to make it possible for Jews to pray at the compound, not merely visit it. He did not repeat that message during his visit in early January 2023, but his presence there, now as a senior member of the government, sent a clear message: things were going to change.

Ben-Gvir's visit to the Temple Mount was denounced by the entire Arab world, including countries like Jordan, Egypt, and the United Arab Emirates, which enjoy close ties with Israel. Hamas was less restrained: it promised to begin another war if Ben-Gvir tried to change the existing arrangements at the site.

But even after this, Netanyahu and his allies remained unimpressed by Sinwar's promise of war, and anyway, they had a higher priority upon their return to power: weakening the Israeli judicial system. This was a decades-long dream of Israel's Far Right and ultrareligious parties, which considered the Israeli Supreme Court a liberalizing force in Israeli society, and for good reason: ever since the 1980s, the court had adopted a series of landmark decisions on women's rights, LGBT rights, and the rights of Israel's Arab minority—rulings that collectively had enshrined Israel's liberal values in its legal system and enraged the extremists now holding the keys to Netanyahu's new government.

Netanyahu himself, for most of his career, had opposed the Far Right's plans to weaken the courts, explaining that the judicial branch held a vital role in restraining the powers of the government, and that limiting its powers would hurt Israel's international standing as a liberal democracy. But now, with the criminal trial endangering his hold on power, Netanyahu was finally willing to let his allies have their way.

On the evening of January 4, 2023, Avishay was bathing his four kids—the three girls now had a baby brother named Tzor—when he received a push notification from a leading news website. "Watch: Justice Minister Yariv Levin Unveils His Judicial Reform Plan," said the headline. Avishay clicked on the link and left the phone on the floor—out of his eyesight, but close enough so he could hear every word of the broadcast. As Levin, a veteran Likud lawmaker and a sworn enemy of the judicial system, began speaking, Avishay felt the ground shaking underneath his feet.

Levin laid out a radical plan to reshape the balance of power between the different authorities in Israel, in a way that would leave almost no checks and balances on the power of the government. His plan included legislation that would allow the smallest Knesset majority to overcome Supreme Court rulings; a new judicial appointments process that would, in effect, allow the government to appoint whoever it wanted to any judicial position; and the cancellation of several judicial standards that had been used by Israeli courts for decades to tackle corruption and government overreach. Even some of the toughest critics of Israel's judicial system within the academic world—conservative scholars who did not like the court's liberal tendencies—found Levin's plan too extreme for their taste and warned that it could severely damage Israeli democracy.

After the girls went to bed, Avishay told Brit they would have to go out and demonstrate. It was something they'd never done before. Avishay had served as a combat officer in the military before pursuing a scientific career; Brit was working for the police. Demonstrations weren't their thing. But Levin's plan left them no choice. "I felt like this man was simply threatening my children's future," Avishay later explained.

That weekend, Miri and I watched the Edris load the kids into their car and drive toward Tel Aviv, where they joined the first protest against the Netanyahu government's judicial plan. More than five thousand people protested with them; a week later, they drove once again to Tel Aviv, and this time close to twenty thousand protesters took out to the streets. The next week, Miri also joined, bringing with her a homemade sign that read: "Don't destroy an entire country for one corrupt man." Like many Israelis, she suspected that the real motivation behind the judicial overhaul was to stop Netanyahu's court cases. I didn't join her—someone had to stay at home with Galia and Carmel—and I preferred it that way, since my work as a journalist was to write about these protests, not participate in them.

Soon, demonstrations began taking place not just in Tel Aviv, but all over the country. Hundreds of thousands of Israelis took to the streets every weekend, from the northern border with Lebanon to the southern port city of Eilat. Miri joined a group of residents from the Gaza border region who organized a weekly protest at the intersection of roads 232 and 34, right outside Sderot. Many drivers who passed by honked and gave them a thumbs-up, expressing their support. Others, however, stopped their cars next to the group in order to curse, threaten, and spit at the demonstrators. One truck driver yelled, "Fucking leftists, I hope Hamas kills your children."

***

By mid-March 2023, Israel was being torn apart from the inside. Netanyahu described the demonstrators as violent anarchists and promised to pursue the judicial legislation as planned, despite their objections. In response, an unprecedented trend began: officers in Israel's reserve forces started announcing that if the legislation were to pass in its current form, they would no longer show up for duty. This was the most severe step taken by the protest movement, and as more and more officers signed onto the ultimatum, alarm bells were ringing in the top ranks of the military.

In addition to conscripts, a large part of Israel's fighting force is made up of reservists—people who have completed their compulsory military service and gone on with their lives but could be called in whenever they're needed for military missions of various kinds. For Israelis who serve in combat roles or in top-secret intelligence units, it is totally normal to have a regular life—a career, a family, a never-ending list of household chores—and at the same time, to know that at any given moment, they could receive a phone call from their unit and have to leave everything behind for a week or two because their country needs them. Most reservists are asked to contribute approximately one month every year to the military; without them, Israel would not have enough manpower to provide basic security to its citizens. In certain parts of the military, the role of the reservists is especially significant—that's the case, for example, in the Israeli Air Force, where reserve pilots can be asked to carry out flight missions on a weekly basis.

As the battle over the judicial legislation kept escalating, thousands of reservists from all parts of the military joined the original group of protesting officers, announcing they would no longer show up for routine missions and trainings in protest of the government's actions.

Avishay, who did reserve duty almost every year, understood why some of his fellow reservists had decided to take this drastic step—but he wasn't ready to join them. He felt it was a bridge too far for him and feared that friends from his unit who didn't share his political convictions would be personally offended if he stopped coming to serve alongside them. Still, he continued to attend demonstrations every week, and his concerns about the direction of the country continued to mount.

On March 25, Israel's defense minister, Yoav Gallant, a member of Likud, organized an urgent press conference. In front of the cameras, he asked Netanyahu and Levin to put the judicial legislation on hold. Israel's enemies, he explained, were closely monitoring the country's internal crisis, and some of them would inevitably see it as an opportunity to launch an attack on Israel while its people were busy fighting one another. Now was the time to stop, he said, before it would be too late.

Netanyahu didn't immediately respond to Gallant's plea; he was out of the country, on a weekend trip to London, where his host, British prime minister Rishi Sunak, also expressed his concerns about the potential damage Levin's plan could cause to Israeli democracy. But the next day, Netanyahu returned to Israel, and shortly before 9:00 P.M. he detonated a political bomb by announcing that he had fired his defense minister.

"This is getting scary," I texted Avishay a short time after the news broke.

"Yes," he replied. "I'm worried that someone bad will sense an opportunity here. The Iranians, Hamas, or maybe Hezbollah."

In Tel Aviv, almost a quarter of a million people took to the streets, blocking highways and staying out until 2:00 A.M. Israel had never experienced such a demonstration before. The next morning, chastened by the out-pouring of public anger, Netanyahu walked back Gallant's firing and placed a temporary freeze on the legislation. The protesters celebrated a partial victory but knew that it wouldn't last for long. Ben-Gvir was now issuing his own threats, saying that if the legislation against the courts didn't get back on track soon, he would bring down the entire government by exiting the coalition and leaving Netanyahu without a governing majority.

Netanyahu agreed to enter negotiations with the largest opposition parties over the content of the legislation, but just like his past negotiations with the Palestinians over a two-state solution, nothing came of the talks with his Israeli opponents over the judicial legislation. He used the same evasion tactics that had frustrated every US administration that had worked with him since the 1990s, wasting time on procedural issues and refusing to offer any real substance in the negotiation room.

Eventually, on July 23, while hundreds of thousands of people protested outside the Knesset, a decisive vote was held on the first component of the judicial overhaul—a bill limiting the court's power to review certain governmental decisions. Specifically, the legislation revoked the court's ability to use a judicial tool known as "the reasonableness standard," which had been used over the decades to assess whether a decision by the government was "extremely unreasonable" and therefore should not be carried out. The biggest fear among the protesters was that once this standard had been canceled, Netanyahu would fire Israel's attorney general—who had been in charge of the prime minister's ongoing corruption trial—and appoint instead a loyal AG who would close his cases. As long as the reasonableness standard was in use, the court had a way to stop this nightmare scenario for Israeli democracy; once the court had been stripped of this ability, they feared Netanyahu would be free to realize it himself.

Inside the Knesset, Gallant desperately tried to convince Levin to stop the vote and allow a few more days for negotiation. He pleaded with Netanyahu to do something, for the sake of Israel's national security, repeating his warning that the country's enemies were watching. But the prime minister, seated right next to him, ignored his requests. The vote took place as planned; after it passed, Likud lawmakers took a celebratory selfie in the chamber.

That evening, I met Avishay while we were both walking our dogs in the neighborhood. He looked devastated. "We've taken our children onto a ship, and now it's out in the deep ocean, and the captain is drunk," he told me, in an attempt to explain his feelings. "I want to get my children off the ship. And I'm scared that it might be too late."

———————

From Gaza, Yihiya Sinwar was closely studying the turmoil in Israel as the divisive, anger-filled summer of 2023 gave way to autumn. Throughout the year, Hamas had increased the number of rockets it launched from the Strip, but it was the West Bank, not the coastal enclave, where the organization was actually inflicting real pain on Israelis. Between January and late September, terror cells in different Palestinian cities—Jenin, Nablus, Hebron, and others—carried out a series of deadly attacks that cost the lives of more than thirty Israelis. The attacks were a constant source of embarrassment for Netanyahu and Ben-Gvir, who had been elected based on a promise to deliver security and were now overseeing a sharp rise in the number of terror victims instead.

In an attempt to put an end to these attacks, the government steadily increased the amount of army battalions in the West Bank, eventually sending close to thirty of them to that region—many thousands of soldiers. Along the Gaza border, meanwhile, only four battalions were left—just several hundred soldiers, not enough to protect the region around Gaza if Sinwar made good on his promise to send a "flood" of fighters into Israel.

In August, one of Sinwar's deputies, Salah Arouri, boasted in a lengthy interview that Israel had been forced to send so many soldiers to the West Bank (he got the number almost right, saying "more than thirty battalions" had been stationed there) because of Hamas's successful attacks. The writing was on the wall—but Netanyahu and the heads of the military continued to insist that the 2021 war had deterred Hamas, and left it uninterested in another round of fighting with Israel. In fact, they insisted,

Hamas was attacking from the West Bank precisely *because* it didn't want a major escalation in Gaza.

But in September, in defiance of that logic, Hamas began organizing protests and riots along the Gaza-Israel border, demonstrations similar to the ones that had taken place in 2018. Thousands of people marched toward the border fence once again. The military used tear gas to disperse them. From our home in Nahal Oz, we heard the daily confrontations, and sensed that things were getting out of hand.

Netanyahu tried to solve the problem using the same tools as before— Qatari money and economic incentives. In briefings to the media, his national security adviser expressed optimism that soon Qatar would funnel more money into Gaza and things would settle down along the border. The top adviser predicted that Ben-Gvir would speak out against this move, but unlike Lieberman in 2018, wouldn't quit the government; after working so hard for so many years to gain real political power, there was no way the Far Right leader would give it up because of some cash payments to Gaza. In addition, this Netanyahu aide said, the government would maintain its aggressive posture in the West Bank, and that mattered more to Ben-Gvir's political base than anything happening along the Gaza border, where he had won very few votes and which, as an issue, did not galvanize right-wing voters elsewhere in Israel nearly as much as the expansion of West Bank settlements.

So Netanyahu went ahead with the plan, facing no significant objections to it inside his Far Right cabinet. The only politician who spoke out against it publicly was Lieberman, now a member of the opposition, who warned during a tour of the border communities in late September: "After a dozen days of violence along the Gaza border fence, the Netanyahu government has decided to bow down to terrorism. They agreed to approach the Qataris and ask them to increase their payments to Gaza. This is what surrender looks like."

On the last weekend of September, my colleague Amos Harel, the long-time defense analyst for *Haaretz*, warned in his column that "Israel seems to be convincing itself of a mistaken assumption that Hamas is committed to long-term quiet." I read his column and realized what he was trying to warn people of—but thought that events on the ground seemed to prove him wrong this time.

By Monday, October 2, quiet had returned along the border. In Israel, the holiday of Sukkot was still in full swing—and Simchat Torah, the next holiday on the Jewish calendar, was just days away. On the Palestinian side of the border, there was no demonstration that afternoon, as there regularly had been for the past several weeks. The weather was beautiful, sunny in the morning with some clouds expected in the afternoon—typical of early autumn in southern Israel. It was the sort of day that reminded me why we had chosen to live here in the first place.

Miri and I were both at home with the girls when Avishay sent me a text message with a pinned location. He and Brit had taken their kids to a large cotton field outside Nahal Oz, situated between the kibbutz and the border fence—only eight hundred feet from Gaza. I knew this cotton field; at this time of year it was like a calm white ocean. "Let's join them," I told Miri. "The girls will enjoy it."

We drove into the fields, and several minutes later we spotted Avishay's white SUV. Not far from it, the Edri family was seated on a blue picnic blanket. We got out and joined them, sharing snacks and watching our kids play together amid the blindingly white cotton bolls. The border fence stretched out in the middle distance, a gray line of metal against the blue sky. We could clearly see a Hamas position situated on the other side of the border, directly across from us: a small building with darkened windows, surrounded by sandbags.

"Do you think someone in there is watching us right now?" Miri asked.

"Probably," I replied.

Gray clouds were coming from the Mediterranean and passing above us, but luckily, they continued east, toward the Negev desert and Jordan beyond it, without releasing any raindrops. The girls had now moved away from the cotton and run to a nearby field that was soon to be planted with potato seeds but for now was empty. They began hopping from one furrow to the next, singing to themselves and urging me to look as they stumbled and laughed together.

Galia and Carmel in the fields of Nahal Oz, five days before the October 7 attack.

At 5:38 P.M., I snapped a picture, catching Galia and Carmel from the back, both of them staring into the horizon, surrounded by nothing but vast open fields. They wanted to keep standing there, to keep looking at the world—the land, the clouds, a far-off line of trees. But it was getting dark, and we needed to get home.

"Girls, it's time to go," I said. "We'll come back here again soon. I promise."

CHAPTER 12

"THE MOST IMPORTANT THING"

OCTOBER 7, 2023, AND AFTERMATH

Y ECHIEL CHLENOV WAS SUPPOSED TO leave Nahal Oz on the same bus that took us out of the kibbutz that night. The eighty-nine-year-old man, one of the founding members of the community, hadn't left his home once during any of the previous rounds of fighting with Hamas. He had stayed in the kibbutz during Operation Cast Lead in 2009 and during the subsequent wars of 2014 and 2021, seeing it as part of his mission to remain in Nahal Oz even under the most difficult conditions. "I don't have young kids anymore," he used to say, explaining this choice. "I like being in my house. No one will force me to leave it."

But when a group of Maglan commandos arrived at his home in the evening hours of October 7 and found Yechiel in the safe room with his girl-friend, eighty-four-year-old Tamar Livyatan, he knew that this time would be different. For the first time in the community's seventy-year history, mehablim had infiltrated the kibbutz. He and Tamar heard the gunfire all day long from inside the safe room. Since their neighborhood, unlike ours, hadn't experienced a communications blackout, they also were painfully aware of the kidnappings, the murders, the families who had been barri-caded inside their own safe rooms for hours, and the other horrors that had happened during the long, endless hours of terror.

The soldiers told Yechiel and Tamar that the entire community was being evacuated, and he nodded sadly, realizing that for the first time since he came to this place as a nineteen-year-old, he was going to have to abandon it—at least temporarily. Without arguing, he began to pack.

Tamar was a relative newcomer to Nahal Oz: she had moved in with Yechiel several years earlier, leaving behind a comfortable life in the Tel Aviv area in order to join the man she loved. She knew as well as he did that they had to go. But she had something else holding her back: the fate of her daughter and granddaughter.

Tamar and Yechiel were both widowers, each having lost their loved ones in the early 2000s. They had known each other since childhood, and miraculously, in their seventh decade of life, they met again and fell in love. After she moved in with him, Tamar's family began to regularly visit them at Nahal Oz. On that Saturday morning, her daughter Judith Raanan, fifty-nine, and granddaughter Natalie, seventeen, were both in the kibbutz: they had come for a weeklong visit that coincided with Tamar's eighty-fifth birthday.

They were both US citizens, living in Evanston, Illinois. Judith had grown up in Israel, but had lived elsewhere for years, and was almost a tourist in her former land during the visit. That Saturday morning, the two of them were sleeping in an apartment at the northwestern part of the community, a freestanding residence often used for housing the kibbutz's guests.

As soon as the barrage of mortars had begun, Tamar called the two women and instructed them to enter the guest apartment's safe room and stay there until further notice. Judith and Natalie went there immediately. The call very likely saved their lives: a short time later, a rocket from Gaza detonated inside the apartment's living room.

For several hours, the mother and daughter barricaded inside the safe room as they listened to gunfire raging right outside their apartment. Natalie was scared, and Judith did her best to calm her down. Then, chillingly, they heard the terrorists trying to break into the residence.

Judith took a deep breath and prepared her daughter for what she was about to see: armed men coming through the door of the safe room. She promised Natalie that no matter what, they were going to be OK. Not long after the promise had left Judith's lips, the terrorists entered the apartment and moments later, broke into the safe room.

Tamar's younger daughter Sarai lived in northern Israel and had spent much of that morning on the phone with her sister, hearing gut-wrenching reports about the terror gripping Nahal Oz. At around noon, she had received a message from Judith indicating that there was gunfire nearby. After that message, no one had heard anything from either Judith or Natalie.

By the time the soldiers appeared at her own safe room door, Tamar was increasingly worried. She asked the soldiers if they had seen her daughter and granddaughter, explaining that they were tourists visiting from the US. The soldiers said they had not, but tried to reassure her that once she and Yechiel joined the rest of the community at the tractor depot, they would surely find Judith and Natalie.

Tamar refused to take their word for it. Instead, she asked the soldiers to take her to the apartment where her loved ones had been staying, a six-minute walk from Yechiel's home. "We can't do that," one of the soldiers explained. "Our order is to bring you to the evacuation point. You can ask the senior commander over there about going to other places in the kibbutz."

Reluctantly, the elderly couple left the house and boarded one of the Humvees that were bringing people to the depot. When they arrived, dozens of people from the kibbutz had already assembled inside—including our family—but Tamar didn't have time to notice anyone else; she was laser-focused on finding Judith and Natalie. And contrary to what the soldier had told her, they weren't there.

Tamar approached the soldiers who were guarding the depot and asked for help, trying to invoke the chain of command. "My daughter and granddaughter aren't here," she pleaded. "Please take me to your commander."

The bus had arrived, and people were beginning to board. The soldiers tried to reason with Tamar, telling her that the evacuation process would last several hours—one busload at a time—and that if her family members weren't here for this round, they would surely come out next.

But Tamar refused to get on the bus. Once again, she asked to speak to someone higher in the chain of command. As one of the soldiers began to answer her, Yechiel cleared his throat and, in a deep voice, released six words into the air: "No daughter and granddaughter—no evacuation!"

For a second the soldiers just stood there, surprised by the strength and conviction in the old man's tone. Then, one of them told Tamar, "OK, come with me."

Leaving Yechiel behind at the evacuation point, Tamar and five soldiers walked in total darkness toward the front gate of the community. The soldiers formed a rough circle around her; after all, they were armed with M16s and wearing helmets, while she was in civilian clothes, wearing the same dress she had been wearing since the early morning, when she had first run to the safe room.

At the end of the five-minute journey, the group met an officer from the Givati Brigade, who was now in charge of the evacuation process. Tamar quickly explained the situation to him, and he asked how close the guest apartment was to the gate. Tamar estimated that it was another five-minute walk. "Take her there," he told the soldiers. "But be careful. There are still mehablim around."

They continued toward the apartment in total silence—Tamar walking in the middle of the road, the soldiers encircling her, guns in hand, anticipating an attack from any direction. The streetlamps had all been shattered, and the homes they passed along the way were all empty and dark. As they walked by the northernmost row of homes in the community, Tamar saw the smashed windows and bullet holes scarring the walls.

Finally, they got to the guest apartment. Its front door was wide open. Tamar immediately realized what had happened.

Two soldiers went in first to sweep the house for terrorists, using their phones as flashlights. Tamar took a deep breath and told herself, *Memorize everything. Every detail.* Then, when one of the soldiers shouted "clear," she followed them inside.

The floor was covered with broken glass; Judith and Natalie's personal belongings were strewn everywhere, a chaotic mess that would not have been made by Tamar's tidy daughter. Their computers and cell phones were still in the apartment, but Judith and Natalie were not.

Tamar stayed focused on the details: The windows were broken. So was a back door leading to a small garden behind the apartment. Tamar etched it all in her brain, but she was looking for something else—something that, gladly, she failed to find: bloodstains. There was no blood anywhere in the apartment.

"Thank you," she told the soldiers. "Take me back to your commander. We need to tell him that my daughter and granddaughter have been kidnapped."

The young fighters were shocked at how calm and cool she was at that moment. But Tamar knew that she had no choice. This was the only way she could help Judith and Natalie. She had to focus, had to think straight—not let her emotions distract her from her mission: to save her daughter and granddaughter, who were now, she was sure, across the Gaza border in the hands of Hamas.

When they returned to the tractor parking area, Yechiel was there waiting for her, a worried look on his face.

"They've been taken," she told him. "We need to call the American embassy."

Ten hours earlier, right where Tamar had been standing, terrorists were pointing their guns at Judith and Natalie inside of their breached safe room.

They yelled at Judith in Arabic and Hebrew and pointed their guns at her daughter, but Judith answered them in English. "We're Americans," she said. She kept repeating that phrase as the terrorists sifted through their personal belongings and continued yelling at her. And she kept insisting that she could only speak English, which wasn't true: Judith spoke perfect Hebrew and had also learned some Arabic in a language course at a community college. But she wanted these Hamas members to internalize the fact that she and her daughter were American citizens.

At this point, Judith had realized, there were only two options: the terrorists were either going to murder them or kidnap them. As American hostages, they could be valuable to Hamas; perhaps the organization could get something in return for releasing them. At the very least, if the Hamasniks knew that they were Americans, perhaps they'd hesitate to murder them—knowing that this could force the US to take tougher measures against the organization in reprisal. It was a desperate bet—but Judith had no other cards to play.

At last, one of the terrorists appeared to accept Judith's repeated claims of only being able to speak English and began addressing her in that language. He asked her what they were doing there, and she replied that they were tourists. He said that if they cooperated with his orders, they wouldn't be killed. Then he told them that they were going to be taken to another house nearby.

A few minutes later, with the terrorists' guns trained on them, Judith and Natalie were led out of the guest apartment and into the Idan family's home, just over a minute away by foot. On the kitchen floor, they saw Gali, the family's mother, hugging her children, all of them in tears. Tzachi, the father, was sitting next to her, silent; he seemed to be in a state of shock. Communicating with the family only in English so as to maintain her identity, Judith learned of the tragedy that had occurred in the home an hour earlier, when the terrorists had shot to death the family's oldest daughter, eighteen-year-old Ma'ayan.

There was another family in the house: Omri Miran and his wife Lishay, with two-year-old Roni and baby Alma, whom Lishay was holding in her hands. They all sat on the floor, surrounded by broken glass and empty shell casings. These children, too, were crying while their parents tried to calm them.

At approximately 1:30 P.M., the terrorists who were guarding these captives started getting nervous. The Israeli military had finally reached the kibbutz, which meant that the Hamas fighters had to get going. But for reasons that the hostages in the house couldn't quite understand, their captors didn't have the ability to take all of them at once into Gaza. So they decided to take just four people from the group: the two Israeli fathers, and the American mother and daughter.

The kidnappers marched these four hostages out of the house, leaving Gali, Lishay, and the children behind; they would wait on the floor in total silence until Israeli soldiers arrived to rescue them hours later. The four hostages, meanwhile, were led by foot toward the fence of the kibbutz, to a spot where the terrorists had breached it earlier that day in order to enter the compound.

An hour prior, another family had been taken along a small segment of this same route: Noam Elyakim, Dikla Arava, and Noam's two young daughters, fifteen-year old Dafna and eight year-old Ela. Noam was badly bleeding from an injury to his foot, leaving a red trail behind him on the asphalt not far from the Idan family's home. Dikla's seventeen-year-old son Tomer wasn't with them; the terrorists had murdered him after forcing him to knock on other families' safe room doors and beg them to open up lest he be killed. Omri and Lishay had agreed to do so, in a futile attempt to save Tomer's life. The terrorists had shot him anyway.

Now, they had led Noam, Dikla, and the girls by foot into a car, still within the kibbutz, and pushed them all inside. Noam's bleeding was getting worse, and it was clear he wouldn't be able to stay alive for much longer without medical care. But the terrorists seemed indifferent to his suffering. They tried to rush him, ignoring the fact that the injury had slowed him down.

Dikla and the girls were holding hands when the car had left the kibbutz through a hole in the perimeter fence and began to head toward Gaza. It was a nightmare—worse than anything they could have ever imagined—but at least they were together. And then, just as they had left the grounds of the kibbutz, Dikla was hit by a stray bullet.

The shot was likely fired by another Hamas team, its fighters misidentifying the car into which the hostages had just been forced. But whoever was responsible, the outcome was a swift and brutal fact: Dikla died on the spot. In the blink of an eye, Dafna and her little sister were left alone with the terrorists who had murdered the rest of their family. Noam and Dikla's bodies were left near the border, while Dafna and Ela were transferred into a second vehicle, surrounded by armed mehablim. Moments later, that car crossed the border fence—and the two sisters disappeared into Gaza.

With the Elyakim girls now inside Gaza, Hamas focused on bringing over the next group of hostages: Judith, Natalie, Omri, and Tzachi. Their hands were secured with zip ties, and each hostage was accompanied by two armed guards. The terrorists threatened to shoot anyone who didn't walk fast enough and fired at the ground to emphasize the point.

After exiting the kibbutz through a hole in the perimeter fence, the group trudged into the fields of Nahal Oz, heading west toward the border. There were no Israeli soldiers in their path, no one to challenge the mehablim as they led their hostages at gunpoint toward the fence. They passed through fields of wheat and potatoes; Judith had only flip-flops on her feet and dreaded the prospect of a snake or a scorpion lurking among the plants. Sounds of gunfire were coming from every direction—from the kibbutz, now behind them, and from the Strip, still ahead of them. Finally, when they got close to the border fence, the four hostages were pushed into a car, which took them into Gaza.

Once inside the Strip, the two American women were separated from Omri and Tzachi and taken into one of Gaza City's largest hospitals. They were led through the hallways by armed Hamas fighters, and saw several nurses cheering and clapping in celebration.

After being examined in the hospital, Judith and Natalie were taken to an apartment somewhere else in the city—where, exactly, they had no way of knowing. Five armed guards stayed with them inside the apartment; the mother and daughter were confined to a single bedroom. Judith thought of her mother Tamar—who, for all she knew, was still in Nahal Oz. Was she dead? Had she also been kidnapped? Judith had no way of knowing and was plagued by terrible thoughts.

As the sun rose over Gaza City on the morning of October 8, it became clear that the horror of the previous day was real and not an awful dream. Judith and Natalie were in the hands of Hamas, held captive in a small room, somewhere in Gaza City; they had no idea if anyone in their family knew what had happened to them or if the US government was aware of their kidnapping. Worst of all, they were completely at the mercy of the armed men who were guarding them, extremists who—as they had seen the day before—had very little mercy to spare.

But Judith, a deeply religious woman, believed she could find a way into their hearts, even after all the atrocities she had witnessed a day earlier. After her initial shock, she decided that she had to try to engage in conversation with them—at least as much as their grasp of English would allow. In one of her first successful attempts, she spoke to one of her captors about the fact that Jews, Christians, and Muslims were all the children of one historical father, Abraham, and asked the man how he could know that one of his great-great-great-grandfathers hadn't been Jewish.

Her tactic seemed to work: their captors, for the time being, were not being violent toward her or her daughter.

In an attempt to calm Natalie, Judith sang songs to her, including Louis Armstrong's "What a Wonderful World." Its idyllic lyrics contrasted starkly with the conditions in which they were being held: except for short walks to the bathroom across the hall, for which they needed to ask authorization from their guards, Judith and Natalie saw nothing outside the four walls of their single room. They were not allowed to shower, and the guards' constant supervision meant that the women had almost no privacy. Food was brought to them once or twice a day—usually bread, cheese, and vegetables. The terrorists also brought them paper, pencils, and markers so that they could draw. They were disconnected from the world—without their cell phones and computers, unable to watch or receive any news updates, unaware of what was happening around them.

But Judith and Natalie could tell that something big was going on beyond the walls of their makeshift prison. Israeli war planes and artillery units began bombarding Gaza, creating a cacophony of explosions and shockwaves that rocked the entire Strip, from Beit Hanoun in the north to Rafah in the south. Just days after the October 7 attack, this had already become the most destructive Israeli attack ever conducted against Gaza. Entire blocks of Gaza City were razed. As the building where they were staying shook from the blasts, Judith and Natalie realized a war was going on—and that Israel, despite the chaos they had experienced on October 7, was now mounting a concerted response to Hamas's attack.

This Israeli counterattack was far from a given, at least from the perspective of the hostages. Hamas had kidnapped more than two hundred people on that day, a mixture of Israeli soldiers, Israeli civilians—including dozens of women and children—and foreign nationals who worked in communities along the border, mostly agricultural workers from Thailand. Many of the hostages didn't know, in the first hours of their kidnapping, if there was even going to be an Israel to fight for their release; they thought that Hezbollah might have joined Hamas's surprise attack and attacked Israel from the north, and feared for their country's very existence. The terrorists exacerbated this fear by feeding the hostages disinformation, saying that Tel Aviv had been destroyed and Israel conquered by its enemies. Only when the bombs started falling on Gaza City did it become clear that Israel not only still existed but also was now taking the fight to Hamas.

Ironically, the same bombs that gave the hostages some hope—providing proof that someone was fighting for them—also exposed them to a new type of peril. Their captors, it seemed, were concerned about their survival in this respect: many of the hostages were moved around between different parts of Gaza in an attempt to avoid the most heavily bombed areas. But these evasive measures were purely pragmatic: Hamas now had a trove of valuable assets—Israelis and some foreign nationals as well—who could be traded for Palestinian prisoners, just like in the 2011 Shalit deal. The organization was determined to keep them alive in order to get the highest possible price—presuming that Israel would still agree to release some Palestinian prisoners in return for a dead hostage, but a significantly lower number than would be offered in exchange for a hostage who was still alive.

Judith continued to communicate in English with some of the Hamas guards. One of the men, after seeing her and Natalie's drawings, asked if they could draw a picture of him. But she feared that it was a test—a way to see if Judith and her daughter, if they were eventually released, would be able to produce a likeness of their captors for the Israeli or American authorities. "We only draw flowers and animals, never people," she replied. Another time, one of the captors asked, jokingly, what she would like to eat that day—as if there was going to be a change to their dull menu. She replied that she'd heard there were great fish restaurants in Gaza, and asked if he could take them to one. These exchanges, however, were rare. Many days passed in total silence, punctuated only by explosions.

In a different area of Gaza City, in an apartment building not far from the sea, Dafna and Ela were also sharing a bedroom. This one was inside the home of a Palestinian family: a father, a mother, and several children, most of them Ela's age or younger. At first, the two sisters were not allowed to interact with any of them; Hamas had armed men in the house watching the hostages' every move. One of these guards snapped a photo of Dafna, sitting on a mattress on the floor with tears in her eyes. Hamas soon published the image on social media, providing a heartbreaking yet invaluable sign of life for at least one of Noam's two daughters.

As the days passed, the Palestinian family in whose home they were being held slowly began to interact with Dafna and Ela, if only to a limited degree. They were allowed to eat dinner together, and Ela could play with the younger children. Still, the sisters were strictly separated from the family most of the time, and even when they were together, Dafna and Ela received no gestures of kindness or support from the parents; the atmosphere in the house remained tense even during dinner time, at least from Dafna's perspective. She felt, through their looks and body language, as if the family blamed her and her sister for the continued Israeli bombardments, which shook the house and woke up everyone in the middle of the night.

Even though just a young girl herself, Dafna acted like Ela's mother the entire time—making sure her little sister had had enough to eat at every meal, knowing that more food might not be available later, and reminding her to be nice to the other kids even if they stole a toy she was playing with, because there was no way to know what would happen if the parents of the family got mad at them.

At night, Ela would often cry and ask about their father, Dikla, and Tomer. Dafna wanted to cry, too, but she couldn't: she had to stay strong and calm. She was the grown-up now.

––––––––––

A hundred miles north of Gaza, on the morning of October 8, the first bus carrying the survivors of the attack on Nahal Oz arrived at a kibbutz called Mishmar Ha'emek. Located in the north of Israel not far from Haifa, the nation's third-largest city, this community of just over 1,200 people had volunteered to welcome the 400-plus members of our kibbutz after what had just been the most terrible day of our lives.

When the first busload of survivors disembarked shortly before 6:00 A.M., they looked to their hosts like living ghosts. Many were still wearing the same pajamas in which they had rushed to their safe rooms a day earlier; some arrived barefoot. The soldiers had given each family only a few minutes to pack one or two bags before leaving their homes under mortar fire; thus, the survivors arrived in Mishmar Ha'emek with very few clothes, no toys for the children, no diapers for the babies. It was up to the host community to take care of all those needs.

One of the unique things about Mishmar Ha'emek was the fact that upon reaching age sixteen, teenagers in the community would leave their parents' home and go to live on a boarding school–like campus on the western side of their kibbutz. When the families from Nahal Oz arrived that morning, the local teenagers were sent back home, and each refugee family received a small dorm room, approximately 180 square feet, to sleep in. While the families from Nahal Oz gathered at the communal dining hall to eat a warm breakfast, volunteers from Mishmar Ha'emek brought mattresses, clean sheets, blankets, pillows, and towels to each room, knowing that we hadn't brought any of those things with us.

As the Nahal Oz survivors settled into their rooms, the most urgent need was to take care of the children. From toddlers to teenagers, every child who got off one of the busses from Nahal Oz was traumatized by what they had just gone through. Many had lost loved ones, some right before their eyes, and many others had members of their family who were missing and who, for all they knew, might be dead—or held hostage in Gaza. More than a dozen psychologists and social workers who lived in nearby communities rushed to Mishmar Ha'emek to offer their help.

Within a day, dozens of volunteers had converted an office complex in the center of the kibbutz into a daycare and kindergarten for the evacuated children of Nahal Oz; a staff of teachers and caretakers was recruited, and on the morning of October 9, a day after our arrival, the children and their parents were invited to an "orientation day" at the new facility. There were toys and puzzles neatly organized on the shelves, large dollhouses on the floor, and hundreds of children's books—everything donated by private citizens from the host kibbutz and surrounding communities who wanted to help.

The Israeli government was supposedly responsible for helping people like us—survivors of a massive terror attack who had been evacuated from their homes. This, at least, was the expectation in the immediate aftermath of the attack—that the ship of state, to which all of us had paid taxes and contributed our sweat, even our blood, during our compulsory military service, would be there for us at our time of need. Israel was founded, after all, in order to offer protection to the Jewish people, a place of refuge and safety in an often hostile and unsafe world. Of course the government would spring into action and help its citizens impacted by the atrocities of October 7.

Yet after the buses—which had been organized by the military the night before—pulled away, the government was nowhere to be seen. Even in the lead-up to our arrival, it had done practically nothing to help resettle us: Mishmar Ha'emek had contacted our community manager directly in the morning hours of October 7, when the attack on our kibbutz had just began and offered to host us whenever we were able to get out of harm's way. The local kibbutz members took care of all our needs out of their own community budget, with no assurances that the government would ever pay them back, and they took it upon themselves to appeal to other communities in their region to donate clothes, toys, shoes, and anything else we needed.

The government's dysfunction in the aftermath of the attack was painfully clear to the entire country, not just to the survivors from the border region. More than thirty communities had been evacuated by the morning of October 8, including Sderot, the largest town along the border. In addition, tens of thousands of Israelis living along the country's northern border feared that after Hamas's surprise attack, Hezbollah would strike next from Lebanon, so they decided to leave their communities, too, without waiting for any official evacuation orders from the government. Literally overnight, Israel was flooded with internally displaced people, more than one hundred thousand in total. It was up to communities like Mishmar Ha'emek to help those refugees, and they were doing it with almost no assistance from state authorities.

Miri, Carmel, Galia, and I received a small room in one of the boarding school buildings. By now, we had said goodbye to my father, who had returned to my parents' home in Tel Aviv. Our family's story—the long hours we had spent in the safe room with our very young girls, the heroic journey my parents took to Nahal Oz in order to save us, and the moment my father knocked on our window and asked us to open our door—attracted endless media attention following his interview on the night of October 7; the next morning, after he'd returned to Tel Aviv, he literally couldn't walk down the street without being stopped by strangers who wanted to thank him for his actions and hear him retell the details of his story.

Brit and Avishay, who had survived the attack with their four children, were in the dorm building right next to us. Carine and Na'ama, with their one-year-old baby Yonatan, were two buildings to our east, as were Dani and Siobhan, Carine's parents. Arie "Daum" Dotan was also staying in that building; so were Oshrit Sabag, her husband Gidi, and their two children.

Nissan Dekalo, the deputy security chief who had battled the terrorists for twelve hours before almost passing out due to dehydration, was in our building, one floor above us, together with his wife Lee and their two teenage children. Nissan, one of the biggest heroes of October 7, was still at war—but now he was fighting his own demons, clearly suffering from early signs of PTSD. He had seen too many bodies, killed too many people, and had been on the verge of death too many times.

Beri Meirovitch, Nissan's partner in that long battle, had also made it out alive and was staying in a building right behind ours, with his wife Roni and their four kids. Eitan and Dganit, our "adoptive parents," were also there. It was during our first day in Mishmar Ha'emek that Eitan told me about how my father and the Maglan soldiers had rescued him and Dganit from their safe room.

Down the hall from our room, Sharon Fiorentino, our next-door neighbor in Nahal Oz, was sharing a room with her three daughters and her mother, who had come from her home in a community thirty minutes to the north of Mishmar Ha'emek to be with them. When we first arrived in Mishmar Ha'emek, there was still no information about the fate of Sharon's husband Ilan, the community's security chief; we all feared that he had died in the fighting, but the fact that his body hadn't been found gave us some sliver of hope that maybe he was still alive and being held hostage in Gaza.

Sharon asked me to speak with the French embassy in Israel; Ilan, it turned out, held French citizenship, due to the fact that one of his grandparents had been born there. I contacted the French ambassador and gave him all the necessary details, out of hope that if he had indeed been kidnapped, the French government would pull its strings to secure his release. We had no such expectation from our own government, after its massive failure on October 7 and deep dysfunction in the days after.

The same logic had guided Tamar Livyatan immediately after she had discovered that Judith and Natalie had been taken to Gaza. Her first reaction wasn't to inform anyone in the Israeli government. Rather, it was to report Judith and Natalie's kidnapping to the US embassy in Jerusalem.

Tamar and Yechiel had done this even before reaching Mishmar Ha'emek. During the three-hour bus journey from the Gaza border to our host community, they had called the US embassy to say that two American citizens had very likely been kidnapped and taken into Gaza. They also updated everyone in their extended family of the situation. In endless phone calls that began on the night of October 7 and continued into the next morning, the family reached a clear decision: the only way to secure Judith and Natalie's release was to involve President Biden and his senior staff; there could no longer be any faith in the Netanyahu government in Israel.

The family sprang into action. One member was given the responsibility for handling the media—doing interviews, providing images and videos to producers, urging reporters to seek information from their sources in the government, and generally making sure that Judith and Natalie remained in the headlines. Another family member was charged with contacting members of the US Congress and prominent figures in the American Jewish community. A third was made the official point of contact with the FBI, which began its own investigation into the kidnapping of Judith and Natalie within forty-eight hours of their disappearance. Tamar, from the little dorm room that she and Yechiel were now sharing in Mishmar Ha'emek, ran the entire global operation from her cell phone—feeling at times as if, at age eighty-five, she had suddenly been appointed CIA director.

Yechiel also helped as much as he could, but on some days, he was nearly incapacitated by grief. He felt an enormous sense of guilt for what had happened: Several years earlier, he'd invited Tamar to come and live with him in the kibbutz; she had agreed, and her family had begun to regularly visit her there. Now, in one of those visits, her daughter and granddaughter had been kidnapped by mehablim. On top of that, for the first time since he had arrived at Nahal Oz as a young soldier to participate in the very formation of the community, he was now displaced from his home—and had no way of knowing when, if ever, he'd be able to go back. When Tamar tried to cheer him up one day, his reply broke her heart: "My life's mission has ended in failure."

––––––––––––

In our small room in Mishmar Ha'emek, my family had struggles of our own. Galia and Carmel refused to let us shut the door before going to bed; they demanded that it be left cracked open, so as to let in light from the hallway. We didn't argue. How could we, after everything they'd gone through?

The four of us slept on mattresses on the floor, something that the girls, to our relief, seemed to enjoy; they could roll over to us in the morning and cuddle. For my wife and me, of course, this was less than ideal—but we realized that we were lucky to have a problem like this, given everything else that had happened.

The girls' trauma manifested in other ways, as well. When we first took Carmel and Galia to their new daycare, where they were reunited with the rest of their friends from Nahal Oz, they seemed to like the place—but they wouldn't let us leave. We couldn't argue with this, either: Miri's workplace in the city of Ashkleon was shut down because of the war—the city was now under constant bombardment from Hamas—and I had told *Haaretz* that I needed two weeks off to deal with our new situation, a request that my bosses immediately approved. So we stayed with the girls every morning until, several days after our arrival, they were finally willing to let go.

They kept asking about Pluto, our black Labrador, whom we had been forced to leave behind in Nahal Oz when we left on the night of October 7. For two long days, the soldiers who had remained in the kibbutz looked after Pluto, making sure to take him out twice a day, give him food, and refill his water reservoir in our bathtub. Originally, we had hoped to be able to get back to pick him up after a day or two, but given how far we had traveled and how badly the girls needed us (not to mention how dangerous the border region remained), that was beginning to seem absurdly optimistic.

Then, on October 9, my uncle Dudi, a dairy farmer who lived outside Jerusalem, traveled to Nahal Oz—still an active war zone at that point—to feed our community's cows. My father had helped him obtain a weapon from the military and an authorization to drive a truck full of straw for the animals into the kibbutz. After feeding the cows and releasing them into a paddock along with their calves so that the little ones would be able to nurse, he stopped by our home, let Pluto out of the house and into his car, and drove him out of Nahal Oz.

I met Dudi at a gas station halfway between Nahal Oz and his own community, and took Pluto from there to my parents' home in Tel Aviv. We would have loved to have him with us, but our dorm room in Mishmar Ha'emek was too small for four people, let alone all of us *and* a rambunctious ninety-pound lab.

The girls still missed their pet and couldn't understand why he hadn't come with us, but Miri and I were relieved to know that he was safe. It was just one more example of our luck, which we felt acutely as we settled into our new existence in Mishmar Ha'emek—knowing that so many others in the border region and beyond it had suffered through much worse.

———

The total number of Israeli deaths on October 7 was hard to determine in the chaotic days after the attack, but most estimates put it at approximately 1,200 civilians and soldiers, a figure that ended up being broadly accurate and was bolstered by the dozens of foreign workers, mostly from Thailand, who had been murdered by Hamas on that day.

More than three hundred of the victims had been murdered at a single site: the Nova music festival in Re'im forest, from which Bar and Lior, the couple my parents rescued, had managed to escape. There were approximately one hundred deaths recorded in Kibbutz Be'eri, a fifteen-minute drive from Nahal Oz, and sixty in Kfar Azza, the kibbutz right next to us. Many people in Nahal Oz had also lost friends and acquaintances in those neighboring communities. Miri was crushed to learn that a friend of hers from one of these communities had lost his daughter-in-law, while his son and three grandchildren had been kidnapped into Gaza; Carine Rachamim was grieving the murder of Nadav Goldstein, her former coach who had influenced her decision, at a young age, to pursue a professional sports career; a resident of Kfar Azza, Nadav was shot to death together with Yam, his twenty-year-old daughter, while his wife and three other children were taken hostage.

The numbers were impossible to comprehend, especially given the diminutive size of Israel—whose population is on par with the state of New Jersey's—and in particular the exponentially smaller size of these communities, some of which only had several hundred residents before the attacks. With every passing day, moreover, the death toll kept increasing, as people who had previously been considered missing were identified among the hundreds of bodies spread in and around the kibbutzim on the border.

On October 11, four days after the attack, we received the news we had all so hoped wouldn't come: Ilan Fiorentino, our neighbor and protector, was dead. His body had been found and identified; we weren't told exactly where or in what condition, but the identification was clear. Our hope died along with this terrible news. I could only think of Sharon: how strong she had been for all those hours in her safe room, with her three daughters; and how, later, she had battled back tears all that afternoon, after the soldiers had brought her to our house with the girls and they kept asking where their father was.

Ilan was a beloved figure in Nahal Oz, a native son of the kibbutz who had made dozens of friends throughout the border region and had won awards from the military for his excellent work as security chief. How, I asked myself, would our community ever recover from this disaster? And a voice in my head answered, *Maybe we won't.*

With Ilan now added to the list of confirmed deaths, the last of our missing had been accounted for, and we could finally sum up our tragedy in numbers. Nahal Oz had lost thirteen members on October 7—the darkest day in our community's history. In addition, two foreigners who lived on the kibbutz—Joshua Mollel, twenty-one, a student from Tanzania who came to Israel to study agriculture and dreamed of opening a small business upon returning home; and Somkuan Pansa-ard, a farm worker from Thailand who found a job in our banana plantation—were also murdered by the terrorists. For a small community of our size—approximately 450 residents—this meant that more than 3 percent of our entire population had been murdered or killed. If it wasn't for the brave members of the special police force, who had defended the kibbutz for hours alongside Nissan and Beri, the number probably would have been significantly higher. The same was true of the Maglan and Givati soldiers, who had arrived just as the small force in the armored vehicle was about to run out of water, gas, and bullets, saving them—and, by extension, many of us—from almost certain annihilation.

In addition to the fifteen people who had died, we now also knew that seven people had been kidnapped from the kibbutz: Dafna and Ela, Judith and Natalie, Omri and Tzachi, and Elma Avraham, a woman in her eighties who was last seen in a Hamas propaganda video being driven into Gaza on a motorcycle with a terrified look on her face. Their lives now hung in the balance, along with those of the 233 other Israelis and foreign nationals who were known to be held inside Gaza. Perversely, we had hoped that number would be one digit higher—that we would end up with fourteen members of our community dead and eight kidnapped. But that hope had been dashed when Ilan's body was recovered.

On Friday, October 13, the Nahal Oz community gathered for the second time in its seventy-year history to bury its security chief. Roi Rutberg had died defending the kibbutz in 1956; Ilan Fiorentino's life ended the same way in 2023. The burial could not take place in our kibbutz's cemetery because of the security situation on the border, where an active war was now raging. Instead, Ilan was buried in a small cemetery not far from Mishmar Ha'emek. His father, Yehuda, who had lived in Nahal Oz for decades, collapsed during the funeral. Sharon promised that when security conditions allowed it, they would bring Ilan back to his home, back to Nahal Oz.

The similarities between Roi and Ilan were impossible to miss: the two men had died protecting their kibbutz and their own families within it. But this time, there was no Moshe Dayan present at the funeral—in fact, no senior member of the government had even bothered to show up.

Ilan Fiorentino standing next to Nahal Oz's armored vehicle; his insistence on procuring it for the kibbutz helped save the community from a larger massacre on October 7.

One leader who did show up—not to the funeral, but to the shiva, the traditional Jewish mourning period during which the family of a dead person sits in their home for seven days and welcomes visitors who want to comfort them—was Naftali Bennett, the right-wing politician and former prime minister whose diverse coalition government had given hope to our community, for a brief moment, before losing power to Netanyahu's Far Right bloc the year before.

Bennett's year in power had been the quietest we had experienced along the Gaza border in more than two decades. After his government had fallen apart and was replaced by the Netanyahu and Ben-Gvir coalition, we all sensed that something bad was about to happen—but no one could have imagined just *how* bad it would be. Bennett, now a former prime minister with no official role, sat with Ilan's family for more than an hour, and apologized on behalf of the State of Israel for how our community had been abandoned by its government during and after the attack.

It was an absurd situation: a man who had been out of power for more than a year before the attack was offering his apology to us, the victims, while those who had actually been in power on that terrible day were nowhere to be seen.

A day after Bennett's appearance at Mishmar Ha'emek, I received a phone call from the US embassy in Jerusalem. On the line was a career diplomat who wanted to ask me a personal question and clarified that the entire call was off-the-record. "President Biden is coming to Israel in two days," she said, "and we're planning to bring a dozen Israelis who have been personally impacted by the October 7 attack to come and meet him." She wanted to know if my father and I could be part of the group.

I said yes on the spot. During my career as a journalist, I'd had the chance to interview prime ministers, presidents, senators, and other senior political leaders, although I'd never been invited before to such an intimate meeting with a president of the United States. But the excitement of meeting a world leader had played no role in my reply. This wasn't about the honor or the experience, about burnishing my journalistic credentials, or even about conducting journalism at all. We were being offered a rare chance to speak with the most powerful man in the world—and we had a message to deliver to him. After I'd gotten off the phone with the diplomat, I called my father to tell him what I'd signed us up for and what I was planning. He immediately agreed.

Biden landed in Israel on October 17, becoming the first US president ever to visit the country while it was at war. By the time he arrived, Israel had been bombarding targets all across Gaza for nine straight days and ground forces were gathering around the Strip, preparing for a large-scale invasion. On our country's northern border, Israel and Hezbollah were trading blows—both sides firing at each other across the fence but neither crossing into their rival's territory, at least not yet.

Biden's number-one goal during his visit was to decrease the likelihood of the Gaza conflict escalating into a wider, regional war—but the White House explained that he also hoped to make progress on a potential deal for the release of the Israeli and foreign hostages in Gaza. Hamas was demanding the release of thousands of prisoners from Israeli jails in return for the hostages, which Israel was sure to reject—but even this outlandish request showed that the organization was at least open to negotiation.

In the immediate aftermath of October 7, Hamas's leadership was in a state of euphoria. They had just successfully conducted the deadliest terror attack in the history of the Israeli-Palestinian conflict, an attack overshadowed perhaps only by al-Qaeda's actions on 9/11. For long hours on the day of the attack, while we barricaded in our safe rooms, there were public displays of celebration in the streets of Gaza City; sweets were handed out to citizens, and Israeli hostages—some of them alive, others dead—were paraded in the backs of pickup trucks to the cheers of hundreds of Hamas supporters.

But in a sense, Hamas's surprise attack had been *too* successful. Hamas was now holding more than a hundred Israeli women and children, including a young baby and several toddlers. Images of these kids from before their kidnappings, with their angelic faces and innocent smiles, were being spread all over the world and were being used extensively—and effectively—in Israeli propaganda efforts against Hamas. The Israeli government was publicly comparing the organization to ISIS, the universally renounced terror group that had murdered tens of thousands of innocent people in Syria, Iraq, and other countries, making itself famous with its exceptionally cruel methods of killing.

While the comparison had some flaws (e.g., if Hamas was as bad as ISIS, why did Netanyahu allow the Qatari government to give more than a billion dollars to the organization over the years?), the fact that it was now holding young children at gunpoint gave credence to such accusations. This helped Israel gain international support for its counterattack on Gaza, which began with a massive aerial assault and was soon followed by a large ground invasion—the kind Netanyahu had declined to pursue time after time in previous rounds of fighting. The images emerging out of Gaza as a result of this counterattack were horrifying and heartbreaking, as thousands of families were fleeing from their destroyed homes and bombs were flattening residential streets. But the outrage of Hamas's kidnapping of young children gave Israel a powerful argument in the battle for global legitimacy and public opinion.

Qatar, too, was facing immense pressure—mostly from the Biden administration, which wanted the country to help get the hostages out of Gaza. For years, the oil-rich kingdom had sponsored Hamas and hosted the organization's senior political leadership in its capital city, Doha; now, the stain of the October 7 attack and the cruel captivity of the young children was becoming a threat to its international reputation.

This was the backdrop to Biden's arrival in Israel and the context that he would try to exploit as he worked to negotiate with regional leaders over the release of the hostages and the containment of the war between Israel and Hamas. For those of us who had a personal stake in all this, Biden's visit could not have been more consequential. And now, at a time when my neighbors from Nahal Oz were still in the hands of Hamas, my father and I were going to have a chance to speak with the American leader directly.

An hour after he landed, Biden was already meeting Netanyahu and other senior members of the government at a hotel in downtown Tel Aviv. While that was happening, my father and I met at my parents' home, where I had traveled in a rental car from Mishmar Ha'emek. Together, we drove to the same downtown hotel, where we underwent a security check ahead of our meeting with the president. With us were ten other Israelis who were also scheduled to meet Biden that afternoon. After passing through security, we were told to wait and informed that it would take several hours until the president would be able to meet us.

As we settled into chairs in a small dining room on the hotel's ground floor, I recognized most of the faces in the group of people with us—the Israelis who, like us, had been chosen by the US embassy to meet the president. The group was mostly made up of people who had become famous for incredible acts of heroism they had displayed on that Saturday. As my eyes worked across the room, I felt humbled to be in their company.

There was Inbal Lieberman, a twenty-six-year-old woman who a year earlier had been appointed to be the security chief of kibbutz Nir-Am, several miles north of Nahal Oz. On the morning of October 7, when she heard the first indications of a cross-border attack on other communities, Inbal realized that her kibbutz was next—and she took quick, decisive action to defend it. She organized the local security team along the community's perimeter fence, and when the terrorists arrived, she led a well-coordinated battle to repel them with the aid of a small military force that arrived from a nearby base. Several members of her team were injured but not a single Israeli in kibbutz Nir-Am was killed that day.

I also spotted Rachel Edri, a woman in her sixties from the town of Ofakim. She had woken up on the morning of October 7 to find five Hamasniks in her living room. They held her and her husband at gunpoint for hours. At some point, Rachel saw Israeli police officers outside her window, getting into firing positions. In order to distract her captors, she started offering them some food—homemade cookies that she'd made the day before, she explained, from a secret family recipe. The terrorists took the bait, turning their back on the large living room window and entering her kitchen to taste the cookies. Seconds later, the policemen fired through the windows, killing several of the Hamas fighters; then the officers quickly broke into the apartment, rescuing the Israeli couple and killing their remaining captors. In the aftermath of the ordeal, as Rachel's story spread across Israel, she was asked again and again for the cookie recipe—but she demurred, insisting that it truly was a family secret.

Elsewhere in the group waiting to meet Biden was Mohammad Darawshe, a leading Arab-Israeli peace activist. I had known him for years through my journalism work. I hadn't known that he had any noteworthy connection to October 7. When I approached him, however, he told me the heroic story of his nephew Awad, who had been working at the Nova party as a paramedic and was murdered by Hamas while trying to save other's lives. Mohammad added that Awad was one of more than twenty Israeli-Arab citizens murdered by Hamas on that day; many had faced especially cruel treatment.

After waiting for almost six hours, we were finally called into a large ballroom and told that President Biden would arrive any minute. Each of us would have sixty seconds to speak with him. I didn't want to take away precious time from others in the group, so I had rehearsed one short line; my father had done the same.

When Biden entered the room, it quickly became clear that he was going to give this group of guests much more attention than his staff had prepared us for. He hugged people, listened to their stories, asked questions, and shared his own experience of grief and loss as a father who had lost two of his children. Not a single eye remained dry as he moved around the room.

When the president got to my father, the chargé d'affaires of the US embassy in Jerusalem, Stephanie Hallett, introduced him to the president as Noam Tibon, a retired general. But my dad told Biden that he was "just a grandfather," to which the president replied, "Well, so am I."

My father thanked the president for supporting Israel; then, as Biden nodded and shook his hand, he segued to the message that he had been preparing for the past few days. It was a request: "Get our hostages back," my father urged Biden. "That's the most important thing. Push all the sides involved to make a deal, even if they don't like it."

His choice of words was carefully calculated. Netanyahu, shocked by the disaster of October 7 and desperate to keep his coalition intact in its aftermath, was showing no urgency to make a deal with Hamas in order to release the hostages. A dozen years earlier, as part of the Shalit deal, our prime minister had agreed to release more than one thousand prisoners for one soldier, but now—with dozens of women and children in the hands of Hamas—he was slow-walking the negotiations. Netanyahu, it seemed, was trapped in the very same Faustian pact that he had struck in order to reclaim power: he was being threatened by Ben-Gvir, his Far Right coalition partner, who was promising to bring down the government if Netanyahu prioritized a deal to return the hostages over a continuation of the fighting. My father urged Biden to push as hard as he could for a deal; people's lives, including those of my neighbors, were at stake.

When it was my turn to speak, I offered a similar message. "Mr. President," I said, "your friend John McCain survived five years in the Vietnamese prison. But he was a soldier. The young girls kidnapped from my kibbutz won't survive even five weeks. Please do everything you can to get them out of there."

President Biden, his eyes still watery after hearing the heartbreaking stories of other members of our group, looked me in the eye and replied with two short sentences: "I'm working on it. I'm really, really working on it."

On Friday, October 19, two days after President Biden's visit, Judith and Natalie Raanan noticed that something unusual was happening. There was a commotion outside of their room: one of the guards received a phone call, and soon, the two women were told that they were about to be released. Judith didn't believe it at first. But soon, they were taken out of the house and placed in a car that began heading south.

The same day, Tamar and Yechiel received a phone call from Adi, a colonel in the Israeli military who had been assigned to update the family on any news related to Judith and Natalie. Up to that point, most of these conversations had been short and uninformative; the officer mostly expressed her sympathy and asked if there was anything the family needed. Now, however, she had real news to deliver: Judith and Natalie were going to be released that evening.

The women's liberation wasn't part of a broader prisoner swap but rather an attempt by Qatar to prove to the Biden administration that it had enough influence with Hamas to actually get hostages out of Gaza. The kingdom had pressured Hamas to release one or two hostages without accepting anything in return from Israel, just so the US would become convinced that Qatar, and not another potential mediator like Egypt or Turkey, was the country best situated to bring about a broader hostage release deal. Qatar badly needed Hamas to give *something*, anything, in order to show the White House that the kingdom could pull the necessary strings for a major hostage deal with Israel.

Hamas, swayed by its Qatari benefactors, chose to release Judith and Natalie, the American mother and daughter who by then had become world-famous due to the efforts of Tamar and her family to publicize their kidnapping. Releasing them early also decreased the likelihood that they would somehow die in captivity—a development that would force the US government to put even more pressure on Hamas and its sponsor, Qatar, and therefore was best avoided from Hamas's perspective.

Tamar wasn't totally surprised by Adi's phone call; their family had been in constant touch with senior officials in the White House and the State Department and had even attended a Zoom call with the president himself at one point along with the families of other hostages. A day before Biden's arrival, my newspaper, *Haaretz*, had published a lengthy interview with Tamar and other members of the family about their efforts to secure the release of Judith and Natalie. Sarai, Judith's young sister, was quoted as saying, "The president of the United States found the time to be humane and to personally contact the family. We have three FBI representatives who are in constant contact with us; we have a liaison from the US Embassy in constant contact. They're there for us. We feel embraced, that there's compassion, that they care. In Israel, except for one amazing officer who's in contact with us, no one has reached out. What happened here is such a tremendous failure that I feel like they're afraid to come forward."

After the US president left Israel, the family had picked up hints of optimism in their conversations with administration officials. But Tamar had refused to believe any of it; there was no room for hope, she had decided, until her daughter and granddaughter were released.

That Friday evening, thirteen days after Judith and Natalie had been kidnapped from Nahal Oz, two convoys made their way south along the Israel-Gaza border. Both were heading toward the southeastern corner of the Gaza Strip, where the Israel-Gaza border intersects with the northern border of Egypt. But one group of vehicles was in Israel, and one was in Gaza.

The convoy driving inside Israel was headed down Route 232 and was composed mostly of military vehicles; the other, driving inside Gaza along the Strip's main highway, Salah al-Deen Road, was made up mostly of white vans, some belonging to Hamas, others to the International Red Cross. The first convoy was going to wait for the two hostages on the Israeli side of the border; the second convoy was ferrying Judith and Natalie to the opposite point on the Palestinian side.

The event was broadcast on live television and viewed by millions of Israelis. For the first time since October 7, two of the hostages were being returned alive. The country was overflowing with excitement as the Red Cross handed the mother and daughter over to Egyptian military officers, who in turn would transfer them into the custody of the IDF.

Tamar was waiting for her daughter and granddaughter at an Israeli Air Force base not far from the border, where they were driven immediately after the Egyptian military had passed them over to Israel. When Judith and Natalie arrived, Tamar enfolded them in a long embrace, shedding tears of joy. Then, suddenly, she was approached by an American embassy staffer with a cell phone in hand, who told her, "President Biden wants to speak to Judith."

Judith took the phone. Tamar couldn't hear much of what the American president was saying, but later she recalled "how warm his voice sounded" and how Judith ended the call by reminding him that there were still many other hostages inside Gaza. The president had promised to work just as hard to get them out of there—and Judith said she was planning on helping him.

Earlier that evening, when Judith and Natalie were already back on Israeli soil and on their way to the air force base to meet with Tamar, Netanyahu's office had also tried to place a call to the family—but Tamar had refused to accept it. "He wasn't there for us when we needed him," she explained. "And then he wanted to celebrate an achievement that he had nothing to do with. I said, no way."

Dafna and Ela heard explosions all around them, all day long. Israel was bombing Gaza City from the air, shelling it from the ground, and sending thousands of troops, reinforced by tanks and armored personnel carriers, into its largest neighborhoods.

The conflict was quickly turning into a war unlike any that Gaza, or Israel, had ever seen. For one thing, it hadn't started like any of the previous Israel-Hamas wars; October 7 was an unprecedented event in the history of the long Israeli-Palestinian struggle, the bloodiest terror attack in Israel's history. But what followed was also very different from any other round of fighting.

Within a handful of weeks, Israel had turned large parts of Gaza City into an expanse of scorched earth. Buildings that hadn't been destroyed from the air were blown up by Israel's ground forces—or, to save time and money, simply set on fire by the soldiers. The city's roads, from the largest highways to the smallest streets, were overrun by Israeli tanks, rendering some of them unusable for normal vehicles. Dozens of public buildings—including schools—were raided by the military. Often, the soldiers found weapons hidden inside or tunnels dug underneath; still, this meant that the city would have no public infrastructure for its residents to return to in the future.

Israel's ground offensive started in the northern part of the Strip, in and around Gaza City; the million-plus people living there were ordered by Israeli forces to leave their homes and move south toward Khan Younis and Rafah, the enclave's other two large cities. Hundreds of thousands of displaced people began making their way on foot, walking in two seemingly endless lines through specific corridors—so-called humanitarian passages—established by the Israeli military. Most refugees brought only what they could carry: blankets, clothes, medicine, food. Those who could afford it used carts harnessed to donkeys.

The pictures emerging from the Strip reminded many Palestinians and Israelis, as well as foreign observers of the conflict, of the Nakba—the defining Palestinian catastrophe of 1948. Back then, hundreds of thousands of Palestinians had left their homes, some forcefully evicted by Israeli troops, others fleeing out of fear for their lives. Many of them eventually found refuge in Gaza. Now, however, Gaza itself was the scene of a massive exodus, as entire families left their homes in the northern part of the coastal enclave and moved south. Hamas, which was still in control of Khan Younis and Rafah, erected several huge tent cities in the Strip's southern area, which would soon be inhabited by more than a million people.

By early November, the UN was starting to warn that a humanitarian catastrophe was unfolding in the Strip: food and water shortages, lack of fuel, overcrowded hospitals, and a real threat of massive disease outbreak among the refugee population. Not enough aid was making its way into the enclave, in part because Israel had shut down both the Erez crossing on the Strip's northern border and the Kerem Shalom crossing in the south, turning the Rafah crossing with Egypt into the Strip's only lifeline.

Hamas, for its part, was still on its feet, firing dozens of rockets at Israel on a daily basis and killing dozens of Israeli soldiers in combat. But the organization was clearly outmatched by Israel's war machine, which had inexorably pushed through Gaza City, neighborhood by neighborhood, destroying almost everything in its path. The destruction was unprecedented, and so was the rising death toll, which had surpassed ten thousand by mid-November.

During the early stages of the war, Dafna and Ela remained in the hands of the family that had been charged with "hosting" them since the day they had been kidnapped. But after spending several weeks—Dafna couldn't tell how many—in that family's apartment, they were moved in the middle of the night to another home and eventually taken to a school building that housed hundreds of families fleeing the Israeli bombardments. Dafna and Ela were forced to cover their faces with headscarves and stay away from other people in order to hide their identities. Meanwhile, the bombings continued.

Dafna was afraid that they wouldn't survive. She couldn't tell how long she and Ela had been held in Gaza or whether anyone in the world was even trying to get them out of there. She could barely communicate with her kidnappers and was afraid to ask too many questions. The only thing she cared about was keeping her sister safe. Nothing else mattered.

On November 24, a month and a half into the fighting, with Israeli tanks now in the heart of Gaza City, Hamas and Israel finally reached a prisoner swap agreement, orchestrated by the Biden administration with the help of Egypt and Qatar. A temporary, weeklong ceasefire was announced, and Hamas agreed to release approximately one hundred Israeli hostages, all of them women and children. In return, Israel would release three Palestinian prisoners for every hostage—a relatively small ratio compared to previous prisoner exchanges. Still, Hamas continued to hold on to more than 130 other hostages—a handful of civilian women, several female soldiers, and dozens of men of various ages, both soldiers and citizens, in addition to two children, whom the organization claimed had died in captivity. The organization declared that these hostages would only be released in a separate deal and for a much higher price.

In the days before the signing of the agreement, the Israeli military had closed in on the school where Dafna and Ela were being held. Hamas decided to move them once again. This time, their captors took them underground—into the tunnels.

As bad as their conditions had been aboveground, it was only when they reached their new destination, deep below Gaza City, that Dafna and Ela realized how much relatively worse the past weeks could have been— and had been, for the hostages who had been brought underground right from the start. The sisters were kept in a locked cell with several other female hostages, in total darkness for long stretches of the day and with no natural light. The ceiling above them was too low for some of the women to fully stand up—Dafna, relatively tall for her age, could barely stand up straight. They received very little food: a bit of rice, a small slice of pita bread, and some water was all they got most days. Hamas said in a statement that the lack of humanitarian aid in Gaza, after more than a month of fighting, was now also impacting the hostages.

It soon became clear, too, that the other female hostages, a mixture of young civilians taken from nearby kibbutzim and the Nova party and of IDF soldiers captured at the Nahal Oz base, had gone through unspeakable horrors. Some of them shared the details with Dafna—describing the sexual violence they had endured at the hands of their captors. Alone together in the darkness, bonds soon developed between them: although Dafna remained laser-focused on protecting her little sister, among these slightly older hostages she herself was once again a child, too. She was treated with empathy and love by the women sharing a jail cell with her— the first real kindness that anyone other than her little sister had shown her for weeks.

Then, on Sunday, November 26, two days after the prisoner swap had been announced, one of the Hamasniks told Dafna that she and Ela were going to be released. At first Dafna refused to believe it, thinking it was a cruel attempt to give her a false sense of hope. But when she realized that it was actually going to happen—that they were preparing to move her and her sister out of the cell—she mostly felt terrible for the other hostages, who were all going to be left behind in the dark tunnel. Before being taken away, she asked if they wanted her to pass any messages to their families in Israel. She didn't have a pen or paper to write anything down, but she memorized every word that they told her and promised that she would deliver the messages to their families once she made it back to Israel. Then she and Ela were led out of the tunnel.

For the first time in days, the sisters saw natural light and breathed fresh air. They were surrounded by destruction and being shepherded through the wasteland by a group of heavily armed men—all of which would have been terrifying for a teenager and an elementary school girl under other circumstances. But at that moment, Dafna felt hope.

Soon, the sisters were loaded onto a white van, along with several other Israeli hostages. Among them was Elma Avraham, Nahal Oz's oldest hostage. She was the woman who had been filmed riding on the back of the motorcycle on October 7, looking terrified; now, she was barely breathing, and her captors had been forced to load her into the vehicle on a stretcher.

As the van drove toward the Gaza-Egypt border crossing, a camera crew for the Qatari-owned Al Jazeera network caught a glimpse of Dafna and Ela through one of the windows. A minute later, the image was broadcast on Israeli television.

Watching with other friends from the kibbutz in the dining hall of Mishmar Ha'emek, I jumped with joy at the sight of the girls' familiar faces. I couldn't imagine what the two of them had been through, but they were alive and on their way home, and in that moment, this was the only thing that mattered.

In the weeks leading up to the release, I had given several interviews to US news networks and often spoke about Dafna and Ela and how important it was to get them out of Gaza. What I didn't disclose in any of the interviews, however, was that Dafna had been Carmel's babysitter for months leading up to October 7 and had watched over her at our home just two weeks before the attack. I feared that if this information became known, Dafna's captors would start interrogating her about her ties to the family of the Israeli general who had fought against them at Nahal Oz—something I didn't want her to have to endure. Now, as she was finally making her way out of Gaza, all of that restraint came crumbling down, and I was overcome with emotion.

From the border crossing where they were released, the girls were loaded into a different van, this one with Israeli license plates, and driven directly to an Israeli Air Force base. Their mother, who had divorced their late father Noam years earlier and did not live in Nahal Oz, was waiting for them. She gave her daughters a long hug, but Dafna said that even then, she wasn't totally convinced that they were safe. "I was afraid that maybe it was just a temporary thing," she admitted later. "That they'd allowed us to meet our mother, but any minute now, a Hamasnik would arrive and take us back into the tunnel."

Elma, meanwhile, was flown in a helicopter directly to the closest Israeli hospital, and rushed into surgery. At the time of her release, her body temperature had been 82 degrees Fahrenheit. The doctors spent days fighting for her life. Had she been released just twenty-four hours later, she wouldn't have made it—but two weeks after her return to Israel, Elma's family was informed that she was going to be OK.

For our community, the return of the five women and girls kidnapped from Nahal Oz—Judith, Natalie, Dafna, Ela, and Elma—was the first cause for celebration since the tragedy that we had experienced on October 7. But the joy was incomplete. Omri and Tzachi remained behind, somewhere in the tunnels of Gaza; so did the female soldiers abducted from the base next to our kibbutz.

As of this writing, July 1, 2024, they are still in the hands of Hamas.

EPILOGUE

IT's A SUNNY MORNING IN the last, mild days of the Israeli winter. A cool wind is blowing from the sea as I walk along the promenade of Bat Yam, a city located just south of Tel Aviv on the shore of the Mediterranean. I'm headed toward two white residential towers, both approximately twenty stories high, rising into the sky right in front of a beautiful strip of golden sand. A small café at the entrance to the tower complex is empty but open; I walk in and buy myself a cup of coffee before continuing toward the elevators.

In late December 2023, seventeen older members of Nahal Oz—most of them in their eighties—moved here, to the Mediterranean Towers retirement community. The living conditions in Mishmar Ha'emek—the small rooms, the noise from the families with young children, the absence of any kitchen space to prepare and store food—had become too difficult for them. They had to go somewhere else, even if that meant decoupling from the rest of us—their friends, neighbors, and often also family members. We could only hope that the separation would be temporary.

Some of these elderly refugees had wanted to return to Nahal Oz. During previous wars, they had never evacuated from the kibbutz. Staying in their homes, even under fire, was part of their identity; their sense of self was tied up in their strong sense of connection to this particular stretch of earth. Among this group of community members who wished to return were several of the kibbutz's original founders who had arrived in 1953 as well as members who had arrived later in the 1950s, back when Nahal Oz was still a remote, isolated spot on the map, without even a proper road connecting it to the rest of Israel. Leaving the place that they had invested so many years of their lives building, strengthening, and expanding was a heartbreaking experience for them, and they hoped to be the first to go back home after the October 7 attack.

But the reality on the ground made returning impossible. The kibbutz was still being heavily bombarded by Hamas, while Israeli tanks and artillery units had taken up positions in the surrounding fields and were attacking targets in Gaza nonstop, day and night; the noise was unbearable, in part because, after the trauma of October 7, it brought back too many bad memories. What's more, none of the homes in the kibbutz had been repaired after the damage they'd sustained that Saturday: the bullet holes, the broken glass, and the destruction from hand grenades and mortars. The local clinic, which even during previous times of war had always continued to provide services to the elderly residents who'd insisted on remaining in the kibbutz, was now shut down. On most days, only a handful of people could be found inside Nahal Oz, working in the cowshed or manning tractors in the fields. At night, the kibbutz was a ghost town, silent and empty.

Sadly, the community's older members had realized that they needed to find a third option. After looking into several possibilities in different parts of Israel, they decided to move to this Bat Yam tower complex, which had offered to host them for at least a year, at which point they all hoped to be able to return to their homes in southern Israel.

As I walk through the lobby of this old-age home, I see Yechiel Chlenov, a member of the original "seed group" that first arrived at Nahal Oz in 1953. His girlfriend Tamar Livyatan—whose daughter and granddaughter have by now returned to their home in the US after being released from Gaza—is staying with him in an apartment in the complex's northern tower. He tells me that they like the place and enjoy the fact that they're now so close to Tel Aviv, the big city where he was born and grew up before moving to Nahal Oz and becoming a kibbutznik.

Tami Halevi, an eighty-five-year-old kibbutz member who moved to Nahal Oz in 1955, in time to attend the famous funeral of Roi Rutberg where Moshe Dayan gave his iconic speech, is now living in the southern tower, in a small but neatly organized room on the fourteenth floor, with expansive views of the ocean. I knock on her door, and she enthusiastically invites me in. It feels good to see her face—those familiar round glasses and her distinctive short brown hair and warm smile, which I have not seen in person since she moved away from Mishmar Ha'emek.

I have my own coffee in hand, but she brings out some cookies, and we sit and talk for a while as the blue sea stretches out before us.

"I miss your daughters," Tami says. "And all the other children of the kibbutz." Her own kids all left Nahal Oz years ago and chose to raise their children elsewhere, but Tami fostered close connections with the young families who had moved to the kibbutz after 2014. She used to love seeing Galia and Carmel on their way to the pool or the grocery store.

I ask her questions about the past—about her husband Tzvika, who replaced Roi Rutberg in 1956 as the community's security chief after his friend's tragic death, and who passed away in 2008, having raised five children and several grandchildren. "I'm happy he didn't live to see what happened to our community," she says, thinking back to that Saturday. "It would have caused him so much sorrow."

"Will you go back to Nahal Oz?" I ask Tami.

She smiles and turns the question around on me. "Will you?"

I have asked myself this very question time and time again since leaving Nahal Oz almost three months prior, but the answer still doesn't come easily. The two of us sit there in silence for what might be a full minute, listening to the distant roar of the surf. Finally, I admit to Tami what has been so hard to admit to myself: that I hope to return but can't say for certain that I will.

I tell her about my four visits to the kibbutz in the weeks before our meeting: once in November, when I returned to our house for the first time since the attack in order to take stock of the damage and retrieve some clothes and beloved toys and books for the girls; and three more times in December, when I went to the community archive to collect materials for this book. Tami asks me if the archive was damaged on October 7, and I explain that the mehablim fired some bullets at its exterior but basically skipped it in their hurry to kill and kidnap our neighbors. The history of the kibbutz, at least, has survived Hamas's onslaught.

"What was it like to go back?" she asks, once again turning the tables on me, the writer so used to interviewing others.

I tell her that my first visit to the kibbutz was very difficult, emotionally—especially seeing our home again, empty now, scarred by bullets and littered with broken glass. But every time I go back, it gets just a little bit easier.

Tami nods and concludes this part of the conversation with one short sentence: "I will probably go back, but I don't know what I'd do if I had children as young as your daughters."

As we speak in her room, a war is still raging an hour south of us, along both sides of the Israel-Gaza border, but mostly on the Palestinian side of it, inside the coastal enclave. After the weeklong ceasefire that brought us back Dafna, Ela, and Elma, the fighting resumed, and Israel moved into Khan Younis, the Strip's second-largest city. Hundreds of thousands of Palestinians who had found refuge there were pushed farther south into Rafah, the last remaining stronghold of Hamas, now the world's largest refugee camp, home to almost two million people. More than thirty thousand people in Gaza have been killed by the Israeli military since the war started. Tami says she doesn't find any comfort or satisfaction in the humanitarian catastrophe evolving there.

"I'm happy about every Hamasnik our soldiers are killing there, but not the citizens, certainly not women and children," she tells me. She supports the war's two declared, overarching goals, as presented to the public by the Israeli government: defeating Hamas and releasing the hostages. But she has no illusions about where this will all lead: more war, more bloodshed. "They will want to seek revenge," she predicts of the Palestinians in Gaza. "I don't think we'll be any closer to peace when this is over."

"Do you sometimes regret it all?" I ask her before leaving. By which I mean: *the decision to come to Nahal Oz as a young woman, to settle down there, to make it your home, to raise a family a stone's throw from Gaza.*

"I don't regret anything. I had the best years of my life there," she replies. "But if I were the same age today?" She pauses, and once again silence fills the apartment as she considers her words. Finally, she answers her own question: "I'm not sure I would have done it."

Tami has so many reasons to be angry—at Hamas for orchestrating this attack and killing so many of our friends and neighbors, at the Netanyahu government for failing so miserably and leaving us at the mercy of our enemies, at the military for being so slow to respond even after it became clear what was happening inside the gates of our community. But she doesn't want to drown in her own anger.

"I have the sea to calm me," she says. I leave her there, smiling, looking out at the dancing waves.

———————

I'm sitting in my car at the roundabout connecting Route 232 with the small, winding road to Nahal Oz. The sea is not as close now, but when I open the window, I can feel a slight breeze from the direction of Gaza, just a couple of miles to the west. It's almost 1:00 P.M., and two bored-looking soldiers are operating a small checkpoint directly ahead of me. Their rifles are slung over their shoulders, their fingers nowhere near the triggers; they look calm, despite the fact that a war is raging not far from their position. I can see why: they're in charge of controlling what little traffic still flows to and from our abandoned kibbutz, which is now surrounded by hundreds of soldiers and has almost no civilian presence inside of it.

I'm waiting for a white Mazda, and at 1:00 P.M. sharp, exactly when we agreed to meet, it pulls up alongside me. Behind the wheel is Roi, the paratrooper who, months earlier, had a chance encounter with my father at this exact spot and ended up following him into a gunfight with Hamas terrorists along the road to our community—the same route that the soldiers ahead of us are now guarding. He has a short military-style haircut and brown eyes. He smiles at me from the driver's seat.

I wave at Roi from my car and then signal to him to follow me, which he does. We steer our vehicles toward the checkpoint, and I show the soldiers a small document proving that I'm a Nahal Oz resident, which allows me to pass through. "The car behind me is with me," I add, and they allow Roi to pass, too.

We connected by accident. Weeks earlier, I was invited to give a speech about Nahal Oz and October 7 in front of the staff of a large tech company in the Tel Aviv area. As I finished telling our story, one of the workers, a man in his late twenties, approached me and said, "I know the commander of the paratroopers who fought alongside your father. He's a very good friend of mine." I asked the man to connect the two of us, and the very next day I called up Roi and introduced myself as Amir Tibon from Nahal Oz. He immediately recognized me and sounded overwhelmed by excitement.

"I have so many things to tell you," Roi said on that first call. "I was so worried about you and your family when we left your father on the road and went into that burning base." We agreed to meet soon, and Roi—despite being a resident of Tel Aviv—suggested that we get together in Nahal Oz so that he could show me exactly where it all happened.

After we pass the bend in the kibbutz's small access road—the same turn that Hen Bukhris, the slain deputy commander of the Maglan unit, had wanted to avoid, correctly suspecting that an ambush could be awaiting them there—Roi flashes his headlights twice, signaling for me to stop. We both pull our cars to the side of the road and climb out. I walk over to Roi to finally shake his hand.

To the left of us is a small wooded area where tall eucalyptus trees create a dense forest. Roi points at a spot between two of those trees, where I can just barely make out a small gravel road. "That's where we saw them," he says, referring to Hen and his four comrades, two others of whom—Yiftah Yavetz and Afik Rosenthal—had also been killed right there, next to their commanding officer, while attempting to reach our community.

For a moment, a look of anguish crosses Roi's face. This is his first time back here, at the spot where he saw so much death, and where he almost lost one of his own soldiers. But then, the paratrooper commander in him is awakened, and he starts walking toward the woods with a fast, confident stride.

"This is where Hamas positioned the ambush," he says, pointing to a secluded spot to the east of the gravel road. Hen had been right in anticipating Hamas's tactic but had been off by just a few a hundred feet, expecting that any ambushers would be waiting for Israeli reinforcements closer to the bend. "There was no way for them to know where exactly the mehablim would be waiting," Roi says, matter-of-factly. "All things considered, he made the best possible decision under those impossible circumstances."

Roi kneels and picks up two shell casings—one of them from an Israeli soldier's M16, the other from a Hamas fighter's AK-47. As I scour the ground, I see dozens more shells scattered around us. The Wrangler and the dead bodies—Israeli and Palestinian—were all removed from the site in the days after October 7. But as we walk around and study the battle scene, we still find plenty of evidence of what happened that Saturday.

At one spot, we find a small crater in the ground. "I remember exactly how this happened," Roi says. "One of them tried to throw a grenade at us."

He starts from the beginning, telling me everything as he remembers it: how he and his men got out of their vehicle and ran toward the bullet-riddled Wrangler, seconds after the two Israelis driving ahead of them—my father and Avi—had done the same; how he himself shot to death at least one of the Hamas fighters; how Yedidia, one of the officers under his command, ran into the line of fire and took a bullet to the stomach; and how, only as the gunfire dissipated and my father agreed to evacuate the heavily bleeding paratrooper and the two wounded Maglan soldiers, did Roi realize that the tall man with the helmet on his head was Noam Tibon, a retired general who had once served in the same battalion in which Roi himself was now fighting.

We are about to move on from the battle site and head toward the kibbutz—I promised to show Roi our house and tell him about my own experience that day—when suddenly we both notice something on the ground. It's a tiny mound of earth surrounded by a circle of small stones. We walk toward it and I feel my heart pounding as my brain processes what my eyes are looking at.

On the mound, inside the circle of stones, are two cloth epaulettes, covered with dust, with a captain's rank on them. Next to them are a small black bracelet with a name inscribed on it; a broken piece of a military radio, black and somewhat rusty; and a sign, impossible to notice from where we had stood moments ago but now clearly visible to me, with a quote on it: "Easy paths won't lead you to special places." Next to the slogan is a black-and-white drawing of Yiftah, one of the three fallen Maglan soldiers who died here on October 7 in an effort to save us.

Roi and I stand next to Yiftah's personal effects in silence for a minute. As we do, I recall reading an interview with Gilad, Yiftah's father and a former Maglan officer himself, in which he said that he had visited the place where his son had died in battle and created a small, plain memorial for him there.

"What's there to say?" I ask Roi, finally.

"Not much," he replies. If they hadn't gotten here first, that same ambush could have killed Roi or my father.

We return to our cars and drive to the kibbutz, passing the junction where, on October 7, Roi had to make one of the most difficult decisions of his entire life—whether to turn right into the base, which was in flames or turn left toward the kibbutz, where more than four hundred residents were in mortal danger. On that day, after some hesitation, he initially decided to turn left toward our community, only to immediately see the larger Maglan force arriving from the fields; he'd promptly rushed right, instead, to aid the soldiers under siege in the barracks.

Now, we both turn left. We drive down the two-lane asphalt road to the kibbutz, and a minute later we pass through the familiar yellow gate and are inside the community. We drive on to the new neighborhood and straight to my home.

I don't need to show Roi the bullet marks—they're impossible to miss the moment we walk through the door. He asks if he can see the safe room, to try to understand what the civilians in the border region had gone through on that fateful day. I lead him through our hallway and turn on the light in the small room, illuminating Galia and Carmel's empty beds. I hear a sharp intake of breath from Roi: he has seen the changing table close to the window and the toys that we brought into the room on the evening of October 7, when at least ten children from different homes sheltered here with their families before we were all evacuated from the kibbutz.

When the tour is over, Roi and I sit on the porch with two cups of coffee, which I've made using the small pod-fed espresso machine that still stands on our kitchen counter—undamaged but unused since we left our home what now seems like a lifetime ago. As we drink the strong, dark blend, I point at the house in front us—Ilan and Sharon's house. I tell him the story of how Ilan saved twelve-year-old Ariel Zohar, whose entire family was later murdered in their home on the other end of the community. "Where is he staying now?" Roi asks and seems relieved to hear that

Ariel is with his uncles in central Israel but has been to at least one community event in Mishmar Ha'emek to see his friends from the kibbutz.

From the porch, I notice a plane flying slowly over Gaza—not an Israeli warplane, but a larger, heavier one, belonging to a foreign government. As it passes over the city on the other side of the border, it releases a series of parachutes that drift slowly toward the ground. Beneath them, I know, are large boxes containing humanitarian aid for the hundreds of thousands of Palestinians stranded in the northern part of the Strip, living in an unimaginable hellscape without normal access to food, water, medicine, or electricity.

I've heard about these airdrops in the news and have watched them on television, but seeing them with my own eyes, from my abandoned home, I am struck anew by how much pain and suffering this war has brought—first on our side of the border and then on theirs.

Roi tells me he has to head back north; his unit is preparing for the possibility of a full-blown war in the north with Hezbollah, and he needs to oversee their training. Before he leaves, however, he has one last thought to share with me.

"My men all fought heroically that day," he says. "They killed a lot of bad people. But when I see what happened inside this kibbutz, I realize that we had it easy. You guys—your community, the people who lived through this horror—you're the ones who truly deserve all the credit. You're the *real* heroes."

———————

After he leaves, I collect several books from the house—two for me, two for Miri, one each for Carmel and Galia—and lock the door behind me. It's my sixth time at home since we left on the night of October 7, and as on each of these earlier visits, leaving the house is still the most difficult part.

I have a three-hour drive ahead of me, back to Miri and the girls and all our friends in Mishmar Ha'emek. But before hitting the road, I decide to make a short stop at a place I haven't been to in a long time. A quiet place, full of tall, beautiful trees, with birds chirping and butterflies drinking the nectar of hundreds of flowers. A perfect place to watch the sun descend slowly over Gaza City and, if there's good visibility, to also catch a glimpse of the Mediterranean.

I exit the kibbutz via its main gate and take a right turn toward a small gravel path, which takes me past the small agricultural side gate through which my father and the Maglan troops entered the community when they came to rescue us on October 7. I continue east, toward my destination: Nahal Oz's hilltop cemetery, which lies to the east of the perimeter fence, separated from the kibbutz itself by a large plot of land. The field is currently used as a parking lot for tanks, but it was a wheat field before the war and maybe will be again someday.

When Roi Rutberg died in April 1956, the young members of the kibbutz had to decide where to bury him. They chose this gentle hill, eight hundred feet to the east of the perimeter fence, offering an unparalleled panorama of neighboring Gaza. Roi was the first person to be buried there. The last time I was in the cemetery was in March 2022, when the entire community gathered for the funeral of an elderly member of the kibbutz who had passed away. Back then, the place was packed. Now, I'm standing here alone, surrounded by people who can no longer speak but only listen.

I walk between the tombstones and think about the friends we lost on October 7, all of whom have been buried in other parts of the country. Will any of them be relocated here in the future, as several of their families have requested? I can't answer that question, just as I can't say, at this point, whether those of us who were lucky enough to survive will ever return to live in the kibbutz below.

I raise my head and look west, toward Gaza. From here, it's easier to see the staggering scale of the destruction—and harder to come to terms with it. The last time I was up here, I saw hundreds of buildings on the other side of the fence; now, there is nothing where they once stood but piles of rubble. Gunfire clatters in the distance, and smoke rises from deep inside the ruined city, the result of an Israeli aerial bombardment that took place minutes ago, while I was driving to the cemetery.

As an Israeli citizen, I supported the war effort, at least in the early months of the fighting. I was angry over what Hamas had done and scared of how Israeli weakness in the face of that attack would be perceived by our other adversaries in the region. But as a human being, I find it extremely difficult to countenance the level of destruction caused by my own country inside Gaza. And as a resident of Nahal Oz who still holds out hope that my family will one day be able to return here, I have to ask myself what will result from all this violence—peace and quiet or more violence?

Almost sixty-eight years ago, Moshe Dayan tried to answer this exact question in the famous eulogy he delivered here. I open my phone and pull up the text. "It is not among the Arabs of Gaza but in our own midst that we must seek Roi's blood," he said back then. The words are a stinging rebuke to Israel's current generation of politicians; our own leadership has failed to take responsibility for the biggest security failure in the history of Israel and has refused to apologize for the blood that was spilled under its watch—not of one young man but of more than 1,200 people, children and seniors, citizens and soldiers, farmers and fighters, men and women, none of whom deserved to die.

I try to imagine what that speech would sound like today, coming from the lips of an Israeli or a Palestinian leader after the atrocities that Hamas committed inside Israel on October 7, followed by the unimaginable destruction that Israel has unleashed on Gaza in the aftermath. Could such a sentiment even be mustered at a funeral of these proportions—not for one human being, but for thousands, let alone tens of thousands? What would our leaders say if, even in the depth of this suffering, they sought to acknowledge each other's points of view—as Dayan had done in 1956—without ceding an inch of their own people's national aspirations?

After a minute or two, I give up, realizing that this thought experiment seems unlikely to be tested anytime soon. There are no leaders in this land these days—not on the Israeli side or on the Palestinian one. In their place are psychopaths and egomaniacs, some of whom dream of endless war and of annihilating the other side, whatever the cost; others are simply too weak and feckless to stand up to those who have dragged all of us into this nightmare.

I continue reading the text, silently, until I reach the final paragraph. There, in the palm of my hand, are Dayan's words about the young man "who left Tel Aviv to build his home at the gates of Gaza" and of those heavy gates, which "weighed too heavily on his shoulders and overcame him."

When Dayan finished speaking on that sad day in April, eight years after Israel's founding, the young kibbutzniks of Nahal Oz were angry at him. They had come to build their homes on the border knowing that war might interrupt their lives at any moment—but they had never seen conflict as an inevitability. They wanted to believe that one day, there could be peace with the people on the other side. Some of them still believe it, even after everything that had happened on October 7 and its aftermath.

Gaza's gates still weigh on our country, as heavily as if Dayan had delivered his speech only yesterday. But as I walk out of the cemetery, I realize that there's more to the story. These gates don't just weigh on our shoulders, as Dayan said back then; in the years and decades to come, they will weigh even more heavily on our souls.

ACKNOWLEDGMENTS

I didn't want to write this book. In the first weeks after October 7, and the disastrous war it had unleashed, all I wanted to do was take care of my family, help those in need in my community, and visit the families of the soldiers who had died trying to save us, in order to show respect for their sacrifice. Writing about it all seemed like a task that would be too difficult and painful.

The person most responsible for my decision to overcome those concerns, and devote myself to this project, is Jessica Kasmer-Jacobs, my talented agent and beloved sister-in-law, who was patient enough to let me think it over again and again, but forceful enough to eventually convince me that this story must be told, and that I was the right person to tell it. She, together with her incredible colleagues at the esteemed Deborah Harris Agency in Jerusalem, made this possible.

Once the project landed with Little, Brown and Company, I found myself working with a magnificent team of professionals, starting with the editor of this book, Alexander Littlefield. For several long months, we exchanged drafts and notes on a daily basis, until I felt that our minds were connected by an invisible thread that went all the way from my room in northern Israel to his office in Manhattan. If you've made it to this part of the book, that's mostly because of his brilliant edits.

I was more than lucky to also work alongside Katharine Myers, the company's senior director of publicity; Bryan Christian, senior director of marketing; production editor Linda Arends; audio producer Melanie Schmidt; and assistant editor Morgan Wu. I am also grateful to Bruce Nichols, who oversaw the book's acquisition by the company. Thank you all for believing in this project and working so hard to bring it to fruition.

ACKNOWLEDGMENTS

The tantalizing cover of this book is the work of cover designer Lucy Kim. It features a photo by Israeli photographer Eyal Bartov, taken inside the home of Varda Goldstein, a neighbor of ours in the Gaza border region. I'm grateful to Lucy for her brilliant design, to Eyal for the powerful image, and to Varda for allowing me to show the world what her kitchen looked like in the aftermath of the October 7 attack.

My friend Adrian Hennigan, a legendary editor at *Haaretz*, the newspaper where we've been working together for years, was the first person to read many of the chapters in this book and offer wise input and helpful feedback. I wish every reporter to work once in their career with an editor like Adrian.

Ron Tuvia, a close friend and a rising star in Israeli journalism, conducted incredible research for the book and helped me answer some questions that I didn't believe we'd ever be able to figure out. A separate story can be written about the long days we spent together at the Nahal Oz archive, with the kibbutz around us abandoned and under mortar fire. Maybe one day he will write it.

I wish to thank several experts whose work was incredibly helpful: Dr. Michael Milstein, whose knowledge of the Israel-Hamas rivalry is unparalleled, and who was kind enough to share some of it with me; Suleiman al-Shafi and Shlomi Eldar, two journalists whose work in and on Gaza opened the gates of the besieged coastal Strip to so many people; and Tareq Baconi, Jean-Pierre Filliu, Dotan Halevy, and Sara Roy, four leading historians whom I found myself reading again and again in the course of my work on the book.

In the same spirit, I'm incredibly grateful to three good friends—Dr. Moran Stern, Grant Rumley and Yasmeen Serhan—who agreed to read early versions of this book and improve its historical accuracy to the best of their ability. Any mistakes that may have still found their way into the manuscript are my sole responsibility; without their generous help, there would have been many, many more.

Lesley Stahl aired a segment about our family's story on *60 Minutes* in October 2023 and was kind enough to return to it months later, read the book, and write a heartfelt endorsement for it. As someone who grew up watching her segments, it's an unbelievable honor to have her name on the back cover of this book. Thank you also to veteran producer Shachar

Bar-On, for putting a spotlight on our story and helping spread the truth, a journalist's most important commitment.

I'm equally grateful to Bianna Golodryga, a rare voice of reason and compassion in her coverage of our part of the world, and to former ambassador Dan Kurtzer, the most interesting man in the world to discuss Middle East diplomacy with, for taking the time to read the book and then encourage others to do the same.

I owe a huge debt to the documentary team at "Project Edut 710" (edut710en.org), who have led an inspiring effort to document and commemorate the events of October 7, which I found immensely helpful throughout the research and writing process. A special thanks to Dr. Shalhevet Dotan-Ofir, who has done so much to document the story of Nahal Oz.

Dozens of people were interviewed for this book: residents of Nahal Oz and neighboring communities, soldiers and policemen who participated in the battles of October 7 in and around our kibbutz (some of whom I have pseudonymized due to security requirements), senior officials in the Israeli government, experts on the Israeli-Palestinian conflict, and others. I'm grateful to each and every person who agreed to contribute their time, open their heart, and share their story or their analysis in order to make this book accurate and interesting.

I also want to thank James Fenelon, the incredibly talented artist behind the maps included in this book, for his patience, commitment, and professionalism. It was a real honor to work with him.

A special thanks goes to the families of Ilan Fiorentino, Ya'akov Karsninsky, Hen Bukhris, Yiftah Yavetz, and Afik Rosenthal, five heroes who put their lives on the line to save our community on October 7. We will never forget their courage, and I'm proud that this book will help commemorate their sacrifice.

And then, there is my family. My compass in this world.

Uri, my brother, of whom I have always been incredibly proud, but never more than now, for his choice to devote his life to helping others, saving lives, and making this a better world.

My parents, who raised us both to fulfill our values, hold onto our faith, and chase our dreams—and were always, always there for us, as the story told in this book clearly demonstrates.

Miri, the love of my life, the woman who came with me to the end of the land, my best adviser, closest friend, and never-ending source of strength. I meant every word I told you on that day. I still do.

Galia and Carmel, the biggest heroes of this story. My smart, strong, beautiful, and brave little girls, whom I continue to learn from every day. Thank you for bringing so much light into this world. You, your beloved cousin Yoav, and all your friends, deserve a better future. I promise that we won't rest until we make it happen.

NOTES

CHAPTER 1

On Our Experience inside the Safe Room

Miri Tibon, interview, Project Edut 710, January 2024.

Omri Assenheim, "The Tibon Family's 7/10 Story," *Yihie Tov*, Kan News, November 15, 2023.

Lesley Stahl and Shachar Bar-On, "Rescue at the Kibbutz," *60 Minutes*, CBS News, October 14, 2023.

*On the 2014 Israel-Gaza War, Iron Dome, and the Postwar
Situation in Nahal Oz*

Tareq Baconi, *Hamas Contained: The Rise and Pacification of Palestinian Resistance* (Stanford: Stanford University Press, 2018).

Itay Maoz, interview by the author, August 2014.

Adam Taylor and Brittany Shammas, "How Israel's Iron Dome Air Defense System Disables Some Hamas Rockets," *Washington Post*, October 9, 2023.

Gabriel Levin, "How Does Israel's Last Invasion of Gaza Compare to Now?," *Voice of America*, October 17, 2023.

Shirly Seidler, "Boy Killed by Hamas Shell Was Son of Local Council Spokeswoman," *Haaretz*, August 24, 2014.

Harriet Sherwood and Hazem Balousha, "Gaza Ceasefire: Israel and Palestinians Agree to Halt Weeks of Fighting," *The Guardian*, August 27, 2014.

Marissa Neman, "20 Families Leave Southern Kibbutz After Gaza Conflict," *Times of Israel*, October 15, 2014.

Sue Serkes, "Despite Rockets, Arson Balloons, Israeli Communities on Gaza Border Keep Growing," *Times of Israel*, May 4, 2019.

NOTES

CHAPTER 2

The Foundation of Nahal Oz and Life in the Kibbutz from 1953 to 1957

Yehiel Chlenov, interview by the author, December 2023.

Tami Halevi, interview by the author, December 2023.

Ofer Aderet, "Israeli Kibbutz's Early Days, Long before Hamas' Attack," *Haaretz*, October 26, 2023.

Kennett Love, "Israeli Settlers Grow with Town: Nahal Oz, Founded in 1953, Has Average Age of 20—and Works Armed," *New York Times*, August 28, 1955.

Expired Strings: The First Piano of Nahal Oz, a short documentary film directed by Arie Dotan (Nahal Oz: 2020).

Has the Flower Withered?, a short documentary film directed by Eitan Wetzler (Tel Aviv: 2000).

Irving Heymont, "The Israeli Nahal Program," *Middle East Journal* 21, no. 3 (Summer 1967): 314–324.

David Ben-Gurion letter to Gaza border communities, March 7, 1957, Jerusalem, Prime Minister's Office, Ben-Gurion Archive, Ben-Gurion University of the Negev.

Moshe Dayan's Eulogy of Roi Rutberg

Chemi Shalev, "Moshe Dayan's Enduring Gaza Eulogy: This Is the Fate of Our Generation," *Haaretz*, July 20, 2014.

Mitch Ginsburg, "When Moshe Dayan Delivered the Defining Speech of Zionism," *Times of Israel*, April 28, 2016.

The 1948 War, the Palestinian Refugee Problem, and the Security Situation along the Israel-Gaza Border in the State's Early Years

Benny Morris, *1948: A History of the First Arab-Israeli War* (New Haven, CT: Yale University Press, 2008).

Benny Morris, *Israel's Border Wars, 1949–1956* (Oxford: Oxford University Press, 1997).

Jean-Pierre Filiu, *Gaza: A History* (Oxford: Oxford University Press, 2014).

Khaled Elgindy, *Blind Spot: America and the Palestinians, from Balfour to Trump* (Washington, DC: Brookings Institution Press, 2019).

Beryl Cheal, "Refugees in the Gaza Strip, December 1948–May 1950," *Journal of Palestine Studies* 18, no. 1 (Autumn 1988): 138–157.

Nur Masalha, *Palestine: A Four Thousand Year History* (London: Bloomsbury, 2003).

Egypt, Gaza, and the 1956 Suez War

Gabriel R. Warburg, "The Sinai Peninsula Borders, 1906–47," *Journal of Contemporary History* 14, no. 4 (October 1979): 677–692.

David Charlwood, *Suez Crisis 1956: The End of an Empire and the Reshaping of the Middle East* (Barnsley, UK: Pen and Sword Military, 2019).

David Nicols, *Eisenhower 1956: The President's Year of Crisis* (New York: Simon and Schuster, 2012).

Mordechai Bar-On, *Moshe Dayan: Israel's Controversial Hero* (New Haven, CT: Yale University Press, 2012).

CHAPTER 3

Events inside Our Safe Room and My Parents' Journey from Tel Aviv

Miri Tibon, interview, Project Edut 710, January 2024.

Omri Assenheim, "The Tibon Family's 7/10 Story," *Yihie Tov*, Kan News, November 15, 2023.

Lesley Stahl and Shachar Bar-On, "Rescue at the Kibbutz," *60 Minutes*, CBS News, October 14, 2023.

Shiri Lev-Ari, "The Author Who Went with Her Husband to Rescue Their Son from Nahal Oz: Difficult Feeling of Betrayal," *Calcalist*, October 22, 2023.

Background on the Construction of Our Neighborhood in Nahal Oz and of Safe Rooms in Israel

"Examination of our Method from a Security Perspective," GSB Systems, retrieved from the company website, March 2024.

Katherine Tangalakis-Lippert, Reem Makhoul, and Lauren Steussy, "IN PHOTOS: What It's Like inside a Typical Safe Room in Israel," *Business Insider*, October 11, 2023.

On Hamas's Use of Attack Tunnels against Israel

Jean-Pierre Filiu, *Gaza: A History* (Oxford: Oxford University Press, 2014).

Tareq Baconi, *Hamas Contained: The Rise and Pacification of Palestinian Resistance* (Stanford, CA: Stanford University Press, 2018).

Joseph Berger and Greg Myre, "Bomb under Gaza Base Kills Israeli Soldier and Hurts 5," *New York Times*, June 28, 2004.

Amos Harel, "How Were Palestinian Militants Able to Abduct Gilad Shalit?," *Haaretz*, October 18, 2011.

NOTES

Daniel Rubinstein, "Hamas' Tunnel Network: A Massacre in the Making," *Jerusalem Center for Public Affairs*, July 2015.

Ari Judah Gross, "'A Wall of Iron, Sensors and Concrete': IDF Completes Tunnel-Busting Gaza Barrier," *Times of Israel*, December 7, 2021.

On the Number of Israeli Troops along the Border on the Morning of October 7 and the Military's Intelligence Failures

"Only 600 Israeli Soldiers Were Guarding Gaza Border on October 7—Report," liveblog, *Times of Israel*, February 26, 2024.

Ami Rojkes Dombe, "The IDF Didn't Invest in the Border Defense Force Due to the Fence," *Israel Defense*, October 15, 2023.

Rory Jones and Dion Nissenbaum, "Israel Was Prepared for a Different War," *Wall Street Journal*, October 9, 2023.

Aluf Benn, "The West Bank Occupation Outweighed Israel's Defense of the Gaza Border on the Eve of October 7," *Haaretz*, February 21, 2024.

Adam Goldman, Ronen Bergman, Mark Mazzetti, Natan Odenheimer, Alexander Cardia, Ainara Tiefenthäler, and Sheera Frenkel, "Where Was the Israeli Military?," *New York Times*, January 3, 2024.

Alice Cuddy, "They Were Israel's Eyes on the Border—But Their Hamas Warnings Went Unheard," *BBC News*, January 15, 2024.

On Ilan Fiorentino's Rescue of Twelve-Year-Old Boy

Sharon Fiorentino, interview, Project Edut 710, March 2024.

Dror Kessler, interview with the author, March 2024.

Adam Geller, "They Fled Nahal Oz after Hamas Attacked on Oct. 7. They Don't Know Whether to Return," *Times of Israel*, March 28, 2024.

CHAPTER 4

On Life in Nahal Oz before the 1967 War

Arie Dotan, interview by the author, January 2024.

Yehiel Chlenov, interview by the author, December 2023.

Nahal Oz community update, May 1967.

On the "Waiting Period" ahead of the 1967 War and the War's Results

William B. Quandt, "Lyndon Johnson and the June 1967 War: What Color Was the Light?," *Middle East Journal* 46, no. 2 (Spring 1992): 198–228.

Tom Segev, *1967: Israel, the War, and the Year that Transformed the Middle East* (London: Picador, 2008).

Gershom Gorenberg, *The Accidental Empire: Israel and the Birth of the Settlements, 1967–1977* (New York: Times Books, 2007).

On the Postwar Reality in Gaza and among the Palestinian Public

Sara Roy, *Failing Peace: Gaza and the Palestinian-Israeli Conflict* (London: Pluto Press, 2014).

Sara Roy, "The Gaza Strip: A Case of Economic De-Development," *Journal of Palestine Studies* 17, no. 1 (Autumn 1987): 56–88.

Yezid Sayigh, *Armed Struggle and the Search for State: The Palestinian National Movement, 1949–1993* (Oxford: Oxford University Press, 2000).

Noura Erekat, "Taking the Land without the People: The 1967 Story as Told by the Law," *Institute for Palestine Studies*, 47, no. 1 (Autumn 2017): 18–38.

Jean-Pierre Filiu, *Gaza: A History* (Oxford: Oxford University Press, 2014).

On the 1968 Land Mine Incident in Nahal Oz

Ehud Doron, interview by the author, January 2024.

Arie Dotan, interview by the author, January 2024.

On Life in Nahal Oz in the 1970s and the Relationship with Gaza

Dani Rachamim, interview by the author, January 2024.

Yehiel Chlenov, interview by the author, December 2023.

Isabel Kershner and David Halbfinger, "Israelis Reflect on Gaza: 'I Hope at Least That Each Bullet Was Justified,'" *New York Times*, May 15, 2018.

On Mizrahi Jews in Israel during the Country's Early Decades

Rachel Shabi, *We Look Like the Enemy: The Hidden Story of Israel's Jews from Arab Lands* (New York: Walker Books, 2009).

Bryan K. Roby, *The Mizrahi Era of Rebellion: Israel's Forgotten Civil Rights Struggle* (Syracuse: Syracuse University Press, 2015).

On the 1973 War and Its Effect on Israeli Society and Politics

Uri Bar-Joseph, "Last Chance to Avoid War: Sadat's Peace Initiative of February 1973 and Its Failure," *Journal of Contemporary History* 41, no. 3 (July 2006): 545–556.

Arnon Gutfeld and Boaz Vanetik, "'A Situation That Had to Be Manipulated': The American Airlift to Israel During the Yom Kippur War," *Middle Eastern Studies* 52, no. 3 (2016): 419–447.

"New Study: One of Every Five Fallen Soldiers in Yom Kippur—From a Kibbutz," *Israel Hayom*, September 11, 2023.

On the Economic Reality in Gaza in the 1970s and 1980s and the Importance of Workers Entering Israel

Sara Roy, "The Gaza Strip: Critical Effects of the Occupation," *Arab Studies Quarterly* 10, no. 1 (Winter 1988): 59–103.

M. K. Budeiri, "Changes in the Economic Structure of the West Bank and Gaza Strip under Israeli Occupation," *Labour, Capital and Society / Travail, Capital et Société* 15, no. 1 (April 1982): 46–63.

On the PLO and Its Shifting Political Agenda

Suleiman al-Shafi, interview by the author, January 2024.

Yezid Sayigh, "Struggle Within, Struggle Without: The Transformation of PLO Politics Since 1982," *International Affairs* 65, no. 2 (Spring 1989): 247–271.

Rashid Hamid, "What Is the PLO?," *Journal of Palestine Studies* 4, no. 4 (Summer 1975): 90–109.

Sameer Abraham, "The PLO at the Crossroads: Moderation, Encirclement, Future Prospects," *MERIP Reports*, no. 80 (September 1979): 5–13, 26.

On the Israeli-Egyptian Peace Agreement and Its Impact on Gaza

Lawrence Wright, *13 Days in September: The Dramatic Story of the Struggle for Peace* (New York: Vintage, 2015).

Eyal Levi, "From the American Proposal to Begin's Insistence: How Israel Got Stuck in Gaza," *Maariv*, June 23, 2018.

Seth Anziska, "How Israel Undermined Washington and Stalled the Dream of Palestinian Statehood," *New York Times*, September 20, 2018.

On the Israeli Settlements in Gaza and the West Bank and How They Were Viewed by the Palestinian Population There

Abdul-Ilah Abu Ayyash, "Israeli Planning Policy in the Occupied Territories," *Journal of Palestine Studies* 11, no. 1 (Autumn 1981): 111–123.

Mohammed Shadid and Rick Seltzer, "Political Attitudes of Palestinians in the West Bank and Gaza Strip," *Middle East Journal* 42, no. 1 (Winter 1988): 16–32.

Akiva Eldar and Idith Zertal, *Lords of the Land: The War for Israel's Settlements in the Occupied Territories, 1967–2007* (New York: Nation Books, 2007).

On the Early Years of Hamas

Tareq Baconi, *Hamas Contained: The Rise and Pacification of Palestinian Resistance* (Stanford, CA: Stanford University Press, 2018).

Ziad Abu-Amr, "Hamas: A Historical and Political Background," *Journal of Palestine Studies* 22, no. 4 (Summer 1993): 5–19.

Shlomi Eldar, *To Know Hamas* (Jerusalem: Keter Books, 2012).

On the First Intifada

Jean-Pierre Filiu, *Gaza: A History* (Oxford: Oxford University Press, 2014).

Avraham Sela, "The First Intifada: How the Arab-Israeli Conflict Was Transformed," *Haaretz*, December 13, 2012.

Helena Cobban, "The PLO and the 'Intifada,'" *Middle East Journal* 44, no. 2 (Spring 1990): 207–233.

Barbara Harlow, "Narrative in Prison: Stories from the Palestinian 'Intifada,'" *Modern Fiction Studies* 35, no. 1 (Spring 1989): 29–46.

CHAPTER 5

On the Battle inside the Kibbutz and the Police Team Involved in It

Nissan Dekalo, interview by the author, December 2023.

Ben [police sniper], interview by the author, January 2024.

Beri Meirovitch, interview, Project Edut 710, January 2024.

Yossi Eli, "They Fought Eight Hours and Killed 100 Terrorists: The Troopers Who Saved Nahal Oz," *Channel 13 News*, October 14, 2023.

Omri Maniv, "The Battle for Nahal Oz," *Channel 12 News*, October 16, 2023.

Lior Veroslavski, "'Yakov Ran Out First and Everybody Else Followed': The Story of the Fighter Who Protected Nahal Oz," *Channel 13 News*, October 22, 2023.

On the IDF Decision to Take Weapons from Local Security Teams

Yaniv Kubovich, "The IDF Took Away Weapons from Gaza Border Communities in Recent Years, and Armed West Bank Settlers in the Thousands," *Haaretz*, October 20, 2023.

"IDF Said to Leave Gaza Border Towns' Security Squads Unarmed for Past Year," *Times of Israel*, September 14, 2021.

On the September 2023 Gaza Border Protests

Nidal Al-Mughrabi, "Israel Bans Workers from Gaza as Border Tensions Escalate," Reuters, September 20, 2023.

Gianluca Pacchiani, "Gazans Abort Border Riots as Israel Reopens Crossing in Reported Egypt-Brokered Deal," *Times of Israel*, September 28, 2023.

On the Murder of Shoshi Brosh and the Rescue of Her Husband Yonatan 'Yonchi' Brosh

Yonatan Brosh, interview, Project Edut 710, January 2024.

"Shoshi Brosh, 75: Grandmother with 'A Blossoming Garden,'" *Times of Israel*, January 25, 2024.

On the Events at the Idan and Elyakim Family Homes

Shany Littman, "'You Start Thinking, Will They Kill the Girls First, or Kill Me First and Then Them?,'" *Haaretz*, December 3, 2023.

Gali Idan, "Hamas Killed My Daughter. My Husband Is Still a Hostage," *Newsweek*, January 5, 2024.

Sheera Frenkel and Talya Minsberg, "Hamas Hijacked Victims' Social Media Accounts to Spread Terror," *New York Times*, October 17, 2023.

Matthew Dooley, "Hamas Terrorists Post Haunting Picture of Kidnapped Israeli Girl as Mum Begs for Release," *Express*, October 16, 2023.

Yigal Mosko, "Live Kidnapping: The Story of the Idan Family," *Channel 12 News*, October 24, 2023.

On the Events at the Home of Micky, Nahal Oz Resident

Micky, interview, Project Edut 710, February 2024.

Rina Matzliah and Akiva Novick, "Saved His Wife and Daughter from Terrorists Who Entered the House," Kan News, October 21, 2023.

On the Events inside Our Safe Room during the Late Morning Hours

Miri Tibon, interview, Project Edut 710, January 2024.

NOTES

CHAPTER 6

On the Rescue of Bar and Lior Metzner

Bar Metzner, interview by the author, February 2024.

Geula Even-Saar, "The Couple Saved from the Nova Massacre: 'Israel Will Never Be the Same,'" *Channel 13 News*, October 10, 2023.

"'This Can't Be Happening to Us, We Have Kids at Home,'" *Mako*, November 20, 2023.

General (ret.) Noam Tibon, interview by Itay Ilani, *Hear a Story*, podcast audio, *Israel Hayom*, February 22, 2023.

On My Parents' Drive into the Border Region

Ilan Lukach, "'Dad Is Here': The Generals Who Joined the War Recount How They Saved the Family," *Channel 12 News*, October 21, 2023.

"The Tibon Family's 7/10 Story," interview by Omri Assenheim, *Yihie Tov*, Kan News, November 15, 2023.

Lesley Stahl and Shachar Bar-On, "Rescue at the Kibbutz," *60 Minutes*, CBS News, October 14, 2023.

Eitan Tuvia, interview by the author, January 2024.

On the Battle in Kibbutz Mefalsim

Roy Reshef, interview by the author, January 2024.

Ami Rojkes Dombe, "How the Security Team of Kibbutz Mefalsim Managed to Stop Hamas' Terrorists," *Israel Defense*, October 13, 2023.

On the Battle in the Gaza Regional Command Center

Gali Weinreb, "The Bedouin Officer Who Pretended to Be a Terrorist and Saved an Entire Base," *Globes*, December 24, 2023.

Yossi Mizrahi, "The Battle for the Gaza Region's Command Center," *Channel 12 News*, October 16, 2023.

Almog Boker, "'Fought for His Home': The Officer Who Pretended to Be a Terrorist—and Saved the Command Center," *Channel 13 News*, January 25, 2024.

Greet Fay Cashman, "Bedouins Who Fought Hamas on Oct. 7 Honored for Bravery and Heroism in Jerusalem," *Jerusalem Post*, February 13, 2024.

NOTES

On Israeli Journalists Trying to Assist Victims of the Hamas Attack

Josh Breiner, "Hundreds of Young People Begged Me for Help; I Called the Police Chief and Begged on Their Behalf," *Haaretz*, November 9, 2023.

Main Newscast, "Tamir Steinman Breaks Down during the Broadcast," video, *Channel 12 News*, October 7, 2023.

Main Newscast, "Tamir Steinman with the Residents of the Gaza Envelope Who Texted Him during the Surprise Attack," video, *Channel 12 News*, October 30, 2023.

CHAPTER 7

On the 1994 Nahal Oz Festival of Peace

Video of the 1994 Nahal Oz Festival of Peace, unknown photographer, August 25, 1994, Nahal Oz archive.

Nahal Oz community update, August 1994.

Dani Rachamim, interview by the author, January 2024.

Carine Rachamim, interview by the author, February 2024.

On Rabin's Return to Power in 1992

Clyde Haberman, "Israel's Labor Party Wins Clear Victory in Election; Ready to Form a Coalition," *New York Times*, June 24, 1992.

Sammy Smooha and Don Peretz, "Israel's 1992 Knesset Elections: Are They Critical?," *Middle East Journal* 47, no. 3 (Summer 1993): 444–463.

Itamar Rabinovich, *Yitzhak Rabin: Soldier, Leader, Statesman* (New Haven, CT: Yale University Press, 2017).

On the Oslo Accords and Creation of the Palestinian Authority

Ann Mosely Lesch, "Transition to Palestinian Self-Government," *Journal of Palestine Studies* 22, no. 3 (Spring 1993): 46–56.

Burhan Dajani, "The September 1993 Israeli-PLO Documents: A Textual Analysis," *Journal of Palestine Studies* 23, no. 3 (Spring 1994): 5–23.

Explainer, "What Is the Palestinian Authority and What Is Its Relationship with Israel?," *Al Jazeera*, October 11, 2023.

On the Deportation of Hamas Operatives to Lebanon

Clyde Haberman, "Israel Deports 400 to Lebanon; Lebanese Deploy to Bar Entry of Palestinians," *New York Times*, December 18, 1992.

David Hoffman, "Kidnapped Israeli Guard Found Slain," *Washington Post*, December 15, 1992.

Shlomi Eldar, *To Know Hamas* (Jerusalem: Keter Books, 2012).

On the Signing of the Oslo Accords and Their Impact

Dennis Ross, *The Missing Peace: The Inside Story of the Fight for Middle East Peace* (New York: Farrar, Straus and Giroux, 2005).

Yossi Beilin, *Touching Peace: From the Oslo Accord to a Final Agreement* (London: George Weidenfeld and Nicholson, 1999).

Martin Indyk, *Innocent Abroad: An Intimate Account of American Peace Diplomacy in the Middle East* (New York: Simon and Schuster, 2014).

Jacques Neriah, "Oslo in the Perspective of 25 Years—The Dream and Its Demise: A Personal View from a Witness," *Jewish Political Studies Review* 30, no. 1/2 (2019): 230–237.

On How the Accords Were Viewed in Nahal Oz

Dani Rachamim, interview with the author, January 2024.

Arie Dotan, interview with the author, December 2023.

Nahal Oz community update, October 1995.

On the Goldstein Massacre and Hamas Suicide Attacks and Their Impact

Chris Hedges and Joel Greenberg, "West Bank Massacre: Before Killing, Final Prayer and Final Taunt," *New York Times*, February 28, 1994.

Robert Paine, "Behind the Hebron Massacre, 1994," *Anthropology Today* 11, no. 1 (February 1995): 8–15.

Clyde Haberman, "Arab Car Bomb Kills 8 in Israel; 44 Wounded," *New York Times*, April 7, 1994.

Clyde Haberman, "5 Killed in Israel as Second Bomber Blows Up," *New York Times*, April 14, 1994.

On Opposition to Oslo among Israelis and Palestinians

Roger Cohen, "The Incitement in Israel That Killed Yitzhak Rabin," *New York Times*, December 4, 2019.

Mona Eltahawy, "Radicals Who Said No to the Accords," *The Guardian*, July 21, 1999.

Yotam Berger, "25 Years Later, Israel's Right Wing Is Still Battling the Oslo Accords," *Haaretz*, September 12, 2018.

Tamar Hermann and Ephraim Yuchtman-Yaar, "Divided yet United: Israeli-Jewish Attitudes toward the Oslo Process," *Journal of Peace Research* 39, no. 5 (September 2002): 597–613.

Paul Cainer, "The Arafat I Knew Was Undermining Oslo from the Very Start," *Jewish Chronicle*, September 7, 2023.

On Rabin's Assassination and Its Impact

Dan Ephron, *Killing a King: The Assassination of Yitzhak Rabin and the Remaking of Israel* (New York: W. W. Norton, 2015).

Uri Savir, *The Process: 1,100 Days That Changed the Middle East* (New York: Vintage, 2010).

Dennis Ross, *The Missing Peace: The Inside Story of the Fight for Middle East Peace* (New York: Farrar, Straus and Giroux, 2005).

Dani Rachamim, interview by the author, January 2024.

On the 1996 Israeli Election and Netanyahu's Victory

Anshel Pfeffer, *Bibi: The Turbulent Life and Times of Benjamin Netanyahu* (New York: Basic Books, 2018).

Don Peretz and Gideon Doron, "Israel's 1996 Elections: A Second Political Earthquake?," *Middle East Journal* 50, no. 4 (Autumn 1996): 529–546.

Benny Morris, "Israel's Elections and Their Implications," *Journal of Palestine Studies* 26, no. 1 (Autumn 1996): 70–81.

Martin Indyk, *Innocent Abroad: An Intimate Account of American Peace Diplomacy in the Middle East* (New York: Simon and Schuster, 2014).

On Botched Mashal Assassination, Yassin Release, and Abu-Marzouk Affair

Amir Bar Shalom, "Begging Royal Mercy: How Israel Recovered from the Botched Mashaal Hit, 25 Years Ago," *Times of Israel*, August 24, 2022.

Andrew Higgins, "How Israel Helped to Spawn Hamas," *Wall Street Journal*, January 24, 2009.

Walter Rodgers and Jerrold Kessel, "Freed Hamas Founder Returns to Gaza," CNN, October 6, 1997.

Adam Raz, "Netanyahu and Abu-Marzouk—The Origins of a Friendship," *Haaretz*, November 30, 2023.

NOTES

On the 1999 Israeli Election, Netanyahu's Loss, and Barak's Rise to Power

Anshel Pfeffer, *Bibi: The Turbulent Life and Times of Benjamin Netanyahu* (New York: Basic Books, 2018).

Nahal Oz community update, May 1999.

Lee Hockstader, "Barak Wins Israeli Vote," *Washington Post*, May 17, 1999.

On Barak's Time in Office and the Lead-Up to the Second Intifada

Gilead Sher, *Within Reach: Israeli-Palestinian Peace Negotiations, 1999–2001* (London: Routledge, 2005).

Jonathan Rynhold, "Making Sense of Tragedy: Barak, the Israeli Left and the Oslo Peace Process," *Israel Studies Forum* 19, no. 1 (Fall 2003): 9–33.

Suzanne Goldenberg, "Rioting as Sharon Visits Islam Holy Site," *The Guardian*, September 29, 2000.

Explainer, "Why the Al-Aqsa Site Is So Important to Muslims and Jews—And the Site of Renewed Violence," Reuters, April 6, 2023.

Nahal Oz community update, October 2000.

On Ariel Sharon's Entry to Office

David Landau, *Arik: The Life of Ariel Sharon* (New York: Knopf, 2014).

Nahal Oz community update, May 2001.

On Mortar and Rocket Fire toward Nahal Oz in 2001

Felix Frisch, "Mortar Fire at Nahal Oz: 'The Rules of the Game Have Changed,'" *Ynet*, March 19, 2001.

Tal Elovits, "Fence against Terrorism: The Examples of the Gaza Strip and the West Bank," *Ma'arakhot* 458 (December 2014): 10–17.

Nahal Oz community update, April 2001.

Nahal Oz community update, July 2001.

Dani Rachamim, interview by the author, January 2024.

Carine Rachamim, interview by the author, February 2024.

On Sharon's Decision to Withdraw from Gaza and Haaretz's Scoop about It

David Landau, *Arik: The Life of Ariel Sharon* (New York: Knopf, 2014).

Elliott Abrams, *Tested by Zion: The Bush Administration and the Israeli-Palestinian Conflict* (Cambridge: Cambridge University Press, 2013).

NOTES

Ari Shavit, "Top PM Aide: Gaza Plan Aims to Freeze the Peace Process," *Haaretz*, October 6, 2004.

Hanoch Marmari, "My Ariel Sharon: Between the Corruption and the Disengagement," *Seventh Eye*, January 21, 2014.

On Views of the Disengagement in Israel—and in Nahal Oz

Yossi Verter, "Poll: Israelis Favor Disengagement, Divided on Referendum," *Haaretz*, January 14, 2005.

Chris McGreal, "Settlers Warn of Civil War over Gaza Withdrawal," *The Guardian*, March 29, 2005.

Greg Myre, "Jewish Settlers Stage New Protests against Planned Gaza Removal," *New York Times*, January 4, 2005.

Jonathan Rynhold and Dov Waxman, "Ideological Change and Israel's Disengagement from Gaza," *Political Science Quarterly* 123, no. 1 (Spring 2008): 11–37.

Dani Rachamim, interview by the author, January 2024.

Eitan Tuvia, interview by the author, February 2024.

The Disengagement in Palestinian Public Opinion

"Hamas Rally Celebrates Gaza 'Victory,'" *Al Jazeera*, August 23, 2005.

Chris McGreal, "Hamas Celebrates Victory of the Bomb as Power of Negotiation Falters," *The Guardian*, September 12, 2005.

Peter Kenyon, "Palestinians React to Gaza Withdrawal," NPR, August 15, 2005.

Israeli and Palestinian Elections of 2006

Shlomi Eldar, *To Know Hamas* (Jerusalem: Keter Books, 2012).

Tareq Baconi, *Hamas Contained: The Rise and Pacification of Palestinian Resistance* (Stanford, CA: Stanford University Press, 2018).

Mahjoob Zweiri, "The Hamas Victory: Shifting Sands or Major Earthquake?," *Third World Quarterly* 27, no. 4 (2006): 675–687.

Scott Wilson, "Sharon's Party Is Winner in Israel," *Washington Post*, March 28, 2006.

Yoel Marcus, "Olmert Zig or Olmert Zag," *Haaretz*, May 17, 2006.

Israeli Blockade of Gaza and Shalit Abduction

Shlomi Eldar, *To Know Hamas* (Jerusalem: Keter Books, 2012).

Tareq Baconi, "How Israel's 10-Year Blockade Brought Gaza to the Brink of Collapse," *The Nation*, July 7, 2017.

Trude Strand, "Tightening the Noose: The Institutionalized Impoverishment of Gaza, 2005–2010," *Journal of Palestine Studies* 43, no. 2 (Winter 2014): 6–23.

Amos Harel, "How Were Palestinian Militants Able to Abduct Gilad Shalit?," *Haaretz*, October 18, 2011.

Lebanon War and Its Political Impact in Israel

Molly Moore, "Olmert Accepts Blame for Operation's 'Failings,'" *Washington Post*, August 15, 2006.

Arie Eldad, "The Lebanon War's Greatest Achievement: What Didn't Happen after It," *Maariv*, June 18, 2016.

Hillel Schenker, "The Tragedy of Ehud Olmert," *The Nation*, August 18, 2008.

Hamas Takeover of Gaza

Tareq Baconi, *Hamas Contained: The Rise and Pacification of Palestinian Resistance* (Stanford, CA: Stanford University Press, 2018).

Shlomi Eldar, *To Know Hamas* (Jerusalem: Keter Books, 2012).

CHAPTER 8

On the First Maglan Force to Approach the Kibbutz

Major S. [brother of Hen Bukhris], interview by the author, December 2023.

Amir Rosenthal [father of Afik Rosenthal], interview by the author, December 2023.

Gilad Yavetz [father of Yiftah Yavetz], interview by the author, November 2023.

Itay Ilnai, "Maglan Unit's October 7, Minute-by-Minute," *Israel Hayom*, February 15, 2024.

General (ret.) Noam Tibon, interview by Itay Ilnai, *Hear a Story*, podcast audio, *Israel Hayom*, February 22, 2023.

On the Attack in Kfar Azza

"Shai-Li Aviani (20), Kfar Aza: 'I Know This Is How My Father Would Have Wanted to Die,'" *Israel Hayom*, November 15, 2023.

Seth Franzman, "Looking into Kfar Aza, Five Months after the October 7 Massacre," *Jerusalem Post*, March 20, 2024.

NOTES

On the Paratrooper Team Led by Roi Rutberg

Major Roi Rutberg, interview by the author, March 2024.

Captain Y., interview by the author, January 2024.

Shmuel Munitz, "The Wounded Fighter Got Married While His Brother Is Missing," *Ynet*, October 19, 2023.

On the Evacuation of the Wounded Soldiers by My Parents

Inbar Twizer, "The Paratroopers' Officer Was Critically Injured—While His Wife Gave Birth," *Channel 12 News*, November 8, 2024.

Itay Ilnai, "Maglan Unit's October 7, Minute-by-Minute," *Israel Hayom*, February 15, 2024.

Omri Assenheim, "The Tibon Family's 7/10 Story," *Yihie Tov*, Kan News, November 15, 2023.

On Yisrael Ziv's Arrival to the Border Region on October 7

General (ret.) Yisrael Ziv, interview by Amir Oren, *Afarkeset*, podcast audio, December 29, 2023.

Ilan Lukach, "'Dad Is Here': The Generals Who Joined the War Recount How They Saved the Family," *Channel 12 News*, October 21, 2023.

On the Arrival of Larger Maglan Force to the Kibbutz

Major Eshel, interview by the author, March 2024.

Eight Maglan fighters, group interview by the author, February 2024.

Itay Ilnai, "Maglan Unit's October 7, Minute-by-Minute," *Israel Hayom*, February 15, 2024.

Yanir Yagna, "'You're the Real Heroes': Commando Fighter to Nahal Oz Survivors," *Walla News*, October 24, 2023.

Major S., interview by the author, December 2023.

On the Process of Clearing the Kibbutz and Rescuing Families

Nissan Dekalo, interview by the author, December 2023.

Beri Meirovitch, interview, Project Edut 710, January 2024.

Ben [police sniper], interview by the author, January 2024.

Major Eshel, interview by the author, March 2024.

Eight Maglan fighters, group interview by the author, February 2024.

David Dalal, interview by the author, March 2024.

Eitan Tuvia, interview by the author, February 2024.

On the Events inside Our Safe Room

Miri Tibon, interview, Project Edut 710, January 2024.

Omri Assenheim, "The Tibon Family's 7/10 Story," *Yihie Tov*, Kan News, November 15, 2023.

CHAPTER 9

On Netanyahu's 2009 Promise to Topple Hamas

Senior Netanyahu aide, interview by the author, February 2024.

Avigdor Lieberman, interview by the author, March 2024.

Yaron Avraham, "'I Will Topple Hamas': Netanyahu's Promise from 2008 Is Still Irrelevant in 2021," *Mako*, May 20, 2021.

On Operation Cast Lead and the 2009 Israeli Election

Camille Mansour, "Reflections on the War on Gaza," *Journal of Palestine Studies* 38, no. 4 (Summer 2009): 91–95.

Haaretz Service, "Hamas Admits 600–700 of Its Men Were Killed in Cast Lead," *Haaretz*, November 9, 2010.

Paola Caridi, *Hamas: From Resistance to Regime* (New York: Seven Stories Press, 2023).

Yehuda Ben Meir and Olena Bagno-Moldavsky, "The Profile of the Israeli Body Politic," in *Vox Populi: Trends in Israeli Public Opinion on National Security 2004–2009*, 31–41 (Tel Aviv: Institute for National Security Studies, 2010).

On the Impact of the War on Nahal Oz

Oshrit Sabag, interview by the author, March 2024.

Arie Dotan, interview by the author, January 2024.

Amos Harel and Yuval Azoulay, "IDF Inquiry into Nahal Oz Raid Highlights Failures," *Haaretz*, April 11, 2008.

On Netanyahu's 2009 Coalition and Political Agenda

Anshel Pfeffer, *Bibi: The Turbulent Life and Times of Benjamin Netanyahu* (New York: Basic Books, 2018).

Isabel Kershner, "Israel's Labor Party Votes to Join Netanyahu Coalition," *New York Times*, March 24, 2009.

On the Gilad Shalit Prisoner Swap and Historical Precedents

Debra Kamin, "The 5 Most Lopsided Prisoner Swaps in Israeli History," *Times of Israel*, June 19, 2014.

Barak Ravid, "Israel Cabinet Approves Gilad Shalit Prisoner Swap," *Haaretz*, October 12, 2011.

Yuval Karniel, Amit Lavie-Dinur, and Tal Samuel Azran, "Professional or Personal Framing? International Media Coverage of the Israel–Hamas Prisoner Exchange Deal," *Media, War & Conflict* 10, no. 1 (2017): 105–124.

Suleiman al-Shafi, interview by the author, January 2024.

Avigdor Lieberman, interview by the author, March 2024.

Shlomo Shamir, "Diplomatic Sources: Shalit Deal Hurt Chances of Renewing Israel-Palestinian Talks," *Haaretz*, October 19, 2011.

On Hamas-Egypt Relationship, including during the Arab Spring

Rory McCarthy, "Under the Border with Egypt, Gaza's Smugglers Return to Work," *The Guardian*, January 21, 2009.

David Kirkpatrick, "In Shift, Egypt Warms to Iran and Hamas, Israel's Foes," *New York Times*, April 28, 2011.

Haaretz Service, "Hamas Chief: Egypt Revolution Brought Us Back to Life," *Haaretz*, March 6, 2011.

On the April 2011 Attack on Nahal Oz School Bus

Oshrit Sabag, interview by the author, March 2024.

Carine Rachamim, interview by the author, February 2024.

Nahal Oz community update, April 2011.

Joel Greenberg, "Missile from Gaza Strip Hits Israeli School Bus, Wounding Teen," *Washington Post*, April 7, 2011.

On Iron Dome

Anshel Pfeffer and Yanir Yagna, "Iron Dome Successfully Intercepts Gaza Rocket for First Time," *Haaretz*, April 7, 2011.

Inbal Orpaz, "How Does the Iron Dome Work?," *Haaretz*, November 19, 2023.

Alex Gatopoulos, "How Successful Was Israel's Iron Dome?," *Al Jazeera*, September 8, 2014.

Yaakov Katz, "Olmert Okays Rafael Anti-Kassam System," *Jerusalem Post*, February 4, 2007.

Oshrit Sabag, interview by the author, March 2024.

On the 2013 Israeli Election

Aviad Rubin, Doron Navot, and As'ad Ghanem, "The 2013 Israeli General Election: Travails of the Former King," *Middle East Journal* 68, no. 2 (Spring 2014): 248–267.

Ben Caspit, "Lapid-Bennett Alliance Shakes Up Israeli Politics," *Al-Monitor*, March 5, 2013.

Dani Rachamim, interview by the author, January 2024.

On Qatari Support for Hamas Starting from 2012

Jodi Rudoren, "Qatar's Emir Visits Gaza, Pledging $400 Million to Hamas," *New York Times*, October 23, 2012.

Ibrahim Barzak and Mohammed Daraghmeh, "Hamas Frets as Relations with Egypt Go South," *Associated Press*, August 3, 2013.

Yaniv Kubovich, "With Israel's Consent, Qatar Gave Gaza $1 Billion since 2012," *Haaretz*, February 10, 2019.

Tal Schneider, "For Years, Netanyahu Propped up Hamas. Now It's Blown Up in Our Faces," *Times of Israel*, October 8, 2023.

On the Lead-Up to 2014 War

Peter Beaumont and Orlando Crowcroft, "Bodies of Three Missing Israeli Teenagers Found in West Bank," *The Guardian*, June 30, 2014.

Nir Hasson, "Unraveling the Murder That's Shaking Jerusalem: The Facts So Far," *Haaretz*, July 4, 2014.

Nir Hasson, "Two Minors Convicted of Abu Khdeir Murder Sentenced to Life, 21 Years," *Haaretz*, February 4, 2016.

Nahal Oz community update, July 2014.

On Hamas's Use of Tunnels in 2014 War

Amos Harel, "Hamas' Terror Tunnels—A National Strategic Failure for Israel," *Haaretz*, July 22, 2014.

NOTES

Ronen Bergman, "How Hamas Beat Israel in Gaza," *New York Times*, August 10, 2014.

Jeffrey White, "The Combat Performance of Hamas in the Gaza War of 2014," *CTC Sentinel* 7, no. 9 (September 2014): 9–13.

Iris Leal, "We Didn't Dare to Know: Seven Years after Hamas Tunnel Attack, Revisiting My Nephew's Death," *Haaretz*, July 28, 2021.

Nahal Oz community update, August 1994.

On Netanyahu's Decision to Avoid Full-Scale Ground Invasion in 2014

Itamar Sharon, "Cabinet Told Purging Gaza of Terror Would Take 5 Years, Cost Hundreds of Soldiers' Lives," *Times of Israel*, August 6, 2014.

Moran Azoulay, "Cabel to Attorney General: Investigate Netanyahu and Government Ministers over Leak of Gaza Invasion Presentation," *Ynet*, August 19, 2014.

Benjamin Netanyahu, *Bibi: My Story* (New York: Threshold Editions, 2022).

Senior Israeli Security Official, interview by the author, February 2024.

Avigdor Lieberman, interview by the author, March 2024.

Haviv Rettig Gur, "The War of the Doves," *Times of Israel*, July 30, 2014.

On the Events in Nahal Oz during 2014 War, including Daniel Tregerman's Death

Oshrit Sabag, interview by the author, March 2024.

Carine Rachamim, interview by the author, February 2024.

Nahal Oz community update, August 2014.

Itay Maoz, interview by the author, August 2014.

"Families Abandon Homes near Gaza Border, Head North," *Times of Israel*, August 23, 2014.

Aloni Mor and Ben Hartman, "At Funeral of Child Killed by Gazan Mortar Shell, Mother Says: We Thought You Would Bring Peace," *Jerusalem Post*, August 24, 2014.

CHAPTER 10

On Events inside Our Safe Room and Home in the Afternoon

Miri Tibon, interview, Project Edut 710, January 2024.

Maglan soldier D., interview by the author, February 2024.

Sharon Fiorentino, interview, Project Edut 710, March 2024.

NOTES

On the Story of Ariel Zohar's Rescue by Ilan Fiorentino

Dror Kessler, interview by the author, March 2024.

Nurit Fiorentino, interview, Project Edut 710, February 2024.

Sharon Fiorentino, interview, Project Edut 710, March 2024.

Merav Sever, "Family's Sole Survivor of Hamas Massacre Managed to Save Tefillin under Fire," *Israel Hayom*, October 19, 2023.

On the Events at the Homes of the Zohar, Idan, and Poslushni Families

Eight Maglan fighters, group interview by the author, February 2024.

Major Eshel, interview by the author, March 2024.

Sharona Poslushni, interview, Project Edut 710, March 2024.

Shany Littman, "'You Start Thinking, Will They Kill the Girls First, or Kill Me First and Then Them?,'" *Haaretz*, December 3, 2023.

On the Events at Our Home in the Evening Hours

Yonatan Brosh, interview, Project Edut 710, January 2024.

Ruti Wagner, interview, Project Edut 710, January 2024.

Beri Meirovitch, interview, Project Edut 710, January 2024.

Maglan soldier D., interview by the author, February 2024.

On Events Elsewhere in the Kibbutz in the Evening Hours

Nissan Dekalo, interview by the author, December 2023.

Major Eshel, interview by the author, March 2024.

Avital Ron, interview by the author, March 2024.

Two Givati brigade soldiers, group interview by the author, March 2024.

Carine Rachamim, interview by the author, February 2024.

October 7th—First Hours, "Noam Tibon Recounts How He Rescued His Family during the Hamas Attack," video, *Channel 12 News*, November 11, 2023.

CHAPTER 11

On the Situation after the End of the 2014 War

Or Heller, "Let's Remember: Gaza Is Our Smallest of Problems," *Globes*, August 27, 2014.

Moshe Steinmetz, "Netanyahu at Memorial to Fallen Soldiers: 'Quiet Will Be Met with Quiet,'" *Walla News*, July 7, 2017.

Oshrit Sabag, interview by the author, March 2024.

Marisa Newman, "20 Families Leave Southern Kibbutz after Gaza Conflict," *Times of Israel*, October 15, 2014.

Nahal Oz community update, November 2014.

Avishay Ben-Sasson, "The Strategic Balance of Israel's Withdrawal from Gaza, 2005–2016," Molad Center, 2016.

Qatari Involvement in Gaza Reconstruction

Emily Harris, "Why Israel Lets Qatar Give Millions to Hamas," NPR, June 18, 2015.

Jack Khoury, "Qatar Announces New Gaza Reconstruction Projects," *Haaretz*, May 30, 2015.

Sigurd Neubauer, "Gaza Reconstruction: Can Norway and Qatar Help Bring Hamas to the Negotiating Table?," *Al Jazeera*, June 30, 2015.

Ahmad Melhem, "Will Qatar-Israel Relations Threaten PA's Relevance in Gaza?," *Al-Monitor*, April 2, 2015.

2015 Israeli Election

Anshel Pfeffer, *Bibi: The Turbulent Life and Times of Benjamin Netanyahu* (New York: Basic Books, 2018).

Jonathan Beck, "Bennett Accuses Netanyahu of Mishandling Gaza War," *Times of Israel*, January 18, 2015.

"Likud Uses Netanyahu Speech to Congress in Campaign Ad," *Times of Israel*, March 13, 2015.

Aluf Benn, "The End of the Old Israel: How Netanyahu Has Transformed the Nation," *Foreign Affairs* 95, no. 4 (July/August 2016): 16–27.

On Demographic Growth of Gaza Border Communities and Our Trips in the Region

Oshrit Sabag, interview by the author, March 2024.

Avishay Edri, interview by the author, March 2024.

Ben Sales, "A Year After Gaza War, Border Communities Are Growing," *JTA*, August 4, 2015.

Tamir Steinman, "One Year after the War: Families Move to Gaza Envelope," *Channel 12 News*, June 15, 2015.

Miriam Feinberg Vamosh, "Israel's Top 10 Ancient Mosaic Discoveries," *Haaretz*, February 27, 2013.

"In PHOTOS: The Ridiculous Beauty of Israel's Ranunculus Flowers during Passover," *Haaretz*, April 13, 2017.

On Trump's Recognition of Jerusalem and Subsequent Escalation on Gaza Border

Mark Landler, "Trump Recognizes Jerusalem as Israel's Capital and Orders U.S. Embassy to Move," *New York Times*, December 6, 2017.

Alexia Underwood, "The Controversial US Jerusalem Embassy Opening, Explained," *Vox*, May 16, 2018.

Yaniv Kubovich, "2017 Saw Highest Number of Rockets Launched from Gaza Since 2014 War, Israeli Army Says," *Haaretz*, January 7, 2018.

On 2018 Gaza Border Protests

Tareq Baconi, "What the Gaza Protests Portend," *New York Review of Books*, May 15, 2018.

Amos Harel, "Gaza Mass Protests Force Israeli Military to Maneuver between Two Contradictory Goals," *Haaretz*, March 30, 2018.

Avi Issacharoff, "Hamas 'Success' on Friday Presages More Protests, More Deaths, in More Places," *Times of Israel*, March 31, 2018.

Isabel Kershner and David Halbfinger, "Israelis Reflect on Gaza: 'I Hope at Least That Each Bullet Was Justified,'" *New York Times*, May 15, 2018.

On the November 2018 Escalation

Avishay Edri, interview by the author, March 2024.

"'Operation Failed': Details Emerge on Israeli Covert Op Gone Awry," *Al Jazeera*, December 4, 2019.

Yaniv Kubovich and Jack Khoury, "Gaza Militants Launch Anti-Tank Missile at Bus, Israeli Soldier Gravely Wounded," *Haaretz*, November 12, 2018.

Avigdor Lieberman, interview by the author, March 2024.

Senior Netanyahu aide, interview by the author, March 2024.

"Defense Minister Lieberman Resigns, Urges Early Elections," *Israel Hayom*, November 14, 2018.

On the Qatari Cash Suitcases

Nima Elbagir, Barbara Arvanitidis, Alex Patt, Raja Razek, Nadeem Ebrahim, and Uri Blau, "Qatar Sent Millions to Gaza for Years—With Israel's Backing. Here's What We Know about the Controversial Deal," CNN, December 12, 2023.

Avi Issacharoff, "Israel and Hamas Cheer Qatar's Gaza Cash Infusion, but Abbas Could Spoil Party," *Times of Israel*, November 11, 2018.

Amos Harel, "Qatari Money Calms Hamas, but Doesn't Guarantee Long-Term Quiet in Gaza," *Haaretz*, January 27, 2019.

Mark Mazzetti and Ronen Bergman, "How Israel Secretly Propped Up Hamas," *New York Times*, December 10, 2023.

Oren Persico, "The Journalistic Sources for Netanyahu's Statement in Favor of Strengthening Hamas," *Seventh Eye*, October 22, 2023.

On the Israeli Election Cycles of 2019–2020

Jonathan Lis, Chaim Levinson, Aaron Rabinowitz, and Jack Khoury, "Israel Heads to New Election After Netanyahu Fails to Form Coalition," *Haaretz*, May 30, 2019.

David Halbfinger and Isabel Kershner, "Israel Heads to Record Third Election, Extending Deadlock," *New York Times*, December 11, 2019.

On Israel-Qatar-Hamas Negotiations for a Wider Ceasefire Arrangement

Shelly Yehimovich, "'Calculated Risk': The Hebrew Note Sinwar Wrote to Netanyahu," *Yediot Aharonot*, April 4, 2022.

"Quietly, Israel Has Been Letting in Thousands of Gaza Workers in Bid to Ease Tensions," Associated Press, October 1, 2019.

"Mossad Chief Visited Doha, Urged Qatar to Continue Hamas Financial Aid," *Haaretz*, February 24, 2020.

Chaim Levinson, "Hamas Leader Yahya Sinwar's Confession Transcript, Reexamined amid a War He Started," *Haaretz*, November 8, 2023.

On the May 2021 War and the Events That Led to It

Mustafa Abu Sneineh, "Sheikh Jarrah Explained: The Past and Present of East Jerusalem Neighborhood," *Middle East Eye*, May 6, 2021.

Nir Hasson, "The East Jerusalem Flashpoint That Could Ignite the Entire Middle East," *Haaretz*, February 14, 2022.

Patrick Kingsley, "Evictions in Jerusalem Become Focus of Israeli-Palestinian Conflict," *New York Times*, May 7, 2021.

"Lapid, Bennett Aim to Form a Government within a Week," 124 News, May 6, 2021.

Shira Rubin and Steve Hendrix, "Netanyahu Turns to Extremist Party That Calls for Expelling Arabs from Israel," *Washington Post*, March 20, 2021.

NOTES

Avishay Edri, interview by the author, March 2024.

Amos Harel, "And Then Hamas Did Two Unexpected Things," *Haaretz*, May 11, 2021.

Michael Hauser Tov, "Bennett-Lapid Coalition Negotiations Suspended Amid Gaza Flare-up," *Haaretz*, May 12, 2021.

Barak Ravid, "11 Days, 8 Calls and a Ceasefire: Inside Biden's Response to the Gaza Crisis," Axios, May 22, 2021.

On Israel's "Government of Change"

"World Reacts as Bennett, Lapid form New Government, Oust Netanyahu After 12 Years," *Times of Israel*, June 13, 2021.

Jeffrey Heller and Maayan Lubell, "Netanyahu Out, Bennett in as Israel Marks End of an Era," Reuters, June 14, 2021.

Reham Owda, "The Bennett Government's Policy towards Gaza," Carnegie Endowment for International Peace, November 4, 2021.

On Carine Rachamim's Wedding and LGBT Acceptance in Nahal Oz

Carine Rachamim, interview by the author, February 2024.

Na'ama Tzadok, interview by the author, January 2024.

Oshrit Sabag, interview by the author, March 2024.

On "The Road to Recovery"—Israelis Driving Palestinians from Gaza to Hospital Treatments

Avishay Edri, interview by the author, March 2024.

Adelle Raemer, "Getting on the Road to Recovery," *The Blogs*, *Times of Israel*, December 5, 2021.

Gal Koplewitz, "An Israeli Charity for Palestinians Grapples with Oct. 7 Attacks," *New York Times*, January 31, 2024.

On 2022 Israeli Election and the Rise of the Far Right

Carrie Keller-Lynn, "Netanyahu Is the Projected Winner, but It Was Ben Gvir Crowned on Election Night," *Times of Israel*, November 3, 2022.

Shaul Magid, "Ben-Gvir Is a Bigger Threat to Israeli Society Than Kahane Ever Was," *Haaretz*, September 9, 2022.

NOTES

On Sinwar's Open Threats of War in December 2022 and Israel's Response

Sally Ibrahim, "Hamas Celebrates Its 35th Anniversary since Its Founding in the Gaza Strip," *New Arab*, December 14, 2022.

"Hamas Marks Anniversary, Predicts Confrontation with Israel," Associated Press, December 15, 2022.

Ben Caspit, "Israel's Pre-October 7 Protocols: Netanyahu Boasted about Hamas Deterrence," *Jerusalem Post*, December 15, 2023.

Shira Rubin, "Israel Was Warned Hamas Was Planning a Major Attack. It Was Ignored," *Washington Post*, December 6, 2023.

On Ben-Gvir's Visit to Al-Aqsa and Hamas's Response

Alec Pollard, "Hamas Warns against Ben-Gvir's Potential Visit to Temple Mount This Week," I24 News, January 1, 2023.

"Hamas Retaliation for Ben-Gvir's Al-Aqsa Visit 'Will Be the Last War,' Far-Right MK Vows," *Haaretz*, January 3, 2023.

On Netanyahu's Judicial Overhaul and Public Opposition to It

Avishay Edri, interview by the author, March 2024.

Bernard Avishai, "Netanyahu's Government Takes a Turn toward Theocracy," *New Yorker*, January 7, 2023.

Jeremy Sharon, "Levin Unveils Bills to Remove Nearly All High Court's Tools for Government Oversight," *Times of Israel*, January 11, 2023.

Maya Orbach, "Thousands Take to the Streets of Rain-Soaked Tel Aviv to Protest against Government," *Jewish Chronicle*, January 15, 2023.

On the Crisis inside the Israeli Military and the Reservists' Protest

"Israel Air Force Reservists to Skip Training in Netanyahu Protest," *Al Jazeera*, March 6, 2023.

Amos Harel, "Over 250 Israeli Air Force Reservists Join Refusal Movement, Will Not Show Up for Training This Week," *Haaretz*, March 19, 2023.

Ronen Bergman and Patrick Kingsley, "Israeli Reservists Threaten Mass Resignations If Judicial Plan Proceeds," *New York Times*, July 15, 2023.

On Netanyahu's Attempt to Fire His Defense Minister

Michael Hauser Tov, "Netanyahu Fires Defense Minister Gallant for Calling to Stop Judicial Overhaul," *Haaretz*, March 26, 2023.

NOTES

Amir Tibon, "'Time to Flood the Streets': How Israel's Historic Night of Pro-democracy Protests Was Born," *Haaretz*, March 27, 2023.

On West Bank Escalation and Israel's Deployment of More Battalions There

Emanuel Fabian, "IDF Sends 2 More Battalions to West Bank after Series of Settler Attacks," *Times of Israel*, June 25, 2023.

"Israel Sends More Troops into Occupied West Bank after Latest Wave of Violence," Associated Press, February 27, 2023.

Aluf Benn, "The West Bank Occupation Outweighed Israel's Defense of the Gaza Border on the Eve of October 7," *Haaretz*, February 21, 2024.

"Exclusive: Al Arouri: Resistance Axis Preparing for All-Out War," *Al Mayadeen English*, August 25, 2023.

On Late September 2023 Border Protests and Their Pacification

Amos Harel, "Israel Hoped a Better Gaza Economy Would Quell Violence. Hamas Has Other Plans," *Haaretz*, September 28, 2023.

Nidal al-Mugrabi, "Israel Reopens Gaza Crossings, Lets Palestinians Back to Work after Two Weeks," Reuters, September 28, 2023.

Amir Tibon, Jonathan Lis, and Yaniv Kubovich, "Amid Border Escalation, Netanyahu Gov't Weighs Aid to Calm Gaza for Sake of Israeli-Saudi Deal," *Haaretz*, October 2, 2023.

CHAPTER 12

On the Kidnapping of Judith and Natalie Ra'anan

Yehiel Chlenov, interview by the author, December 2023.

Tamar Livyatan, interview by the author, December 2023.

Elizabeth Vargas, "Hamas Hostage Says Life in Captivity was Like 'Russian Roulette,'" NewsNation, March 14, 2024.

On the Kidnappings of Omri Miran, Tzachi Idan, and Dafna and Ela Elyakim

Shany Littman, "'You Start Thinking, Will They Kill the Girls First, or Kill Me First and Then Them?,'" *Haaretz*, December 3, 2023.

Shany Littman, "Hamas Abducted Her Daughters: 'I'm Sorry, but I Don't Believe God Exists,'" *Haaretz*, October 16, 2023.

Senior Shin Bet official, interview by the author, March 2024.

NOTES

Yigal Mosko, "Live Kidnapping: The Story of the Idan Family," *Channel 12 News*, October 24, 2023.

Michal Peylan, "I Thought Nobody Even Cares If We Come Back," *Channel 12 News*, January 31, 2024.

On Israeli Hostages' Reactions to Israeli Bombings of Gaza

Ran Shimoni, "They Were Held Captive by Hamas, but Their Biggest Fear Was Israeli Airstrikes," *Haaretz*, December 11, 2023.

Anat Schwartz, "Apology, Tears and Terror: A Former Hostage Recounts a 7-Week Ordeal," *New York Times*, December 15, 2023.

Tamar Livyatan, interview by the author, December 2023.

On Israel's Internally Displaced Population and Nahal Oz's Arrival to Mishmar Ha'emek

Dani Rachamim, interview by the author, January 2024.

Oshrit Sabag, interview by the author, March 2024.

Avishay Edri, interview by the author, March 2024.

Chen Maanit, "How Mishmar Ha'emek Adopted the Evacuees of Nahal Oz," *Haaretz*, December 18, 2023.

"About 200,000 Israelis Internally Displaced amid Ongoing Gaza War, Tensions in North," *Times of Israel*, October 22, 2023.

On the Death Toll in Israel at Large and in Nahal Oz Specifically

Aaron Boxerman, "What We Know about the Death Toll in Israel from the Hamas-Led Attacks," *New York Times*, November 12, 2023.

"Death Toll from Nova Music Festival Massacre on Oct. 7 Raised by 100 to Over 360," *Times of Israel*, November 18, 2023.

On Ilan Fiorentino's Funeral and Shiva

Dror Kessler, interview by the author, March 2024.

Nurit Fiorentino, interview by the author, March 2024.

Naftali Bennett (@naftalibennett), "Friends and family told me about Ilan Fiorentino, the security coordinator who saved the lives of residents," X (Twitter), October 15, 2023.

NOTES

On President Biden's Visit to Israel

Betsy Klein, "Biden Speaks with Families of Americans Unaccounted for in Israel," CNN, October 13, 2023.

Jennifer Hansler, Kevin Liptak, M. J. Lee, and Kayla Tausche, "President Joe Biden Will Visit Israel in High-Stakes Trip," CNN, October 16, 2023.

Shany Littman, "American Hostages Released by Hamas: This Is Their Story," *Haaretz*, October 20, 2023.

On the Israelis Selected to Meet President Biden

Judith Sudilovsky, "Inbal Rabin-Liberman: The Heroine of Kibbutz Nir Am," *Jerusalem Post*, October 12, 2023.

India Today World Desk, "Joe Biden Meets Israeli Granny Who 'Beat' Hamas Terrorists with Tea and Cookies," *India Today*, October 18, 2023.

Pamela Sampson, "An Arab Paramedic Who Treated Israelis Injured by Hamas Militants Is Remembered as a Hero," Associated Press, October 15, 2023.

On Hamas and Qatar's Incentive for Accepting November Prisoner Exchange

"Gaza Hostage Videos an 'Outrage on Personal Dignity,'" Human Rights Watch, November 10, 2023.

Camilla Turner, "Israeli Hostage Paraded through Gaza like a 'Trophy,'" *The Telegraph*, March 13, 2024.

Jacob Magid, "Qatar Pressing Hamas to Release Women, Children and Elderly Hostages—Official," *Times of Israel*, October 15, 2023.

Ishaan Tharoor, "Israel Says Hamas 'Is ISIS.' But It's Not," *Washington Post*, October 25, 2023.

"Full List of Israeli Hostages in Gaza," Mako, accessed October 2023, http://www.mako.co.il.

On the Release of Judith and Natalie Ra'anan

Tamar Livyatan, interview by the author, December 2023.

Jacob Magid and Emanuel Fabian, "Hamas Releases Two Hostages, Mother and Daughter Judith and Natalie Raanan," *Times of Israel*, October 20, 2023.

Isabel Keane, "Freed Hostages Judith Raanan, Daughter Natalie 'Kept Each Other Safe' While Captive, Family Says," *New York Post*, October 23, 2023.

NOTES

On Death Toll and Widespread Destruction from Israeli Attack on Gaza

Senior IDF officer—southern front, interview by the author, March 2024.

"Nearly a Fifth of Gaza's Building Destroyed or Damaged: UN Estimate," Reuters, December 12, 2023.

Evan Hill, Imogen Piper, Meg Kelly, and Jarrett Ley, "Israel Has Waged One of This Century's Most Destructive Wars in Gaza," *Washington Post*, December 23, 2023.

Tareq Baconi, "What Was Hamas Thinking?," *Foreign Policy*, November 22, 2023.

"Lethal Combination of Hunger and Disease to Lead to More Deaths in Gaza," World Health Organization, December 21, 2023.

Mohammed Mhawish, "'A Second Nakba': Echoes of 1948, as Israel Orders Palestinians to Leave," *Al Jazeera*, October 14, 2023.

On the November Prisoner Exchange and the Release of Dafna Elykaim, Ela Elyakim, and Elma Avraham

Jason Burke, Ruth Michaelson, and Julian Borger, "Israel and Hamas Agree Deal for Release of Some Hostages and Four-Day Ceasefire," *The Guardian*, November 22, 2023.

Michael Bachner, "Released Hostage, 15, Says She Acted as Mother to Her Younger Sister in Captivity," *Times of Israel*, January 31, 2024.

Michal Peylan, "The Hostage Who Returned in the Most Difficult Condition Tells Her Story," *Channel 12 News*, January 17, 2024.

ILLUSTRATION CREDITS

1. Ben Gurion in Nahal Oz:
   IDF and Israeli Defense Ministry Archive, photographer: Avraham Vered.
2. Maglan fighters: Courtesy of Buchris and Yavetz families.
3. Wrangler: Amir Tibon
4. Bullet holes in home: Amir Tibon
5. Noam Tibon with gun: Amir Tibon
6. Carine and Dikla at wedding: Courtesy of Carine Rachamim
7. Girls in field: Amir Tibon
8. Ilan Fiorentino with armored vehicle: Courtesy of Tom Danenberg.

INDEX

INDEX

INDEX

ABOUT THE AUTHOR

Amir Tibon is an award-winning diplomatic correspondent for *Haaretz*, Israel's paper of record, and has previously served as the paper's correspondent in Washington, DC, and as a senior editor for its English edition. He is the author of *The Last Palestinian: The Rise and Reign of Mahmoud Abbas* (coauthored with Grant Rumley), the first-ever biography of the leader of the Palestinian Authority. Tibon, his wife, and their two young daughters were evacuated from their home in Kibbutz Nahal Oz after the October 7 attack and are currently living in temporary housing in north-central Israel.